AMSTERDAM — NEW YORK

Previously published in this series:

23. Multiculturalism and the Canon of American Culture,1993
24. Victorianism in the United States, 1992 *
25. Cultural Transmissions and Receptions,   1993
26. Modern American Landscapes, 1994
27. Fair Representations, 1994
28. Hollywood in Europe, 1994
29. American Photographs in Europe, 1994
30. American Culture in the Netherlands, 1996
31. Connecting Cultures, 1994
32. The Small Town in America, 1995
33. 'Writing' Nation and 'Writing' Region in America, 1996
34. The American Columbiad, 1996 *
35. The Insular Dream, 1995 *
36. Brave New Words, 1995
37. Social and Secure? 1996
38. Living with America, 1946-1996, 1997 *
39. Writing Lives, 1998
40. Through the Cultural Looking Glass, 1999
41. Dynamics of Modernization, 1999
42. Beat Culture, 1999
43. Predecessors, 1999
44. Ceremonies and Spectacles, 2000 *
45. The American Metropolis, 2001
46. Transatlantic Encounters, I en II, 2000
47. Federalism, Citizenship, and Collective Identities in U.S. History, 2001
48. Not English Only, 2001
49. "Nature's Nation" Revisited, 2003 *
50. Straddling Borders, 2004
51. Dreams of Paradise, Visions of Apocalypse, 2004
52. Religion in America, 2004
53. Public Space, Private Lives, 2004
54. First Nations of North America, 2005
55. Post-Cold War Europe, Post-Cold War America, 2004
56. Working Sites, 2004
57. The Cultural Shuttle, 2004 *
58. Frontiers and Boundaries in U.S. History, 2004
59. Amsterdam-New York, 2005 ***
    Nation on the Move, 2002 **

*   These volumes have been produced for the European Association for American Studies (E.E.A.S.).
**   This title is not a volume in the series, but closely connected with it.
***   This volume is produced with assistance of the Historical Documentation Center for Dutch Protestantism, Vrije Universiteit Amsterdam.

AMSTERDAM - NEW YORK
Transatlantic Relations and Urban Identities Since 1653

edited by
George Harinck and
Hans Krabbendam

VU Uitgeverij
Amsterdam 2005

EUROPEAN CONTRIBUTIONS TO AMERICAN STUDIES

This series is published for the Netherlands American Studies Association (N.A.S.A.) and the European Association for American Studies (E.A.A.S.)

General editor:
Rob Kroes
Amerika Instituut
Spuistraat 134
1012 VB Amsterdam

VU University Press is an imprint of
VU Boekhandel/Uitgeverij bv
De Boelelaan 1105
1081 HV Amsterdam
The Netherlands
E-mail: info@vu-uitgeverij.nl

ISBN 90 5383 955 0 (ECAS no 59)
NUR 686

Design cover: De Ontwerperij (Marcel Bakker), Amsterdam
Typesetting: Hans Seijlhouwer
Printer: Wilco, Amersfoort

CONTENTS

PREFACE

We often only discuss those issues that divide us. This volume is an opportunity to step back for a moment and not discuss current events, but examine our past. Through such an examination, we can develop a better understanding of our shared values and history and focus on what we have in common.

Like most Americans, I already had a positive image of The Netherlands as a peaceful nation with a rich culture and a strong tradition of international trade before I became Ambassador. It is because of the research done by many Dutch institutions that I have recently been able to get a much broader perspective on how profoundly our countries have influenced one another over the centuries – politically, culturally and financially. The extent of these historical ties is not commonly known outside of intellectual circles and this book is a welcome contribution to the spread of this knowledge.

As Ambassador, I frequently refer to key points in our common history: the founding of New Amsterdam, the departure of the Pilgrims from Leiden and the Ambassadorship of John Adams. After completing my visits to the provinces in 2001, we were able to host all twelve Queen's Commissioners at our residence for a dinner. I was pleased that we could resurrect an old theatrical show focused on the richness of John Adams' letters to Abigail during his tenure here. The Queen's Commissioners were fascinated with John Adams' remarks: that the Dutch would be our 'everlasting friends' and that he looked 'upon his success in Holland as the happiest event, and the greatest action of his life, past or future.' The Commissioners also understood and accepted Adams' references to negotiating America's first loan when he described his situation as that of 'a man in the midst of the ocean, negotiating for his life among a school of sharks.' Many Americans may know that the Dutch loan of five million guilders at 5 per cent arranged in July 1782 was America's first loan. What I am sure many people do not know even today, except perhaps through your research, is that the loans provided by Dutch bankers formed the backbone of the American economy in the following years. Foreign loans, the majority of which were raised in the Netherlands, comprised more than 40 per cent of revenues for the American government until 1791 and over 25 per cent until 1795. The United States could not repay the loan until 1809, but the Dutch were more than willing to accommodate by refinancing the loans, of course at a higher interest rate.

In the years to come, the Dutch played a significant role through direct investment in our country. They were behind the establishment of our banks, railroads, canals and many other large infrastructure projects. In fact, I'm told it's documented that between 1825 and 1840, Dutch financiers provided 90 per cent of funds for many of our canal projects.

Given the history of Dutch investments in the United States, I guess it is no surprise to many of you that the Netherlands, a country of 16 million people, is quickly becoming the second largest investor in the United States, surpassing Japan; and second only to the United Kingdom.

A century before John Adams came on the scene, the seeds of the intertwined Dutch-American relationship had been sown with the establishment of the first Dutch colony in North America at New Amsterdam.

This volume celebrates 350 years of that fateful decision to establish a colony. That is when the Dutch became Americans, and we, as Americans, inherited a Dutch legacy. Recently I was at a function at our residence where one of the speakers quoted a *Ladies' Home Journal* article of 1903 declaring that we owed more of our history and traditions to the Dutch than to the British. I will leave that intellectual pursuit to the readers of this volume.

This volume looks back at the extraordinary relationship between our two leading cities—our ports, banking centers, and our centers of art and music that have served as a magnet for immigrants from around the world. Our relationship is one of trade and immigration, but also of learning, culture and shared values. The scholarly contributions are important in sustaining this relationship for the future.

My first encounter with the Roosevelt Study Center was at the Four Freedoms awards. Those awards, and programs like this continually reinforce our common roots. It is the bedrock of our relationship that we draw upon and should continue to strengthen.

I am pleased with a proclamation from the Office of the Mayor of the City of New York commemorating February 2 as the date of the establishment of New Amsterdam. In conclusion, I would like to quote from this proclamation:

> The meaning of February 2, 1653 is the expression of the steadfast vitality of all the citizens of New York City in their search to create a community which reaches ever upward, a community where seven million inhabitants from all corners of the world build their hopes and dreams.

Clifford M. Sobel
62nd Ambassador of the United States to the Kingdom of the Netherlands

Hans Krabbendam and George Harinck

AMSTERDAM–NEW YORK:
PARALLELS AND REVERSALS IN AN
ENDURING RELATIONSHIP

In 1890 a young author and budding politician, who had just published his first volume of the *Winning of the West* and had made an unsuccessful bid to be mayor of New York four years earlier, produced a history of the city of New York as part of a series on (Anglo) historic towns. This was Theodore Roosevelt (1858-1919) who had yet to become the greatest American of his age. As most nineteenth-century genteel historians who romanticized the city's early history as a haven for the upper and middle classes, he also drew a lesson from the past: 'that he among us who wishes to win honor in our life, and to play his part honestly and manfully, must be indeed an American in spirit and purpose, in heart and thought and deed.' As his patrician peers had done, he encouraged the masses of new immigrants to quickly assimilate, as the Dutch settlers had done on Manhattan in the seventeenth and eighteenth centuries. Though he came to represent Mr. America, a visitor later in life described his physical appearance as 'some conservative banker of Amsterdam...'[1] Roosevelt did not shy away from addressing the faults of the city – as civil service commissioner, he was keenly aware of corruption and mismanagement – but he extolled its virtues and expressed his deep respect for his home town, emphasizing the humble origins of 'a little Dutch trading-hamlet' which its inhabitants had transformed into a 'huge American city.' To him one of the key features of the city was the easy mingling of Dutch, English and other nationalities, a model for his own time of massive immigration. The mother city of Amsterdam played no part in his narrative, because he was mainly interested in the American identity and was convinced that the interests of the American citizens had been ignored and damaged by the stingy Dutch and the treacherous English in Europe. But without old Amsterdam, the new one would not have come into existence.

The official bond between the two cities began on 2 February 1653, when Nieuw Amsterdam installed its first court on Manhattan Island. This court was granted by the commercial authorities of 'old' Amsterdam and marked the beginning of Nieuw Amsterdam as a separate community. From that date on a tale of two cities can be told. Thanks to the durable commercial networks and the close ecclesiastical ties the exchange between the two cities continued long after the turnover of 1664. While the colonial history of Nieuw Amsterdam received attention, most of it was devoted to the West India Company. Only a few historians were interested in the relationship between the two cities, while the continued connections between Amsterdam and Nieuw Amsterdam were fully ignored after the latter had become New York in 1664.

The essays in this volume show how the position of the two cities was gradually reversed. Until the early 1800s Amsterdam was the dominant factor: overshadowing New York in size, prestige, wealth, and power. The shift can be located in the 1830s. Massive immigration boosted New York, while Amsterdam's population stalled and declined after 1750. By 1835 New York surpassed Amsterdam in size.

Table 1: Population Size of Amsterdam and New York, 1400-2000[2]

	Amsterdam	New York	Metropolitan area
1400	5,000	–	–
1600	30,000	–	–
1650	200,000	2,000	2,000
1700	220,000	5,000	10,000
1750	210,000	13,000	25,000
1800	200,000	60,000	80,000
1850	230,000	515,000	700,000
1900	500,000	1,850,000	3,440,000
1950	840,000	1,960,000	7,900,000
2000	740,000	1,537,000	8,000,000

The parallels between the cities are numerous. Both cities were commercial centers with strong maritime traditions, both citizenries were strong cosmopolitan communities from an early date on, financial centers, hotbeds for artistic and academic innovation, battlegrounds of religious and political influence, and offered windows to the wider world. However, the center of gravity changed from the old to the new world. Since the 1960s their special relationship resurfaces when New York and Amsterdam function as icons of the modern world, in which history shapes identity. Amsterdam and New York derive their identity not only from their own local history, but they also attune it to each other. Each city pretends to be unique as a warehouse of the world.

This collection of essays deals mainly with the political, commercial, and intellectual relationship of the cities. It does not deal with a comparison of the cities as ports and immigrant destinations or with the arts, which deserve separate treatment, but it does examine the historical identity of both cities.

Identity Politics and a Recognized Date
In 2003 the 'New York City 350th Anniversary Committee' proclaimed February 2nd as the day of the incorporation of the town, a date worthwhile to remember as a proper local birthday with national reverberations because of its multicultural legacy.[3] The organizers had invited author Russell Shorto to the 2004 celebration to portray a Dutch Manhattan as the early American embodiment of an open society rooted in free trade. Shorto concluded 'February 2, 1653, New York City's birthday as Nieuw Amsterdam, is one of the most im-

portant dates in American history and leads directly to the Declaration of Independence in 1776'.[4]

A century earlier Robert B. Roosevelt, former American minister to the Netherlands, founding member of the Holland Society and uncle to President Theodore Roosevelt, used the commemorative year to scold New York for its submission to the corrupt bosses in Albany. He placed the antecedents of the Dutch heritage to claim the city's 'birthright of independence and self-reliance.'[5] However, the historical significance was lost to a larger audience. The celebration of New York's world fair 'The Exhibition of the Industry of All Nations' which opened on July 15, 1853 in the Crystal Palace, put the bicentennial of the Nieuw Amsterdam charter in the shade. The Dutch were represented with pieces of art and industrial products at the fair, but they did not utilize the historic year. The only memorable contribution that year was the publication of the first volume of John Romeyn Brodhead's *The History of the State of New York*, covering the colonial years of the city. This publication was a result of the commission which Brodhead received from the state of New York to collect documents from European archives dealing with the history of New York. Old Amsterdam was a reality for Brodhead. This son of a Dutch Reformed minister joined his uncle Harmanus Bleecker as his secretary in 1839 when the latter became the American chargé d'affairs in the Hague, but this exploration of the historical cords did not trigger a revival of the urban relationship. The New York elites of the nineteenth century were not interested in Amsterdam as a point of reference to the development of their city, nor were Amsterdammers concerned with New York. Only recently has Nieuw Amsterdam grown into a motto for modern New York, as part of a longer tradition.

In recent years Nieuw Amsterdam has captivated the historical imagination for fiction. Maan Meyers, the author duo Martin and Annette Meyers, have published in the 1990s a mystery series set in historical New York. Starting with *The Dutchman*, set in Nieuw Amsterdam in 1664, the story follows Pieter Tonneman, the last Dutch sheriff of Nieuw Amsterdam and the first sheriff of New York and his descendents. A scholarly biography by Donna Merwick, *Death of a Notary: Conquest and Change in Colonial New York* deals with Adriaen Janse van Ilpendam of Beverwijck/Albany, who lived in Nieuw Amsterdam for several years. Beverly Swerling published in 2001 *City of Dreams: A Novel of Nieuw Amsterdam and Early Manhattan.*[6]

Apart from offering exotic sceneries and excuses for celebrations, the Dutch presence in North America is an uphill battle against academic neglect, lack of language skills, and Anglo dominance. In a review of Benjamin Schmidt, *Innocence Abroad: The Dutch Imagination and the New World, 1570-1670*, Peter C. Mancall claims: 'With the exception of a small group of specialists who have studied New Netherland, American historians have not examined Dutch history in much depth.'[7] The small band of scholars affiliated with the New Netherland Project has generated a growing body of literature on the Dutch presence. One of the recent products is Janny Venema's *Beverwijck: A Dutch Village on the American Frontier, 1652-1664.*[8] Following the leads of others her study confirms the Dutch identity, visible in civil organization, church and social arrangements in Beverwijck/Albany. The greatest service rendered to the Dutch heritage in New York was the publication of Russell Shorto's *The Island at the Center of the World The Epic Story of Dutch Manhattan, the Forgotten Colony that Shaped America*, which quickly appeared in a Dutch translation.[9]

Old World Order for the New World
Fortunately, not only American and Dutch scholars, but also British and German historians are interested in the American Dutch colony as part of the Atlantic community. Together they prevent a chauvinistic treatment of the subject, as presented in this volume.

Jaap Jacobs explains that despite the limited innovations, Nieuw Amsterdam passed a threshold in the year 1653. The city benefited in two ways: the 1653 arrangements clarified the relationship between the inhabitants and the authorities which helped to diminish the sources of conflict between the two sides. Secondly, the charter recognized Nieuw Amsterdam as the capital of the colony, which prepared its role for future growth. Its subsequent development to greater independence was not so much an 'American' desire for freedom, but a natural order which young cities in Europe followed.

Boudewijn Bakker argued that the self-government of Nieuw Amsterdam was almost inevitable, given the fact that Amsterdam and the elites in other Dutch cities in the seventeenth century did not dream of a large empire. Their ideal was a peaceful world, filled by nations that gained wealth, status, and power by the fruits of free trade, protected by an occasional war. Not surprisingly it was the Amsterdam Chamber of the West India Company that was responsible for the state of affairs in the colony.

Simon Middleton cut several specific ties between old and new Amsterdam, since often references to Amsterdam precedents were made by people with no actual connection to Holland's capital. Rulers and ruled worked together to create a society that was familiar to live in. They grew attached to the world they had created and were willing to defend it against disturbing regulations. This interpretation harmonizes two conflicting views of the Dutch legacy, one of which claims its tenacity under English rule, while the other emphasizes the ethnic variety of the citizens. The different groups justified their plans by referring to an enduring and idealized Dutch way of operating. This common point of reference tied the heterogeneous community closer together.

Claudia Schnurmann broadens Middleton's thesis to include Anglo-Dutch relations in and around seventeenth-century Nieuw Amsterdam/New York, since the city took into account American as well as European constellations. Their operations were not hindered by national boundaries, regulations, or ethnicity. The British colonies used their Dutch neighbors to their own advantage usually detrimental to Britain, which explains the hostility of the British authorities against the Dutch colony. Her reconstruction of colonial relations questions the usefulness of traditional national(ist) perspectives on history.

Religious Ties, Tolerance, and Independence
Joyce Goodfriend explored religious pluralism in the transition from Dutch to British rule. She asserts that ethnic diversity in Nieuw Amsterdam did not automatically lead to religious pluralism. As in Old Amsterdam, the Reformed Church was privileged and dominant, though liberty of conscience allowed other faiths to operate in the margin. In fact Stuyvesant wanted to minimalize religious diversity and was whistled back by the Amsterdam authorities. The transfer of power to the British actually extended religious freedom to include Anglicans (of course), but also Lutherans, Quakers, and (temporarily) Catholics, not completely surprising during the reign of a Catholic governor. The subsequent Catholic-Protestant strife in the Old World led to restrictions in the new. Jews had to wait longer for equal treatment. In fact the state constitution of 1777 endorsed religious freedom.

Dirk Mouw zoomed in on the changes in the Dutch Reformed ministry in the same period. He discovered that the Reformed Protestant Dutch congregations called ministers who differed from the candidates selected by the Classis of Amsterdam. New means to recruit ministers resulted in a pietist impetus. This desire for more variety put pressure on the mother church for more local control. However, this did not mean that the relationship between new world and old world Reformed was characterized by opposition. The New York Dutch Reformed maintained their loyalty to the Dordt church order and practices and continued to receive support from the Classis of Amsterdam.

Robin A. Leaver supports Mouw's conclusion of maintaining Dutch practices in the New World by concentrating on the practice of singing, which was done in Dutch till the end of the eighteenth century. He presents evidence for the longevity of the Dathenus psalter. As in the Netherlands, the Dutch in the new world presented alternative rhymes and tunes. Only in 1763 did the first English-speaking Reformed dominee arrive in New York City, an event which coincided with the call for English psalms. The modernization of psalm singing in the Netherlands after the acceptance of the new psalter in 1773 came too late for the American believers to gain ground. The dominant place of the Dathenus version, at that time two centuries old, was a clear sign of the Dutch tongue becoming archaic.

Goods and Images
Hymn books, bibles, devotional publications, and religious treatises formed the majority of the books imported from the Netherlands. Marika Keblusek made a detailed investigation of the book trade from Amsterdam and Leiden to New York. The market for Dutch books in the New World was small and the need was filled via private channels. The main commercial activity was the trade in antiquarian books, which was part of the growth of intellectual life in the young American Republic. James Eastburn's business with the Leiden Luchtmans firm via his Amsterdam agent was part of the growing market for scholarly works, in which the Dutch participated. However, despite the importance of this trade for the intellectual bildung of America, it also strengthened the focus on the past, not on the future.

Among the antiquarian books shipped by Amsterdam and Leiden book traders to New York were the sources that Washington Irving used for his Knickerbocker's history of New Netherland, as Elisabeth P. Funk's research shows. This book was the target of much scorn among the Dutch New Yorkers, but was much more than cheap fun at the Dutch expense. The book was both a register of the strong presence of Dutch folklore in New York and a critical commentary of Irving's early nineteenth-century New York. Moreover, the book inspired generations of historians to search for the real Dutch life in New York.

Trees and the shade they cast was one of the influences of Amsterdam on the physical environment of New York, as Henry Lawrence demonstrates in his essay comparing urban green spaces in both cities. The Amsterdammers practice of planting trees along the streets and canals in the seventeenth century was adopted in New York. In contrast to the planned planting in Amsterdam, New York authorities did not guide the process, but left it to the initiatives of its citizens. During the subsequent eighteenth and early nineteenth centuries the two cities diverged till at the end of the nineteenth century both became part of a cosmopolitan trend on both continents to use tree-lined streets and large public parks to ornament the cities and make them more attractive for their inhabitants and for visitors.

When the United States became independent, the Dutch Republic started official diplomatic relations with its sister Republic. The commercial interests were delegated to the consuls, which allowed the two cities to be closer connected. However, despite the important role of commerce and diplomacy, Hans Krabbendam demonstrates that the cities did not develop a special relationship. During the nineteenth century Amsterdam maintained its grip on the New York consulate. In New York similar commercial interests soon gave way to political agendas, making the Amsterdam consulate a desirable reward for political services. After the turn of the century both services were professionalized, which removed the last mutual local connections and revealed the growing dominance of American shipping in the transatlantic trade of Amsterdam. The consular relations in both cities contributed to the integration of the economic and political sectors, but the original local connections were replaced by national relations.

Part of the consuls' duties was to take care of the citizens in the host country. This task increased with the arrival of American tourists in the Netherlands. George Harinck investigated the expectations of the American travelers who flooded into the Netherlands around the turn of the century. The cause of the sudden popularity of Amsterdam and Holland was that its archaic structure allowed the modernized American to escape to an open air museum, which must have resembled New York's origins.

Journalist Tracy Metz brings the argument full circle. In her tour of the cities in search of urban identity and historical architecture, she notes the differences between contemporary New York and Amsterdam in dealing with the past, and the similarities in their coping with the question of authenticity.

Conclusion

How should the relationship between the two cities be characterized? In fact, it was not the cities themselves that had a relationship. In the seventeenth century it was the intertwined political and commercial elites, while in the eighteenth century religious ties proved strong, due to the central position of the Amsterdam classis. In the nineteenth century the balance shifted to New York. Five conclusions can be drawn from these essays on the relationship between the cities. The first conclusion is that New Netherland was not a colony of the Dutch Republic. The civil administration of Nieuw Amsterdam took shape in 1653 as part of a continuous process of delegating civil authority conforming with the model of urban development that took place in the low countries since the late Middle Ages. Secondly, the continuity of the Dutch commercial network greatly enhanced the independent position of New York City. Thirdly, the pluriform religious constellation of New York City in the eighteenth century originated in the immigration of a variety of religious groups, which had settled there during Dutch control in the previous century. Fourthly, the relative late interest of the New Yorkers for their Amsterdam roots in the nineteenth century served political purposes: to provide the established Dutch-Americans with a higher status compared to recent immigrants and to press for political agendas separate from the Albany bosses. Finally, the mythological status of Amsterdam contributed more to its reputation as 'founding mother' of New York City than actual exchanges between both cities.

Comparisons between the cities are not only interesting for the past. Current problems which plague Western cities encourage comparisons and the exchange of potential solutions. New York social geographer John Mollenkopf compared the fate of the immigrants in Amsterdam with the developments in New York.[10] He argued that the two cities make a suitable pair for comparison, since their economic pasts contain similar ingredients, such as their port and financial facilities, their magnetic attraction for the young and upcoming generations, their heavy regulation of housing, strong presence of civil servants and social services, and their large immigrant populations, forcing changes on existing neighborhoods. Other urban issues, such as disaster management and security, brought delegations from the Amsterdam city council to visit New York to learn lessons.[11] There are abundant reasons to expect that the longstanding relationship between Amsterdam and New York will endure.

Notes

1 Julian Street, 'Roosevelt, Citizen of New York', *The Works of Theodore Roosevelt* 20 vols. (National edition), vol. 10: 360. Preface, p. 362. Clifton Hood, 'Journeying to 'Old New York': Elite New Yorkers and Their Invention of an Idealized City History in the Late Nineteenth and Early Twentieth Centuries', *Journal of Urban History* 28 (September 2002): 699-719.
2 Sources: Dienst Ruimtelijke Ordening Amsterdam, and Kenneth T. Jackson, ed., *Encyclopedia of New York City* (New York 1995), 920-923. New York, is basically Manhattan, and figures for the metropolitan area are inclusive of Manhattan.
3 *New York Sun*, 23 January 2003.
4 http://www.nyc350.org/feb204birthdayrecap.html
5 Robert B. Roosevelt, 'The Oldest Charter of New York,' Theodore M. Banta, ed., *Yearbook of the Holland Society of New York* (1903), 234.
6 (New York: Simon & Schuster, 2001).
7 'Amsterdam's America,' *Reviews in American History* 31 (2003): 14-23. Benjamin Schmidt, *Innocence Abroad: The Dutch Imagination and the New World, 1570-1670* (New York 2001)
8 (Hilversum: Verloren, 2003).
9 (New York: Doubleday, 2004).
10 John Mollenkopf, 'Assimilating Immigrants in Amsterdam: A Perspective from New York,' *The Netherlands Journal of Social Sciences* 30.2 (2000): 126-145.
11 *De Volkskrant*, 30 september 2004.

Jaap Jacobs

'TO FAVOR THIS NEW AND GROWING CITY OF NEW AMSTERDAM WITH A COURT OF JUSTICE.' THE RELATIONS BETWEEN RULERS AND RULED IN NEW AMSTERDAM

The director general and council of New Netherland hereby make known that the honorable *bewindhebbers* [directors] of the chartered West India Company, chamber at Amsterdam, lords and patroons of this province, have thought fit, under the high authority of their director general and council of New Netherland, to favor this new and growing city of New Amsterdam and the inhabitants thereof with a court of justice, to be constituted as far as possible and as the situation of the land allows according to the laudable customs of the city of Amsterdam, name-giver to this newly developing city, however, in such a way that all judgments shall remain subject to reversal by and appeal to the director general and council, to be by them finally disposed of....

Thus, until further amplification, provisionally done at the meeting of the honorable director general and council of New Netherland, this 2nd day of February anno 1653, in New Netherland. Was signed: P[etrus]. Stuyvesant, [Johannes] La Montagne, Brian Newton and Cor[nelis]: van Tienhoven.[1]

In this way the municipal charter of New Amsterdam was promulgated in 1653. The quotation comes from a document of which a copy has been preserved in the handwriting of Hans Bontemantel.[2] This document was rediscovered in 1911 and published in translation by Isaac Phelps Stokes in his monumental *Iconography of Manhattan Island* a couple of years later. In importance it must rank just below the famous Schagen letter of 1626, which contains the information that Manhattan had been bought for the sum of sixty guilders. The 1653 document is important as it is the municipal charter of New Amsterdam, outlining its form of government. Yet focusing only on its content may lead us astray if we try to evaluate its importance. The political and institutional developments in New Amsterdam both before and after 1653, as well as the context of the development of cities and towns in medieval Holland, are essential in understanding municipal government in New Amsterdam.

The Political Background of the 1653 Charter
The chartering of New Amsterdam came relatively late in the history of New Netherland. In several towns much smaller than New Amsterdam inferior courts of justice had already been established: some English and Dutch towns on Long Island, for instance, as well as

Beverwijck in 1652. The tardiness of authorities to allow New Amsterdam its own court must be explained by examining the relations between the West India Company and the colonists from the 1640s onwards. Within the historiography of New Netherland this topic has drawn much attention. More often than not, the conflicts that erupted have been interpreted as typical examples of freedom-loving colonists being suppressed by the local representatives of an authoritarian commercial company. As Edmund B. O'Callaghan wrote in 1846 in his *History of New Netherland*:

> The high-handed and dictatorial manner in which Kieft wielded his power, brought him into collision, at an early period, with the democratic spirit inherent in the breast of Dutch Republicans.[3]

Doubtless O'Callaghan's own experience as a journalist agitating against British rule in Canada in the 1830s played a role in his choice of words here. Even so, similar perspectives can be found in other nineteenth-century works, such as Brodhead's or Van Rensselaer's.[4]

Yet, it is surprising to find remnants of these views persisting at the end of the twentieth century. In their impressive book *Gotham*, Edwin Burrows and Mike Wallace also describe the relations between director general Stuyvesant and the inhabitants of New Amsterdam. They do this by illuminating just about every incident that Washington Irving used to create his caricature of Stubborn Pete in his *Diedrich Knickerbocker's history of New York*. That may be amusing to the unaware general reader, it nevertheless does not help our understanding of these relations. And yet Burrows and Wallace point to what, in my view, is the crux of the matter, when they write:

> Stuyvesant's expectation of obedience from the residents of New Amsterdam quickly ran up against their own expectation, derived from conventional Dutch practice, of a proper municipal government. The Netherlands had no landed aristocracy to speak of, urban capital dominated its agricultural production, and a decentralized political system ensured the power of merchant oligarchies over its cities.[5]

They are quite right in their statement that the expectation of the colonists derived from the situation in the Dutch Republic. But they disregard the fact that it was not just the colonists, but also the rulers of New Netherland who looked towards the Dutch Republic for their examples.[6] Also, Burrows and Wallace neglect to take into account how conventional Dutch practice in the seventeenth century originated, and their interpretation goes awry when they compare, as they implicitly do in the above quotation, the very elaborate state system of the Dutch Republic, in which cities over the course of centuries had obtained considerable power, with that of a fledgling colony in which local government was only just in its prime. In many aspects, the way in which relations between the city government of New Amsterdam and the provincial government of New Netherland developed can be compared with the situation in the Netherlands, not in the seventeenth century, but in the late middle ages, when towns and cities gained importance.

The conflict between colonists and Company had its origins in the early 1640s. After the lifting of the fur trade monopoly, the West India Company, as far as New Netherland was concerned, was no longer a commercial company and was left only with its governmental role.[7] It appears that the Company's *bewindhebbers* and their local officials had difficulty in adapting to their new role. At the same time, the abandonment of the fur trade monopoly attracted a new group of colonists who no longer depended on the Company for their livelihood. This group had resolved to build up a life in New Netherland and the conflicts with the Indians that had been brought about by Director Willem Kieft threatened their interests. The result was that a number of them turned against the Company and its officials. Some of the tension was alleviated by the recall of Kieft and his main adversary, the *predikant* [minister] Everardus Bogardus, but when Stuyvesant took office in 1647 the conflict flared up again. The role of spokesman for the populace was taken over by Adriaen van der Donck, well known for his 1655 *Description of New Netherland*.[8] In 1649, he was one of the three delegates of the colonists to the States General. One of the requests of the delegates was the institution in New Netherland of 'a competent civil government, such as your High Mightinesses will deem advisable to apply to this province, having something in common with the laudable government of our fatherland.'[9]

The States General as usual delegated the matter to a committee, which on April 11, 1650 produced a 'Provisional order respecting the government, preservation and peopling of New Netherland,' which was very much in favor of the colonists. The committee advised the States General to recall Stuyvesant and to establish in New Amsterdam, 'a civil government, consisting of a *schout*, two *burgemeesters* and five *schepenen*.'[10] For several reasons, treatment of the document was delayed by more than two years.[11] On April 27, 1652, the States General did however, decide to issue an order to recall Stuyvesant, which is a clear indication of its intentions. Both this measure and the final ratification of the 'Provisional Order' were thwarted by the outbreak of the First Anglo-Dutch War a month later. Many historians have nevertheless presumed that the decision to erect a court of justice in New Amsterdam was taken by the States General.[12] I do not agree, although it can not be denied that pressure from their High Mightinesses played a role. Three weeks earlier, on April 4, 1652, the two *bewindhebbers* of the Amsterdam chamber charged with keeping the correspondence, David van Baerle and Jacob Pergens, wrote in a letter to New Netherland:

We have resolved hereby to approve your honors's proposal that your honors establish there a bench of justice formed as much as possible after the laws of this city. For this purpose we are sending printed copies relating to all benches of justice and the entire government. For the present, we believe that it will be sufficient to elect one *schout*, two *burgemeesters*, and five *schepenen*.[13]

There are several interesting points in this excerpt. First, it indicates that the decision was taken by the Amsterdam chamber prior to the decision of the States General to recall Stuyvesant. It is also clear that in taking this decision, the Amsterdam chamber, which after 1645 was solely in charge of New Netherland, followed a suggestion from the colony. In an earlier publication, I have attributed this suggestion to Stuyvesant.[14] I no longer think this is correct. The letter is clearly addressed 'Aende Hr. Directeur ende Raden van Nieu-Nederlant' [to the Lord Director and Council of New Netherland] and that indicates that it was this body of men that actually made the suggestion. Also, the wording in the original letter for 'your honor' is 'uE,' the abbreviated form which can either be singular or plural, even though in this letter it has always been translated in the singular. I think it possible that the suggestion was made by director general and council in a letter sent to the *bewindhebbers* in September 1651, which has not survived.[15] By that time relations between the Company officials in the colony and the Nine Men, an advisory body of the populace, had considerably improved. In 1650, most of the Nine Men were still opponents of the Company. But at the end of that year, the director general and council had not accepted their nomination and appointed six new members more favorable to them.[16] Of the members of the Nine Men from 1647 through 1650, none were left in office by 1652. This deliberate policy of the director general and council to purge the Nine Men of opponents of the Company had created a new political atmosphere in which it was considered safe to grant New Amsterdam further prerogatives. Of the nine new members of 1652, five were appointed a year later in the new seven-man body of *burgemeesters* and *schepenen*.[17]

A second point deriving from the letter of April 4, 1652 concerns the form of the government: 'one *schout*, two *burgemeesters*, and five *schepenen*.' This follows the suggestions made to the States General three years earlier. The similarity in itself should not surprise us. This form of government was usual in Holland and it would have been surprising if another form had been chosen, especially as throughout the history of New Netherland the fatherland was always the example to be followed. The suggestion of the director general and council did not so much concern the form of the future government of New Amsterdam, but rather the timing of its establishment.

The third point concerns the order to follow 'as much as possible ... the laws of this city,' meaning Amsterdam. When we look closer at the municipal charter the similarities between Amsterdam and New Amsterdam become even clearer.

The Municipal Charter

As indicated above, the charter was promulgated on 2 February 1653.[18] The choice of date itself is significant. Since 1399 and perhaps even earlier February 2nd, Candlemas had been the traditional day on which the *burgemeesters* in Amsterdam took office, having been elected the night before.[19] The director general and council took their instruction to follow Amsterdam customs very literally in choosing this day to establish a court of justice in New Amsterdam.

The first *burgemeesters* and *schepenen* were selected by the director general and council. For the city government only persons qualified who were 'honorable, reasonable, intelligent' and 'well-to-do.' Opponents of the Company were explicitly excluded. Candidates had to be either native born, which of course very few were in the colony at this stage, or had to have been burghers for at least seven years, following the laudable customs of Amsterdam. A third possibility was that they had been born in the Dutch Republic. Also, magistrates had to be 'promoters and professors of the Reformed religion, as in conformity to the word of God and the regulations of the synod of Dordrecht it is at present taught in the churches of the United Netherlands and here in this country.'

A difference between local courts elsewhere in New Netherland and the new court in New Amsterdam was the division of duties between *burgemeesters* and *schepenen*. The *burgemeesters* had administrative and legislative, rather than judicial, duties, and their tasks included the oversight of building regulations, and 'public buildings, such as churches, schools, a court house, weigh house, charitable institutions, dock, pier, bridges' et cetera. To pay for the upkeep the city government was allowed to levy reasonable taxes, which had to be approved by the director general and council. If the *burgemeesters* saw the need for such offices as orphan masters, church masters, surveyors, and fire wardens, they could report to director general and council, and, if approved, could submit a double nomination from which the higher authority would select new officers.

The *schepenen* were in charge of judicial matters. Although in Amsterdam *burgemeesters* had no judicial authority, in New Amsterdam they were to preside over the meetings of the *schepenen* in which they had a casting vote. The judicial authority of *burgemeesters* and *schepenen* included civil jurisdiction, such as cases of debt or of slander. This was in fact a continuation of the previous situation with the Nine Men, who had since 1647 meted out civil justice.[20] Appeal to the director general and council was possible in civil cases exceeding a hundred guilders,[21] except when the parties had agreed to subject themselves to arbitration, which in essence was an out-of-court settlement, presided over by the two *burgemeesters* with whomever they invited to join them.

In criminal matters, the power of *burgemeesters* and *schepenen* was limited to lower jurisdiction, 'consisting of acts, threats, fights or wounding.' Again, appeal to the director general and council, who also dealt with more severe criminal cases, was possible. The charter specifies the procedures to be used, including regulations for defaults and fines. The *burgemeesters* and *schepenen* would render justice 'according to the written laws of our fatherland, especially, as far as is possible and the nature of the case will permit, according to the laudable customs and ordinances of the city of Amsterdam and the ordinances issued by the director general and council.' In criminal cases tried before the New Amsterdam court, the *schout* would conduct the inquiries and act as prosecutor. When erecting the court in New Amsterdam, director general and council decided that 'until further order,' the *fiscaal* would represent the *schout* of the city. The troubles arising from this were manifold, as I will show later.[22]

The delegation of administrative duties to the *burgemeesters* was an extension of the previous situation with the Nine Men. When instituted in 1647 they were allowed to advise on the erection of public buildings and on the required taxes, but they played no further role. By 1653, New Amsterdam acquired the authority to manage its own affairs, albeit within the limits circumscribed by director general and council. That director general and council were the higher authority is also indicated by the fact that they appointed the first *burgemeesters* and *schepenen*. Historians who attributed the decision to erect a court of justice in New Amsterdam to the States General have seen in this first appointment a violation of the 'Provisional order' of 1650. Again, I do not agree. The 'Provisional order' did not call for any nomination or reference to popular opinion, and, in any case, it was never ratified. Although in many cities in Holland the magistrates had obtained the right to nominate and sometimes even appoint their successors, withholding that right from New Amsterdam, at least for the time being, makes sense when we take a closer look at how city rights in Holland had developed.

City Rights in Holland
In medieval times, most of the provinces in the Netherlands were ruled by noblemen, like the Count of Holland and the Duke of Gelderland. Their power was considerable, but it was also limited by the legal thinking of their age. The prerogatives of the overlord en-

ded where the rights of the subjects began. Needless to say, the boundaries were rather fuzzy and subject to adaptation according to changes in the balance of power. Generally speaking, the laws promulgated by the higher authority could not conflict with existing rights. New rulers, when sworn in, had to take an oath to uphold the privileges and freedoms previously granted. This applied for instance to matters of finance, taxation requiring the consent of the subjects. Foreign policy, war and peace, protection of the church and some parts of criminal and civil jurisdiction were also regarded as the exclusive domain of the overlord.

Although the rituals surrounding the swearing in of new sovereigns included affirmations of the obedience of the subjects and of the upholding of privileges by the overlord, privileges were by no means sacrosanct. The city of Ghent discovered as much, when revolting against Charles the Bold in 1467 and against Charles V in 1540. Ghent was stripped of its privileges and had to endure a citadel with a garrison within its city walls. This development, the ebb and flow of relations between higher and lower authorities, has been termed the 'Great Tradition of urban revolt' by Boone and Prak in their 1995 article, in which they juxtapose it with a 'Little tradition,' the revolts of burghers against urban elites.[23]

Nevertheless, the general trend, kindled by the growing economic importance of cities, was of a gradual devolution of powers from higher to lower authorities. Yet, within the seventeen provinces of the Netherlands, supreme sovereignty remained in the hands of the overlord. By the sixteenth century, all of the overlordships had been assembled in one hand: that of the house of Burgundy/Habsburg. The Dutch Revolt, in which protection of local privileges played an important role alongside religious considerations, changed this situation. As a result of the abjuration of Philip II by the States General in 1581, sovereignty over each of the provinces devolved to the States of this province, at least theoretically. In a practice contested over the course of years, sovereign powers rested for a part with the States General and for a part with the provincial States of which in most cases the largely autonomous cities were voting members.[24]

The exemptions and privileges these cities had acquired were an amalgam accumulated over time, covering a multitude of topics, such as powers of local government, the right of yearly markets, or the freedom to erect city defenses. Commonly, the overlord kept some influence on the composition of city governments by directly appointing the magistrates, sometimes from a double nomination. But there were exceptions. For instance in Amsterdam the *burgemeesters* were appointed by a body comprised of previous *burgemeesters* and *schepenen*. In other cities the *burgemeesters* were appointed by the city council. The *schout*, the chief judicial officer, was in most cases still directly appointed by the sovereign. So, the *schout* of Leiden was appointed by the States of Holland from a nomination drawn up by the *burgemeesters*. 25

Although the rights granted to cities are usually called city rights, it was not the grant that made the city. Rights were only granted to communities that in some way were distinct from the surrounding villages. The size of the population, the density of buildings, and the economic and military role were important factors. So, the granting of rights was a formal recognition of the existing urban character of a locality. Another important point is that the rights were acquired over a number of years. The formation of cities in Holland was a development that took place over the course of several centuries.[26]

New Amsterdam

How does this translate to New Amsterdam? For Dutch colonies, sovereignty rested with the States General. The States General had, by granting a charter in 1621, delegated some of its power to the West India Company, which in turn transferred some of its administrative powers to their appointed officials, the director general and his council. Finally, director general and council appointed the magistrates of New Amsterdam, to whom they also transferred some prerogatives. In principle, the whole situation was the same as in other places in New Netherland with its own bench of justice. 27 But New Amsterdam was different, not just in the size of its population and its economic importance as the main harbor and staple of the colony, but also in the extent to which the city was granted privileges over the years. These privileges cover a multitude of subjects: civil and criminal jurisdiction, nomination and appointments of city magistrates and officials, taxation, economic policy and matters of defense, for instance. But the two subjects which were most essential to the relation between city and province are first, that of the appointment of *burgemeesters* and *schepenen* and the division of tasks between them, and, second, the thorny issue of criminal jurisdiction, and the problem of the *schout* and the *fiscaal*.

First then, appointments in New Amsterdam. In 1653, the power to appoint *burgemeesters* and *schepenen* was retained by director general and council, as outlined in the charter. The first body of magistrates was selected directly by the provincial government. Unlike most of the villages in New Netherland, *burgemeesters* and *schepenen* had not even been granted the privilege of nominating a double number from which their successors would be chosen and it is clear that they did not like the situation. They submitted several petitions to the director general and council, but these were turned down for several reasons. When, in 1656, the privilege of nomination was finally granted, it was on the condition that 'fit persons ... who are acceptable rather to the high administration than to opponents' would be nominated.[28] Another condition was that nominations would be drawn up in the presence of a representative of director general and council. Both conditions turned out to be bones of contention.

The general procedure was as follows. At the end of January each year a day was fixed for the meeting on which the nomination would be made. Prior to that day, each of the *burgemeesters* and *schepenen* would compile his own nomination, without any communication about it with others. At the meeting, all votes were counted in the presence of a representative of director general and council and the definitive nomination would be relayed in writing to the provincial government, which would make the appointment on the 2nd of February, Candlemas, the same day as in Amsterdam.

But the first time things went wrong. The nomination drawn up on 18 January 1656 in the opinion of director general and council listed some people 'who because of previous discord may not be acceptable either to the director general and council or the lords superiors.' Hence, the nomination was refused in its entirety, and only an appointment for the two vacant *schepenen* places was made. The city government was not informed of the true reasons for this. Instead they were told that director general and council had taken the decision 'for important reasons inducing them thereto.' By not fulfilling the conditions, the city government had rendered the nomination invalid.[29]

The same decision was taken two years later, but in that year the circumstances were different. The nomination had been drawn up in the absence of *schout* Nicasius de Sille as representative of the provincial government. Worse still, the representative had not even been officially invited. So director general and council returned the nomination, ordering *burgemeesters* and *schepenen* to draw up a new one. The city government was slightly surprised, but nevertheless did as requested. In the presence of the *schout* exactly the same nomination was drawn up and subsequently appointments were made.[30]

Such squabbles over the correct procedure may seem petty to the modern mind, but they were an essential way of delineating power in the seventeenth century. For the provincial government acknowledgment of the procedure meant acceptance of its overlordship, whereas for the city government it implied recognition of the privileges it had obtained. It is also important to realize that such formalistic and ritualistic struggles were a far cry from the much more vehement conflict that was raging between Kieft and the community in the 1640s. This is emphasized by the fact that in the 1640s the conflict encompassed every possible subject, whereas in the 1650s run-ins were confined to specific topics and both parties cooperated in relative harmony in other matters.

Jurisdiction
The same development as in the matter of nomination and appointment (a gradual devolution of privileges from higher to lower authorities) can be found in the bounds of the jurisdiction of New Amsterdam. In criminal matters, the power of the city government was confined to the low jurisdiction. This meant that *burgemeesters* and *schepenen* acted as a *kleine bank van justitie* [lower bench of justice] and tried cases of slander, insults, minor injuries et cetera. Cases of adultery, theft, blasphemy, serious injuries and manslaughter were tried before the director general and council.

In 1656 the *burgemeesters* and *schepenen* petitioned for wider powers and in response their jurisdiction was widened to include middle jurisdiction. This meant they could try all criminal matters, with the exception of capital cases, as the provincial government reserved so-called high jurisdiction for itself. The city government also obtained the privilege of corporal punishment, such as lashing and branding. In the years after that there occasionally was confusion about the extent of their jurisdiction, but whenever *burgemeesters* and *schepenen* hesitated whether a case was theirs to try, they explicitly asked the director general and council for permission, which was usually granted. The city government also received advice on the exact procedure and proper punishment.[31] Thus we have the typical early-modern situation of a single geographic area with split jurisdictions: low, middle and high. The division was emphasized by the fact that low and middle cases were brought before *burgemeesters* and *schepenen* by the *schout*, while high cases were tried by the director general and council, with the *fiscaal* acting as prosecutor.

The position of *schout* and *fiscaal* has given rise to considerable confusion, not just in the seventeenth century, but also with historians of New Amsterdam and New York City. Yet the difference is essential in understanding the relation between the provincial government and the city government. The *fiscaal* was one of the councilors, charged with defending the rights of the West India Company. That included breaches of Company regulations, such as smuggling, or contraventions of the *artikelbrief* [letter of articles, which gave rules for the behavior of Company servants]. As the income of the West India Company was derived from these rights, the *fiscaal* has sometimes been called 'a fiscal officer.' While not incorrect, this is incomplete. The rights of the Company also comprised criminal jurisdiction over New Netherland, which had been granted by the States General. When establishing local courts, parts of the criminal jurisdiction were transferred, and a *schout*, subordinate to the *fiscaal* and acting as a representative of higher authority, was appointed. Sometimes a Company official, such as a vice-director, carried out the duties of the *schout*, although he was then usually called *officier* [officer]. In appointing the *fiscaal* of New Netherland, residing in New Amsterdam, to the position of *schout* of New Amsterdam, the director general and council combined in one official two positions of different levels, with different judicial competencies.[32]

The people of New Amsterdam were confused by this, but the *burgemeesters* and *schepenen* understood it quite well and were not at all pleased, the more so because the position was occupied by the notorious Cornelis van Tienhoven, who was not much loved, to put it mildly. Already in 1653, *burgemeesters* and *schepenen* petitioned for their own *schout*, but the two positions were not separated until 1660.[33]

How difficult and sometimes intricate relations between the city government and the provincial government were can be illustrated by the incident of pulling the goose in 1654. This rather cruel pastime involved hanging up a goose between two trees with its greased neck and head downwards. Riders on horseback then attempted to pull its head off. Director general and council were opposed to the folkloric ritual, which was associated with pagan Shrovetide activities. Thus, the director general and council turned down a request of farmhands within the jurisdiction of New Amsterdam to pull the goose. The city government, on the other hand, was of the opinion that since the ritual was connived at in the Dutch Republic, it could be allowed. Even more important, *burgemeesters* and *schepenen* regarded the prohibition by director general and council as contravening their authority. They received a stern rebuke for this:

> the establishment of a lower court of justice under the name and title of either '*schout*, *burgemeesters* and *schepenen*' or 'magistrates' does in no way infringe upon or diminish the power and authority of the director-general and council to pass ordinances or issue interdicts especially if they are for the glory of God, the welfare of the inhabitants or the prevention of sin, vice, corruption and misfortunes, and the correction, fine or punishment according to the law of those who wantonly disobey them.[34]

A year later, the chance of a recurrence of the conflict was taken away in advance. Cornelis van Tienhoven, both *schout* and *fiscaal* at that time, reported to *burgemeesters* and *schepenen* that he had received intelligence that some farmhands had the intention to pull the goose. As this was forbidden by director general and council, Van Tienhoven asked the city government to act. *Burgemeesters* and *schepenen* decided that *fiscaal* Van Tienhoven would *ex officio* inform the farmhands of the prohibition. It is only one line in the minutes of the city government, but it is full of meaning. First, it is of importance that Van Tienhoven informed the city government beforehand, even though issuing a prohibition of pulling the goose was the prerogative of director general and council. By informing the city government and giving it the opportunity to act, possible aggravation was avoided, while at the same time it was subtly made clear what the division of power was: the city government did not have the power to prohibit or allow pulling the goose, but it could take action and put the prohibition of the director general and council into practice. The answer of *burgemeesters* and *schepenen* makes clear that they declined to do so. They did not ask Van Tienhoven to act in his capacity of *schout*, but specifically as *fiscaal*, thus representing the director general and council. It is a small incident that illuminates the thinking on privileges and authority in New Amsterdam.

Conclusion

For Langdon Wright it was very simple: 'New Amsterdam was controlled by the director and council anyway.'[35] This statement ignores the distinct development that was going on in the largest town of New Netherland. The institution of a municipal government in New Amsterdam marked a watershed in the relations between the citizens and the provincial government. The situation prior to 1653 had been unclear, inviting measures from both sides which were bound to antagonize the opposition and gave cause to bitter and often personal conflicts. After 1653, however, the institutional framework was much clearer and it thus provided traditional and recognized avenues for disagreements to be solved. It was by no means a situation of perfect harmony, but both parties accepted their opposite roles in the struggle between towns and overlords, handed down to them from medieval times in the 'Great tradition of urban revolt.' The gradual development of cities in the Netherlands in the late middle ages provided a recognizable model, which both the colonists and the authorities could follow.

If we take this perspective, the importance of the municipal charter New Amsterdam received in 1653 becomes clear. The upgrading of the Nine Men to a court of *schout, burgemeesters* and *schepenen* was a significant step in the development of the government of New Amsterdam, since it was the formal recognition of its status as city. In the following years, its powers and prerogatives were gradually enlarged, following the model of the development of city rights in Holland. The terminology used in 1653 already indicated the course of the development. Especially the introduction of the office of *burgemeester*, a typically urban functionary, points to the role New Amsterdam was to have in New Netherland: it would be its main city, its capital. The importance then of the 1653 charter does not lie so much in the powers it bestowed, but rather in the fact that it recognized the special role New Amsterdam would have in New Netherland, which formed the basis for the subsequent importance of New York City.

Notes

1 New York Public Library, New Netherland Papers (hereafter abbreviated as NYPL, NNP), box 1, folder 'Official promulgation of New Amsterdam as a municipality, 1653,' which contains two copies, one in the hand of Jacob Kip, the other in the hand of Hans Bontemantel. Translated in I.N. Phelps Stokes, *The Iconography of Manhattan Island 1498-1909* (New York: Robert H. Dodd, 6 vols., 1915-1928), 4: 133-135. Here and further on, the quotes from the original Dutch have in some cases been slightly modified from the published translations. I have chosen to translate the Dutch term 'directeur-generaal en raden' as 'the director general and council'.

2 On Bontemantel, see G.W. Kernkamp, ed., *De regeeringe van Amsterdam, soo in 't civiel als crimineel en militaire (1653-1672) ontworpen door Hans Bontemantel*, Werken uitgegeven door het Historisch Genootschap, derde serie, 7 ('s-Gravenhage: Martinus Nijhoff, 2 vols.,

1897), xx, lxxxvi-ciii, cxxxix.

3   E.B. O'Callaghan, *History of New Netherland, or New York under the Dutch* (New York: D. Appleton & Company, 2 vols., 2nd ed., 1855), 1: 393-394.

4   A.P.G.J. van der Linde, 'De 'Remonstrantie van Nieu-Nederlandt' (1649) en haar bijzondere betekenis voor Edmund Bailey O'Callaghan' In: E.F. van de Bilt and H.W. van den Doel, eds., *Klassiek Amerikaans: Opstellen voor A. Lammers* (Leiden 2002), 92-102 [Leidse Historische Studiën 7]; John Romeyn Brodhead, *History of the State of New York. First period, 1609-1664* (New York: Harper & Brothers, Publishers, 2nd ed., 1859), 447: 'that irrepressible spirit of civil liberty which ever animated the descendants of the Batavians.' Mariana Griswold Schuyler van Rensselaer, *History of the City of New York in the Seventeenth Century* (New York: The Macmillan Company, 2 vols., 1909), 1: 220: 'Although no people surpassed the Dutch in the love and liberty ....'

5   Edwin G. Burrows and Mike Wallace, *Gotham: A History of New York City to 1898* (New York: Oxford University Press, 1999), 62.

6   Of course, Burrows and Wallace are not alone in holding these views. See for instance Michael Kammen, *Colonial New York: A History* (New York: Oxford University Press, 1975), 51-57, and Philip L. White, 'Municipal government comes to Manhattan,' *New-York Historical Society Quarterly* 37 (1953): 146-157. Much more to the point, though less elaborate, is Alice P. Kenney, *Stubborn for Liberty: The Dutch in New York* (Syracuse: Syracuse University Press, 1975), 69-70.

7   Jaap Jacobs, *Een zegenrijk gewest. Nieuw-Nederland in de zeventiende eeuw* (Amsterdam: Samenwerkende uitgeverijen Prometheus/Bert Bakker, 1999), 132-133. This point has been made earlier by Oliver A. Rink, *Holland on the Hudson: An Economic and Social History of Dutch New York* (Ithaca, NY: Cornell University Press, 1986), 136.

8   Adriaen van der Donck, *Beschryvinge van Nieuw-Nederlant (gelijck het tegenwoordigh in staet is)* (Aemsteldam: Evert Nieuwenhof, 1655, 2nd. ed. 1656). On the conflict between Kieft and Bogardus, see Willem Frijhoff, *Wegen van Evert Willemsz. Een Hollands weeskind op zoek naar zichzelf, 1607-1647* (Nijmegen: SUN, 1995), 657-762.

9   Nationaal Archief, archives of the States General (hereafter abbreviated as Nat. Arch., SG), loketkas WIC, inv. no. 12564.30A 'Naerdere aenwijsinghe ende observatien' (26 July 1649; translated in E.B. O'Callaghan and B. Fernow, trans. and ed., *Documents Relative to the Colonial History of the State of New York* (Albany: Weed, Parsons and Company, 2 vols., 1853-1883), 1: 262-270 (hereafter abbreviated as *DRCHNY*).

10 Nat. Arch., SG, loketkas WIC, inv. no. 12564.30A 'Provisionele ordre over de regieringe, conservatie ende populatie van Nieu Nederlant' (11 April 1650; *DRCHNY* 1: 387-391).

11 For an examination of the causes of the delay, see Jaap Jacobs, 'A hitherto unknown letter of Adriaen van der Donck,' *De Halve Maen* 71 (1998): 1-6.

12 See O'Callaghan, *History of New Netherland*, 2: 192; Kammen, *Colonial New York*, 54; Dennis Maika, 'Commerce and Community: Manhattan Merchants in the Seventeenth Century' (Ph.D. dissertation, New York University 1995), 71; White, 'Municipal government,' 152.

13 New York State Archives, New York Colonial Manuscripts (hereafter abbreviated as NYSA, NYCM) 11: 53 (4 April 1652, translated in Charles T. Gehring, trans. and ed., *Correspondence 1647-1653*. New Netherland Documents Series, vol. 11 (Syracuse, NY: Syracuse University Press, 2000), 149.

14 Jacobs, *Een zegenrijk gewest*, 146.

15 In their letter of April 24, 1650, the bewindhebbers refer to letters they received 'of the 21st, 29th, and 30th of September of last year.' NYSA, NYCM 11: 53 (4 April 1652; Gehring, *Correspondence 1647-1653*, 144).

16 Nat. Arch., SG, loketkas WIC, inv. no. 12564.36 (12 September 1651; *DRCHNY* 1: 452).

17 Arent van Hattem, Marten Kregier, Paulus Leendertsz. van der Grift, Allard Anthony and Willem Beeckman. Jacobs, *Een zegenrijk gewest*, 483-484.

18 All the references to and quotes from the charter in this paragraph are from NYPL, NNP, box 1, folder 'Official promulgation of New Amsterdam as a municipality, 1653' (2 February 1653; Stokes, *Iconography*, 4: 133-136).

19 B.R. de Melker, *Oorkondenboek van Amsterdam tot 1400: supplement* (Hilversum: Verloren, 1995), 92-97. I thank Margriet de Roever for this reference. See also O. Dapper, *Historische beschryving der Stadt Amsterdam* ... (Amsterdam: Jacob van Meurs, 1663, repr. Amsterdam: Buijten & Schipperheijn, 1975), 98.

20 NYSA, NYCM 4: 335-336, 'Instruction for the Nine Men', 26 September 1647; translated in Arnold J.F. van Laer, trans. and ed., *Council Minutes, 1638-1649*. New York Historical Manuscripts: Dutch. Vol. 4 (Baltimore: Genealogical Publishing Co., Inc., 1974), 440-441.

21 This amount is twice that mentioned in the document of 11 April 1650.

22 This passage has benefitted greatly from discussions with Dr. Martha Dickinson Shattuck.

23 M. Boone and M. Prak, 'Rulers, patricians and burghers: the Great and the Little traditions of urban revolt in the Low Countries,' in K. Davids and J. Lucassen, eds., *A Miracle Mirrored. The Dutch Republic in European perspective* (Cambridge: Cambridge University Press, 1995), 99-134. The term was first used by Blockmans in 1988. See also H.G. Koenigsberger, *Monarchies, States Generals and Parliaments: The Netherlands in the Fifteenth and Sixteenth Centuries* (Cambridge: Cambridge University Press, 2001), 1-15, 20-24.

24 Jonathan I. Israel, *The Dutch Republic: Its Rise, Greatness and Fall, 1477-1806* (Oxford: Oxford University Press, 1995, 2nd ed. 1998), 276 ff. Cf. D. Merwick, *Possessing Albany, 1630-1710: The Dutch and English Experiences* (Cambridge: Cambridge University Press, 1990), 4, who claims that 'the people of the Netherlands had vested sovereign power in great trading cities.'

25 Christopher R. Friedrichs, *The Early Modern City 1450-1750* (London: Longman, 1995), 51-58; Steven Rowan, 'Urban communites: the rulers and the ruled,' in Thomas A. Brady Jr., Heiko A. Oberman, James D. Tracy, eds., *Handbook of European History, 1400-1600. Late Middle Ages, Renaissance, and Reformation. Vol. 1 Structures and assertions.* (Leiden: E.J. Brill, 1994), 197-229; S. Groenveld et alii, *De kogel door de kerk? De Opstand in de Nederlanden 1559-1609* (Zutphen: Walburg Pers, 2nd ed., 1983), 14-15, 21-23; Antheun Janse, 'Een in zichzelf verdeeld rijk. Politiek en bestuur van de tiende tot het begin van de vijftiende eeuw,' in Thimo de Nijs and Eelco Beukers eds., *Geschiedenis van Holland. Vol 1. Tot 1572* (Hilversum: Verloren, 2002), 69-102, there 91-95.

26 J.W. Marsilje, 'Bestuur en rechtswezen,' in J.W. Marsilje, ed., *Leiden. De geschiedenis van een Hollandse stad. Deel I. Leiden tot 1574* (Leiden: Stichting Geschiedschrijving Leiden, 2002), 59-93, there 59-61. See also Reinout Rutte, *Stedenpolitiek en stadsplanning in de Lage Landen (12de-13de eeuw)* (Zutphen: Walburg Pers, 2002).

27 For local government in New Netherland in general, see Langdon G. Wright, 'Local government and central authority in New Netherland,' *New-York Historical Society Quarterly* 42 (1973): 7-29; Albert E. McKinley, 'English and Dutch towns of New Netherland,' *American Historical Review* 6 (1900): 1-18; Martha Dickinson Shattuck, 'The Dutch and English on Long Island: an uneasy alliance,' *De Halve Maen* 68-4 (1995): 80-85. Shattuck's article is a revision of the earlier work of Wright and McKinley.

28 NYSA, NYCM 6: 222-223 (18 January 1656; translated in Charles T. Gehring, trans. and ed., *Council Minutes 1655-1656*. New Netherland Documents Series, vol. 6 (Syracuse, NY: Syracuse University Press, 1995), 182-183.

29 NYSA, NYCM 6: 266-267 (1 and 2 February 1656; Gehring, *Council Minutes 1655-1656*, 213). Unfortunately, the names of these unacceptable people were not recorded.

30 New York Municipal Archives, Old Dutch Records 2: 172-174 (31 January and 1 February 1658; translated in Berthold Fernow, trans. and ed., *The Records of New Amsterdam from 1653 to 1674 anno domini*. 7 vols. (New York: Knickerbocker Press, 1897, repr. Baltimore: Genealogical Publishing Company, 1976), 2: 322-323).

31 NYSA, NYCM 8: 299 (20 December 1656; untranslated); NYSA, NYCM 8: 300 (21 December 1656; translated in E.B. O'Callaghan, trans., *Laws and Ordinances of New Netherland, 1636-1674* (Albany: Weed, Parsons and Company, 1868), 268-269). Copies of these documents can be found in NYMA, ODR 2, p. 101 (20 and 21 December 1656; *RNA* 2: 251-252). See also: NYMA, ODR 2, p. 455 (23 January 1660; *RNA* 3: 110-111); NYSA, NYCM 9: 29 (15 January 1660; untranslated); NYSA, NYCM 9: 33 (15 and 21 January 1660; untranslated).

32 To complicate matters further, in New Netherland historiography, though not in the sources, the term *schout-fiscaal* is often used, both prior to 1653 and after 1660. It is only for the years 1653 through 1660, when one man combined the positions of *fiscaal* of the province and *schout* of New Amsterdam, that any justification exists for using the term *schout-fiscaal*. Even then, the sources do not use the combination but refer to either *schout* or *fiscaal*, according to the capacity in which he was acting.

33 The *burgemeesters* and *schepenen* preferred to appoint their own man, but were willing to settle for the privilege of nominating two candidates. Director general and council referred this request to their superiors in Amsterdam, who quickly dismissed it with the argument that 'here in this country all Lords of Manors reserve such patronage to themselves.' NYSA, NYCM 12: 3 (18 May 1654; *DRCHNY* 14: 262. Cornelis van Tienhoven remained as *schout* and *fiscaal* until 1656, when he was succeeded in both positions by Nicasius de Sille. New Amsterdam did not get its own *schout* until 1660, when Pieter Tonneman was appointed as *schout*. Nicasius de Sille remained *fiscaal*.

34 NYSA, NYCM 5: 221-223 (26 February 1654; translated in Ch.T. Gehring, trans. and ed., *Council Minutes, 1652-1654*. New York Historical Manuscripts Dutch, vol. 5 (Baltimore: Genealogical Publishing Company, 1983), 119).

35 Wright, 'Local government,' 14.

Boudewijn Bakker

EMPORIUM OR EMPIRE?
PRINTED METAPHORS OF A MERCHANT METROPOLIS

In the previous contribution to this volume, Jaap Jacobs gives a highly informative analysis and a convincing interpretation of the famous charter of February 2, 1653, in which the 'town' of Nieuw Amsterdam was granted self-government to a certain extent by the installation of a board of *burgemeesters* and *schepenen*. In this essay Jacobs focuses on the contents of the charter, after a detailed account of its antecedents. However, not only the content deserves special attention, but also the procedure which led to this charter, a procedure in which the self-image of 'old' Amsterdam plays an interesting role.[1] I think this – primae facie rather strange – procedure can be better understood when we take into account the general attitude of Amsterdam as mother-city towards her American daughter-town as well as the attitude of the Dutch Republic towards her overseas possessions.

Amsterdam's seventeenth-century self-image as an international power was not only expressed in official and semi-official written documents such as city-histories and laudatory poems but also in pictorial form. An unusual but highly interesting visual source is a particular type of picture which was very popular at the time, especially in Amsterdam: 'self-portraits' of the city in the form of three-dimensional maps, birds' eye views and especially so-called *stadsprofielen* or 'city profile views', views of the whole city in its full grandeur, not from the top down, as in maps, but from the front. These self-portraits of the city could be painted or drawn, but most of them have been preserved as large-scale prints, consisting of four, six, or even twelve different wood blocks or copper plates. The more ambitious issues of these maps and profiles bore impressive titles and allegorical decorations which in fact form part of the whole portrait concept and which are meant to underline the rhetorical function of the print as a city portrait.[2]

Government and Private Interests
The opening words of the charter reveal a peculiarity about the granting agency: 'The director general and Council of New Netherland hereby make known that the Hon. directors of the chartered West India Company, chamber at Amsterdam, lords and patroons of this province, have thought fit... to favor this new and growing town of New Amsterdam... with a court of justice... according to the laudable custom of the city of Amsterdam, name-giver to this new-developing town...' The charter does not state the director general in New Netherland, Petrus Stuyvesant, as the favoring institution, nor the central directors

of the Company, nor the States General of the Republic in The Hague, but the Amsterdam chamber of the Company.

Formally, the administrative relations between the so-called mother-city and daughter-town were indirect, complex, and not transparent. The Company was a chartered trade company, to which the States General in The Hague had granted the monopoly on trade in the Western hemisphere. The company was administered by directors or *bewindheb-bers*, who were delegated by the different local *kamers* or chambers that constituted the company. The most powerful chamber was that of Amsterdam, since Amsterdam was the most powerful city in the States of Holland, and the States of Holland the most influential within the States General. The original *octrooi* of the West Indian Company granted the company not only the monopoly on trade, but also commissioned it to keep law and order in the factories and settlements of the company. In the case of New Netherland, however, the central management of the Company, the *Heeren XIX*, delegated this right and task to the Chamber of Amsterdam, the city which from the beginning had invested more than any other town in the commercial exploration of New Netherland.[3] Within the Amsterdam Chamber, New Netherland matters and the correspondence with the local government in the colony were delegated to a more or less permanent commission consisting of two or three *bewindhebbers*. They probably prepared the decisions made by the Chamber and by the *Heren XIX*, but in commercial and political affairs of minor importance they could intervene immediately in New Netherland.[4]

This laborious construction may explain the complex pre-history of the charter. Since 1639, director Willem Kieft's harsh and ill-judged dealing with the Indians had provoked a series of bloody and devastating confrontations between native Americans and the colonists, which fanned the flame of tension between the colonists and the director as representative of the WIC and the States General.

In 1643, the council of *Acht Man* (Eight Men), which had been installed by Kieft as a representative body to negotiate with the colonists, started to bypass Governor Kieft and wrote several letters to the *Heeren XIX*, the States General and the Amsterdam Chamber, begging for military and financial support against the Indians. Amsterdam repeatedly refused to come to their aid, claiming lack of financial means. Eventually, pressed by the States General, the *Heeren XIX* decided to recall Kieft and to replace him by Pieter Stuyvesant, who arrived in 1647. Within a short period of time, however, the story repeated itself: The college of *Nine Men*, representing the colonists and appointed by Stuyvesant, first wrote letters to The Hague and Amsterdam and then, in 1649, even sent a delegation to Holland headed by Adriaen van der Donck. They pleaded their cause directly before the States General and requested a civil government in New Netherland, which was specified as a government 'corresponding to the government of our fatherland.'

This time, the States General delegated the matter to the permanent committee for West Indian Affairs. In 1650, they advised to recall Stuyvesant and to establish a new and broader advisory board or *Raad* (Council) next to the Director general, consisting of company officials and colonists. Apart from this, they advised to install also a local administrative body with some degree of self-governing competence. This was to be established, however, not in the colony as a whole – as was requested – but only in New Amsterdam. The board should consist of *burgemeesters*, *schepenen* (aldermen) and a *schout* (sheriff).

No documents about the next two years of the case have been preserved, but in April

1652 two important letters were sent. First, the States General officially informed the Amsterdam Chamber in a short letter that they had decided to recall Pieter Stuyvesant. The reason for this single action probably was that in this way, the States General hoped to realize at least part of the governmental changes that they wished to introduce in the colony. In fact even this reorganization was never effectuated, partly due to systematic and secret obstruction by the Amsterdam Chamber, partly caused by the outbreak of the First Anglo-Dutch War.

An earlier letter, which the Amsterdam Chamber had sent three weeks before to director general Stuyvesant and his council had much more effect. This letter begins with the statement (I paraphrase): 'We have resolved to approve your honor's proposal to establish a bench of justice after the laws of this city.' It is the announcement of the local government, which would be officially installed about one year later, in February 1653.

The combination of these two letters is highly interesting. It seems to imply that Stuyvesant and his Council of WIC-officials on one side, and the Amsterdam Chamber on the other, who both had systematically opposed any form of official self-government in the colony (as since several years had been the wish of the States General), now had agreed about creating a most limited independent body[5] One gets the impression that in this way, they tried – and in the end, succeeded – to prevent the realization of the much more 'democratic' solution suggested by the States General West Indian Committee two years before.

This procedure may seem strange but is in fact understandable and in accordance with the rules and practices in the Republic. Recalling the director general in the colony was thought to be a matter of general importance and the prerogative of the States General, but the decision about installing some form of home rule was in fact left to the Company, which in its turn delegated it to its most influential member, the Amsterdam Chamber. And yet, the situation was remarkable. In short: The central government of the Republic, directly or indirectly, delegated a matter of purely political character related to one of the largest colonies within the power radius of the Republic to just one local chapter of a private commercial organization.

A second fact of interest is that there is no indication whatsoever that any local Amsterdam political institution was in any way involved in this affair. Also this is a remarkable feature, since the question at stake concerned the political organization of a rather large community, which at that time was the only direct colonial daughter of Amsterdam. Even the judicial form of the new local government in New Amsterdam, which was expressely based on that of 'Old' Amsterdam, seems to have been not much more than an expression of local patriotism of one or two interested local managers of a commercial enterprise.

This seems all the more strange considering that it happened at the very moment that the Republic, with Amsterdam as its undisputable center, was reaching the position of an international political power. In 1648 the Treaty of Munster had formally institutionalized this position. How can we explain the paradox of a relatively influential political power like Amsterdam showing so little interest in controlling and developing the colony that was most closely related?

Competing Ideals

To understand this, we have to realize that right from the beginning, the Republic of the United Netherlands was characterized by a permanent and even structural tension between two different political ideals. One of these ideals aimed at an unified nation with one national church, a strong army, permanent boundaries and a size as large as was necessary to guarantee peace, welfare and security for all its inhabitants. This ideal, which also implied advocating international missionary work and religiously founded colonization, was embraced by the House of Orange, many immigrants from the Southern Netherlands, most members of the nobility, and the leaders of the Reformed Church.[6] The other ideal aimed at the maintenance of the traditional rights or privileges of the cities and at freedom of trade, enterprise and religion, to guarantee peace, welfare and liberty at least within the central and most influential towns and provinces. Instead of military power they trusted in power based on wealth. This second ideal was mostly represented by the ruling classes in the bigger cities and towns of Holland, with Amsterdam as their undisputed leader.

Not only in the States General but also in the international companies did these two ideals cause permanent tension at least during the first half of the century, not only within the central board of directors but also in the different chambers. In the Amsterdam chamber, the first ideal was – roughly speaking – represented by the 'colonization party', the second one by the 'trade party'.

The colonization party among the Amsterdam *bewindhebbers* advocated a policy of encouraging and subsidizing the settlement of farmers and associated professions, in order to furnish not only food for the Dutch community but after some time also cereals for other colonies and wood and wheat for the European homeland. Probably it was in this same vein that the original charter stipulated that the director in New Netherland had to treat the Indians with politeness and to grant equal justice to Indians and Europeans, in civil as well as in criminal cases.[7]

The trade party wished to concentrate on commercial activities, especially on the fur trade. As a consequence, it tried to maintain the Company's fur trade monopoly as long as possible, to get the largest return on its investments within the shortest possible period of time. Given the high costs of long-term investments in systematic colonization, the trade party wished to limit the Company's local presence to a few small forts to secure safe trade between the company merchants and the Indians. If this minimum protection meant that the colony could be rather easily conquered by the English, it also meant that in that case the financial loss would be low.

About 1630, the acute conflict between these parties was temporarily soothed by the founding of *patroonschappen*, which functioned as a kind of private colonies within the Company's territory. However, most of these failed and at the same time the colonization party in the Amsterdam Chamber lost its seats to the trade party.[8] After 1645 the *Heeren XIX* completely delegated the administration of New Netherland to the Amsterdam Chamber, so that, the colony was managed in the spirit of the commercially thinking share-holders and directors even more than before.[9] In daily practice this meant the strong support of a high-handed central administration and little consideration for the interests of the colonists, let alone those of the Indians. It is true that in 1656, under direct pressure of the outbreak of the Scandinavian War, the city of Amsterdam founded the *patroonschap*-like colony Nieuwer Amstel on the Delaware, to provide the city with wheat and masts, but after three years the city government already regretted its own thoughtlessness and tried to sell the city-colony back to the Company.[10]

Amsterdam's Self-Image

To understand this policy of extreme restriction in colonial affairs, we have to return in time to the early history of Amsterdam. In the thirteenth century, a small group of merchants and craftsmen settled on a small strip of land in the middle of a large area of nearly uninhabitable wetlands, at the mouth of the river Amstel. Amsterdam was, and for several centuries stayed, a water-town in the most literal sense of the word. As a place to live, this island between sea and fens was highly uncomfortable, but in commercial terms it turned out to have been a golden choice. In 1275, the count of Holland granted the citizens of this young settlement the privilege to travel everywhere within the province of Holland without having to pay toll. During the sixteenth century, thanks to her maritime trade, Amsterdam grew from a prosperous provincial town to one of the most important

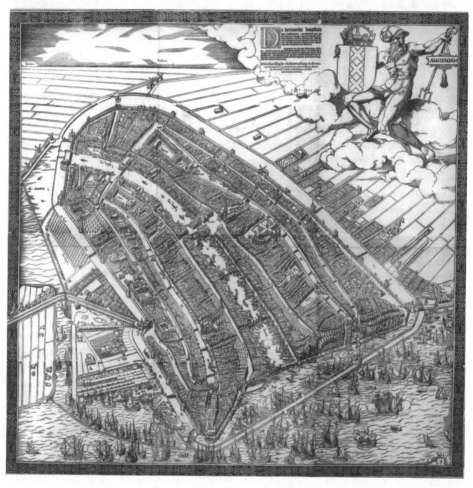

1. Cornelis Anthonisz, *Bird's eye map of Amsterdam*, wood cut, 1544.
Amsterdam, Gemeentearchief

2. Willem Jansz Blaeu (publ.), *Profile view of Amsterdam*, engraving, 1606 (detail).
Amsterdam Gemeentearchief

commercial centers of the world, and around 1600 she outstripped even her most famous rivaling cities, Venice and Antwerp.

Of these two cities, Venice was by far the oldest and also the most famous one. The young and inconspicuous but highly ambitious provincial town in Holland deliberately chose the old and venerable city of Venice as her 'role model'. This is easily understandable, for apart from the scale, the similarities between the two were conspicuous indeed, not only in geography, but also in political, economical and cultural respects. Just like Venice, Amsterdam was founded not by a prince or king but by the people and that in the middle of marshlands near the sea. Both cities based their wealth and power on a free-trade privilege from their political superior. Both were real water cities, with canals instead of streets. Both cherished a famous local school of painting. Moreover, both cities were the center of a republic in a world dominated by kingdoms, 'foxes among wolves', as the saying went. And last but not least, both cities boasted that their wealth and fame was founded not on territorial expansion by military force, but on 'peaceful' maritime trade and transportation.

'Just like Venice, Amsterdam has been drawn with great costs out of the marshes, and therefore she is very strong by her natural condition and situation,' an anonymous chronicler wrote already shortly before 1500. In 1526, a civil servant of Emperor Charles V remarked: 'that the town of Amsterdam is a young and daily growing Venice in commerce.' From the late sixteenth century onwards, Amsterdam figured in the semi-official city chronicles and city guides as 'the new Venice' or 'Venice of the North'.[11]

It is this image that we see reflected in the decorations of the large and monumental self-portraits in the shape of printed city plans and city profile views, which were published in large quantities from about 1550 until far into the eighteenth century. In the famous map of Cornelis Anthonisz from 1544 (ill. 1), Amsterdam is portrayed from the sea side, with numerous ships in the foreground and with the sea-god Neptune as a kind of secularized patron saint.[12] In the text, Amsterdam is advertised as 'the vermaerde coop-stadt', that is

3. Claes Jansz Visscher, *Profile view of Amsterdam*, etching, 1611. Amsterdam, Gemeentearchief

4. Idem, detail

'the famous town of commerce'. This picture was most probably inspired by a large bird's eye view of Venice dated 1500, in which Neptune is placed in the waters in front of this city but in which the air is dominated by his colleague Mercury, the god of transportation and commerce.[13]

In 1606, three years before the voyage of Henry Hudson to the West and the discovery of Manhattan, Willem Jansz Blaeu published a highly ambitious profile view of Amsterdam, measuring more than two meters.[14] The composition gives an impressive view of a city that seems to rise out of the waters, but more interesting to us is what we see in the air. On the left and right side, beautifully framed Latin poems by the well-known humanist

5. Joost Danckerts (publ.), *Profile view of Amsterdam*, engraving, ca. 1670.
Amsterdam, Gemeentearchief

6. Balthasar Florisz, *Map of Amsterdam*, engraving, 1625 (detail).
Amsterdam, Gemeentearchief

7. Jacopo de'Barbari, *Bird's eye map of* Venice, wood cut, 1500 (detail).
Amsterdam, Rijksmuseum

BASILICÆ AMSTELADAMENSIS *confpectus posterior.* | t Stadhuis van Amſteldam van achteren.
Pet: Schenk exc: Amsteled: cum Privil

8. Petrus Schenk (publ.), *The West façade of the Amsterdam Town Hall*, engraving, ca. 1690. Amsterdam, Gemeentearchief

Petrus Scriverius praise the various virtues of the city. In the center, under the Latinized name *Amstelodamum*, the maiden of Amsterdam is sitting with a ship in her right hand, surrounded by several anonymous water gods and nymphs and flanked by Mercury and Neptune (ill. 2). From both sides, merchants and other people from all over the world offer her their precious products. Among them we can discern at least two West-Indians, recognizable by their typical feather head-dress. A profile from 1611, by Claes Jansz Visscher, shows again two Indians among the international crowd, but this time the accompanying text stipulates exactly the products that they present to Amsterdam: sugar, dying wood, tobacco, gold and silver, pearls, precious stones, feathers and parrots (ill. 3, 4).[15]

These two prints belong to one of the two main types of large city profiles, the one that we could call the 'allegorical' type. The other one could be called the 'textual' type. That second type is characterized by a monumental title banner running above and parallel to the picture. The first example dates from 1614, but the one reproduced here dates from the third quarter of the century (ill. 5).[16] The usual form of the title text is more or less like this one. In translation: 'portrait of Amsterdam, the most famous *emporium* (or 'staple-town') of entire Europe and the first city of Holland.' Both traditions were fused by the Amsterdam engraver Balthasar Florisz in his enormous plan dated 1625 and counting 1.40 x 1.60 cm. This map is titled *Amstelredamum emporium Hollandiae primaria totius Europae celeberrimum* ('Amsterdam, first city of Holland, the most famous *emporium* of entire Europe'), and one of the cartouches again shows the city maiden being honored by – among other people – West Indians (ill. 6).[17]

The key word in these titles is *emporium*, which literally means 'staple-town', but in a

9. Hubert Quellien, *The West pediment of the Amsterdam Town Hall*, etching, 1665-1669 (detail).
Amsterdam, Gemeentearchief

wider sense 'the center of an international commercial network'. Just like the allegorical figures of Neptune and Mercury, this title band with the term *emporium* already had a long tradition when it was first introduced in the Amsterdam city portraits. The first time it was used in this connection was in the famous city portrait of Venice from 1500, where it envelops the figure of Neptune (ill. 7). The text reads *Mercurius preceteris huic fauste emporiis illustro*, that is: 'I Mercury shine favorably on this *emporium* above all other *emporiums*.'[18] The second time, we read it on the first city portrait of Antwerp, dated 1515. Here, the text reads *Antverpia mercatorium emporium*, that is 'Antwerp, the *emporium* of the merchants.'[19]

We may conclude from these few examples that at least from about 1500 Venice advertised itself not as the capital of an empire but as an *emporium*. The tradition was soon to be shared by Antwerp. Somewhat later, also Amsterdam admiringly adopted the so-called 'myth of Venice' as its commercial and political ideal. In the course of the seventeenth century, however, when Amsterdam had surpassed Venice in wealth and power, Venice gradually became less popular as an ideal image of Amsterdam. And at last, around mid-century, Amsterdam adopted – apart from Venice – another and a much more illustrious role model: the republic of ancient Rome. In 1648 the Treaty of Munster marked the end of eighty years of war and the formal acceptance of the Republic and Amsterdam as an international political identity. In the same year the city began the building of the new and magnificent Town Hall. In 1653, the year of the municipal charter of New Amsterdam, building and decorating were booming.[20] The front and back façades were being crowned by enormous tympanums, sculptured in stone, in which Amsterdam's position in the world was illustrated in the form of solemn allegories in strictly classical style (ill. 8). But a careful look reveals that the message of the allegories had not essentially changed. The front tympanum still shows the city maiden between Neptune and lesser sea gods, the back tympanum shows the same lady in front of a medieval trading vessel and surrounded by people of all types and kinds who pay homage in the shape of a variety of products. Here again, we discern a West Indian sitting on a half-open reed box and peacefully smoking a tobacco pipe, the pipe of peace (ill. 9). The overall theme of this central allegory is apparently to be read as *peace by trade*.

Conclusion

I return to my initial question why Amsterdam showed so little commitment to the political administration of its American daughter town and in general with its colonies and semi-colonies all over the world. The answer is that Amsterdam and also the ruling classes in the other Dutch cities had never had any serious territorial aspirations. Here the general political ideal was a world of nations peacefully living together, a world in which wealth, respect and power were the result of trade on a *mare liberum*, a worldwide network of free trade routes without tolls of any kind. In this view, war had to be accepted as a necessary evil, but only in order to secure trade and not to obtain a larger territory.

The West and East India Companies were trade companies. To secure free trade, they founded factories which had to be defended against so-called unwilling or treacherous natives. In the course of time, Europeans founded settlements in the land behind and around these trade centers, but the founding of real colonies was certainly not acclaimed by most company managers, particularly those from Amsterdam. When in due course the companies were forced by reality to administer these larger settlements and to protect them against intruders, this was done reluctantly and without any serious territorial aspirations. The more or less official pictorial self-portraits of Amsterdam show that this typical merchant's attitude was not limited to the merchant managers of the WIC and the Company's officials on the spot, but that it was shared at least by the local political government in New Amsterdam's mother city.

Notes

1 Jaap Jacobs, "To favor this new and growing city of New Amsterdam with a court of justice'. The Relations between Rulers and Ruled in New Amsterdam.' For the reconstruction of the course of events, I have used Jacobs' present essay and his book *Een zegenrijk gewest. Nieuw Nederland in de zeventiende eeuw* (Amsterdam: Bert Bakker, 1999), esp. chapter 3 (105-172).

2 Boudewijn Bakker, 'Amsterdam nell'immagine degli artisti e dei cartografi, 1550-1700,' in Cesare de Seta, ed., *Città d'Europa: Iconografia e vedutismo dal XV al XVIII secolo* (Napoli: Electa, 1997), 86-100.

3 The Reformed Church in New Netherland belonged to the *classis* of Amsterdam.

4 Jacobs, *Zegenrijk gewest*, 105-108.

5 See Jaap Jacobs essay in this volume.

6 Henk den Heijer, *De geschiedenis van de WIC* (Zutphen: Walburg Pers, 1994), 21-28.

7 Jacobs, *Zegenrijk gewest*, 110.

8 Jacobs, *Zegenrijk gewest*, 118-129.

9 The most spectacular effect of Amsterdam's and Holland's flagrant disinterest in colonisation was the loss of the rich colony of Brazil in 1654.

10 Jacobs, *Zegenrijk gewest*, 129-132.

11 E.O.G. Haitsma Mulier, *The myth of Venice and Dutch republican thought in the seventeenth century* (Assen: Van Gorcum, 1980); Boudewijn Bakker, 'Amsterdam en Venetië. Twee steden verbeeld,' in Margriet de Roever, ed., *Amsterdam: Venetië van het Noorden* (Amsterdam/The Hague: SDU Uitgeverij, 1991), 10-27; E.O.G. Haitsma Mulier, 'Aandacht voor het staatsbestel. Overeenkomst en verscheidenheid in het Republikeinse denken van de zeventiende eeuw,' in Idem, 46-65.

12 A.E. d'Ailly, *Catalogus van Amsterdamsche plattegronden* (Amsterdam: Gemeentearchief

Amsterdam, 1934), nr. 30-33.

13 Illustrated in Bakker, 'Amsterdam en Venetië,' 10.

14 A.E. d'Ailly, *Repertorium van de profielen der stad Amsterdam en van de plattegronden der schutterswijken* (Amsterdam: Gemeentearchief Amsterdam, 1953) nr. 10.

15 D'Ailly 1953, nr. 17.

16 D'Ailly 1953, resp. nr. 29 en nr. 143.

17 The map was updated and republished in 1647. D'Ailly 1934, nrs. 117, 134.

18 Juergen Schulz, 'Jacopo de' Barbari's View of Venice: Map Making, City Views, and Moralized Geography Before the Year 1500,' *The Art Bulletin* 60 (1978): 425-474.

19 Jan Van der Stock, ed., *Antwerp: Story of a Metropolis, 16th-17th century* (Gent: Snoeck-Ducaju, 1993), 154, with ill.

20 Katharine Fremantle, *The Baroque Town Hall of Amsterdam* (Utrecht: Haentjens, Dekker & Gumbert 1959); Saskia Albrecht, Otto de Ruyter, Marijke Spies e.a., eds., *Vondels Inwydinge van 't Stadthuis t'Amsterdam* (Muiderberg: Coutinho, 1982).

Simon Middleton

THE IDEA OF 'AMSTERDAM' IN NEW AMSTERDAM
AND EARLY NEW YORK

Introduction

The theme of this volume – parallel cities; the 'multifaceted relationship between Amsterdam, New Amsterdam/New York' – in many ways touches on my own research, which consist of a study of tradesmen, skilled work, and politics in New Amsterdam and early New York City. For part of this study I have investigated the ties that bound New World subjects to distant colonizing powers, such as the Dutch West India Company, at the local level of daily life and work. In New Amsterdam, and following the establishment of the municipal government in 1653, these ties comprised, amongst other things, the heterogeneous schedule of municipal regulations, privileges, and duties which developed out of the settlers' civil and judicial administration that nurtured local commercial ambitions as described in other contributions to this volume. When creating this civic order, I will argue, the Company and the settlers were in engaged in the conscious reproduction of an idealized Old World urban order – a project and an intentionality disclosed by the routine invocation of Dutch precedents and practices as justification for their actions.[1] Indeed, at different times various – and on occasion opposing – individuals and groups invoked the practices of Amsterdam, the province of Holland, and the 'fatherland' or *Patria* to justify their position or claim. Thus the topic that suggested itself to me was to inquire what might have been implied by this invocation of 'Amsterdam' and by the settlers' fascination for an idealized Old World order in the later years of New Amsterdam and early English New York.

On the face of it, pondering what the settlers in New Netherland's leading port might have meant by their invocation of Amsterdam might strike some as superfluous. New Netherland was a Dutch colony; New Amsterdam, to all intents and purposes, a Dutch town. In this respect, the settlers' adherence to the practices and precedents of Amsterdam and the United Provinces logically represented what we might call the 'Dutch influence' in early New York. However, the question becomes more complicated when one contemplates the unresolved historiographical division concerning the source and precise nature of this 'Dutch influence.'[2]

For some, the records of New Amsterdam and early New York betray ethnic Dutch sensibilities in diverse areas of colonial life, ranging from land usage, trade, legal and political practices, to attitudes towards architecture, cuisine, and fashion. Provincial patricians in

New Netherland, these scholars argue, emulated the traditions, values, and behavior of wealthy Low Countries merchants; ordinary settlers, to quote Alice Kenny, 'recreated the way of life of Dutch burghers.'[3] Moreover, others have argued, that in the decades following the 1664 English conquest this ethnic influence not only endured – influencing inheritance practices, choices of marriage partner, and devotional loyalties – but also grew stronger as 'Dutch' residents refined their ethnic sense of themselves under an, at times, oppressive English administration. According to some scholars, by the late seventeenth-century, these ethnic antipathies were such that – in the wake of England's Glorious Revolution in 1688 – Dutch city residents rose up and threw out their Stuart-appointed governors in favor of an administration headed by Jacob Leisler, a German Calvinist zealot.

So far so good. However, these findings sit uneasily with the conclusions of others who have asked, as David Cohen did first some twenty years ago, just 'How Dutch were the Dutch of New Netherland?'[4] Cohen's study of some 900 immigrants who came to the colony during the upsurge in immigration in the 1650s and '60s, found that fully half of all migrants declared their origins as outside the Netherlands – mainly from towns and rural villages laying in modern-day Germany, France, Belgium, and Denmark; moreover, only a fifth of settlers coming from the Netherlands declared Amsterdam as their origin or previous place of residence. Thus, although many immigrants passed through Amsterdam, most came from elsewhere, were of middling to low status, and had little or no experience of the Republic's greatest city and its municipal procedures and practices. Looking beyond the English conquest, other scholars of a similar mind, find that significant sections of the Dutch community – and particularly the wealthy merchants who had earlier been the most vociferous advocates of 'Dutch' liberties – quickly recognized the advantages of working with rather than against their conquerors and adapted to English legal and political ways. As A.G. Roeber has argued, although these merchants continued to worship, eat, speak, and dress, in Dutch ways, their key concern was with commerce and maintaining order amongst the lower ranks, rather than preserving their Dutch identity.[5] Thus when considering the 'multifaceted relationship between Amsterdam, New Amsterdam/ New York' and the 'Dutch influence' in the mid-Atlantic region of North America we cannot assume a putative connection between the settlers' geographic origins, their ethnic loyalties and their invocations of Amsterdam and the fatherland as ideals upon which to base colonial practice.

Here we are helped by scholars who have grappled with the problem of essentialism and proposed a less geographically-determined notion of ethnicity within which historical contingency and individual agency play their part. As Joyce Goodfriend has argued in the years leading up to the 1664 conquest 'persons of widely varied ancestry, including English, French, and African slaves owned by Dutch masters became culturally Dutch in the years before 1664' and this process, whereby settlers from disparate origins identified with Dutch ethno-cultural practices continued during early decades of English rule.[6] The shifting and contingent nature of ethnic identity is particularly evident in the work of Donna Merwick – a leading exponent of the 'Dutch influence' school who has also produced some of the most exciting and conceptually stimulating work on Dutch New York in recent years. Merwick's reading of anthropological theory and her use of the present continuous tense in the titles of her major books and articles – *Possessing Albany*, 'Becoming English,' 'Being Dutch' – indicate her commitment to a notion of ethnicity which is less inherent in an individual's past and more fashioned in the process of their making sense of their experience in relation to cultural predispositions or 'metaphors' that can, within limits, be picked up, put down, appropriated, and shaped to suit present needs. Our modified question, then, is what light does the invocation of 'Amsterdam' and an idealized urban Dutch civic order throw upon the choices and agenda of various individuals and groups and shifting loyalties in New Amsterdam and early New York?[7]

Company and Government
As described by Jaap Jacobs in his contribution to this volume, the earliest comparisons between the administration of New Netherland and New Amsterdam and the provinces and towns of the Dutch republic were drawn not by the settlers but by the West India Company in reforms that aimed to attract settlers to the colony. In the early 1620s, the West India Company had established the colony of New Netherland under the terms of a charter that granted it a monopoly on trade and shipping and authority to govern it – subject, of course, to the States General's oversight and the 'Dutch Roman Law, the imperial statutes of Charles V, and edicts, customs, and resolutions of the United Netherlands.'[8] New Amsterdam soon emerged as the main port, but the colony failed to attract immigrants and prosper. By the late 1630s the States General feared, presciently as it turned out, that the burgeoning English settlements to the north would soon squeeze the Dutch off the continent and pressured the Company to introduce reforms. Under the 1640 Revised Freedoms and Exemptions the Company relinquished its trade monopoly, hoping that private enterprise would encourage commercial expansion and increased revenues derived from duties and taxes. It also undertook to govern New Netherland 'according to the style and order of the province of Holland and the cities and manors thereof… [and] as far as possible, the ordinances received here in Amsterdam.'[9]

What this implied in practice, however, was not always clear and many of the subsequent disputes between settlers leaders and Company arguably revolved around differences of opinion regarding the implications of Old World precedents for colonial practice. For example, despite its undertaking to govern the colony according to the practice of Dutch towns, the Company vacillated on the question of local administrative and commercial privileges and protections, although such measures were a common enough feature of urban government in the United Provinces and, according to scholars such as Jacob Price and others, underpinned the claims for autonomy and communal liberty in even smaller towns. Thus the Amsterdam chamber of the WIC struck down measures designed to exclude non-residents from the provincial fur trade, on the grounds that the itinerants essential for its sought-after free-trade expansion.[10] The chamber also disapproved of restrictions on artisan working practices, advising against monopoly grants for the local production of bricks and salt as 'very pernicious and impracticable' and struck down orders fixing the prices of wine and bread, arguing that 'in so tender beginnings of a now emerging country ... which rise must be sought and promoted rather in encouraging and unlimited freedoms rather than forced regulations.'[11] Yet the same chamber was prepared to countenance some measures that provided for local needs and stability, affirming the regulations on coopering and the butchering of cattle, and an order restraining brewers from retailing liquor in taverns as it was 'pursuant to the ordinances and customs of Holland.'

If one were to characterize the Company's position it would be one of understandable and self-interested indecision. The Amsterdam directors were concerned, not unreasonably, to encourage private enterprise and expansion yet they also appeared to seek the stability of an adapted urban order that, they hoped, would provide for the settlers' deference to the local administration. Thus the Company invoked the example of Amsterdam and the fatherland as a governing ideal, while dragging its feet when it came to granting leading settlers the administrative and regulatory remit they would have liked and to which they felt entitled on the basis of their own reading of Old World precedents. This left Stuyvesant in a tricky position, having to negotiate between the policy objectives of his distant employers and the demands of a local merchant lobby for protective measures that would favor residential trade.[12] A predicament acknowledged but unresolved by the Company's shareholders who exhorted their Director to 'act strictly in accordance with the laudable customs and ordinances of this city… [of Amsterdam] at least in so far as the nature and condition of the country and its inhabitants may admit.'[13]

Unfortunately for Stuyvesant the switch to free trade brought increasing numbers of independent settlers and their families who were not satisfied with the Company's partial adaptation of government according to the 'style and order of the province of Holland and the cities and manors thereof.' They sought, in turn, their own version of a 'suitable municipal (*borgerlycke*) government… resembling the laudable Government of our Fatherland' to the States General in Holland.[14] Indeed in the absence of such an administration the New Amsterdammers feared 'the establishment of an Arbitrary Government' and – in keeping with the rhetorical excess of early modern republicans – likened their condition to that of slaves living under the Company's 'tyrannical power.' In 1649, a well-organized settler pressure-group – the Nine Men – launched a successful campaign for commercial advantages and administrative authority – or as they had it privileges and exemptions – that they argued would be the 'mother of population' and prosperity.[15]

Now as Jaap Jacobs has informed us, we have to be careful not to be seduced by the rhetoric of nineteenth-century translators and to cast this campaign in Whiggish terms as a struggle between liberty-loving colonists and an oppressive commercial company. However, if the municipal government was in fact the brainchild of Stuyvesant and his council it is curious that he was so set against the reformers whom he once denounced as 'rascals, liars, rebels, [and] usurers.'[16] It is also not clear why the reformers went to the trouble of producing a lengthy and detailed Remonstrance in 1649 which they dispatched with delegates to Amsterdam; delegates, it is worth noting, who took on a difficult mission involving a perilous sea voyage, the risk of considerable personal expense and status, and in the case of the lead delegate, Adriaen van der Donck, an extended and enforced absence from his New Netherland family and farm.

I am more persuaded by Jacobs' suggestive reading of the municipal administration's earliest days and the determination of Stuyvesant and his council to purge the magisterial bench and to control the newly established city government. This would seem to carry an implied acknowledgement by Stuyvesant and his associates that the city government did indeed constitute a new and important source of local influence that needed to be monitored and as far as possible contained. Thus the Court of *Burgemeesters* and *Schepenen* afforded city traders and landowners a role in local affairs subject to Stuyvesant's oversight and municipal and provincial branches of government collaborated on various measures such as the establishment of a public weigh house with reliable scales, and gaugers and assizers of barrels, and the inspection and quality control of tobacco coming into and exported from New Amsterdam. However, when the two sides fell out, as they did over responsibility for the collection of excise, deployment of the militia, and regulations pertaining to baking and brewing, the merchant leaders held fast to their determination to administer New Amsterdam according to customary Dutch practice and 'after the manner of the Fatherland.'

For this newly established governing group of traders and farmers, then, the claim of adherence to Old World practices provided a platform upon which to challenge the administrative purview – and by implication the authority –of the West India Company and its Director and a foundation for their own authority over the ordinary burghers living and working in New Amsterdam. Although Stuyvesant routinely asserted his on-paper, vice regal authority in practice (and like generations of colonial American governors who came after him) the Director found himself having to negotiate and compromise with the burgomasters who enjoyed the support of leading business interests and the commonalty and who added incrementally to their administrative authority over the town's affairs. In 1656, for example, the burgomasters persuaded the Director to adopt the metropolitan practice of selecting new appointees from a list of nomination of double the number of candidates; they secured the authority to try criminal cases punishable by branding or whipping; they also launched the first full scale survey 'according to which the Streets' were 'set off and laid out with stakes.'[17] The following year the municipal and provincial governments collaborated on the introduction of the burgher right, limiting trade to registered locals. In this fashion the reformers realized their ambition of a burgher government that accorded with other Dutch towns for their own community or the 'City of Amsterdam in New Netherland' as they had taken to calling their town.[18]

The introduction of the burgher right in 1657, modeled directly on Dutch practice, capped a decade of municipal reform and affirmed the status and authority of the merchant elite over their residential charges. The burgomasters hailed the measure, which was modeled directly on the practice of Amsterdam, as 'one of the most important privileges in a well governed city.' Lessor burghers now bore formal civic duties. A burgher was obliged to contribute to the city's defenses and serve in the militia, obey orders relating to the maintenance of property and the conduct of commerce, and respect municipal officers.[19] In 1658, the burgomasters sought further controls over local residents proposing that Stuyvesant 'fix certain hours of the day when working-people should go to their work and come from their work, as well also their recess for meals,' and requesting that 'the Director General and Council… establish Guilds.' The following year the spiraling costs of local necessaries prompted a second petition from the municipal leaders, this time recommending that 'all bakers, brewers, shopkeepers… sell their goods at reasonable prices to the people.' Stuyvesant obliged them with revised rates for *zeewan* exchange and an order requiring brewers, bakers, tapsters, shop keepers and ships chandlers to sell 'daily household commodities' at fixed prices.[20]

Given these and similar municipal resolutions, it is perhaps not surprising that scholars have generally considered the burgher right as a tool in the hands of a governing elite who were intent upon securing the benefits of long-sought-after commercial protections.[21] Yet the administration of New Amsterdam remained a far from top-down affair and whatever authority the burgher right afforded the ruling elite depended to a great extent on the deference of ordinary residents whose expectations of their municipal leaders rested on their own reading of the Old World precedents in New Amsterdam.

The duties required of ordinary burghers were balanced by compensatory privileges which were claimed and asserted by local tradesmen. Registered burghers were protected from seizure of goods for debt, providing they appeared in court; as we have seen they also enjoyed exclusive access to the handicraft and retail trades. In addition to this general prohibition on strangers trading, residents secured supplementary privileges, such as an exclusive right to tap beer and wine at the ferry station, which they expected the city to defend from encroachment by residents and non-residents alike. Between the general privileges enjoyed by all burghers and the idiosyncratic liberties secured by some lay the supplementary privileges claimed by artisans in behalf of their particular trades. Just as the burgomasters held city tradesmen to occupationally-specific duties – such as the manufacture of bread and barrels of the correct weight and size – so skilled workers claimed reciprocal privileges they deemed essential for their trades and over and above the preferences enjoyed by all and in accordance with Old World practices. Thus in 1652 the town's surgeons complained of the damaging competition (and occasionally hazardous service) offered by ship-based and transient practitioners and successfully petitioned for a monopoly of public shaving services, although the townspeople reserved the right to shave each other 'for friendship's sake, [or] out of courtesy and without receiving payment.' Or the 1660 petition by six local butchers secured a monopoly on slaughtering in return for an undertaking to work at regulated rates, supervise the quality of meat offered for local consumption and export, and collect a municipal excise calculated on the value of slaughtered beasts 'in accordance with the laudable custom of our Fatherland and for the accommodation of the Burghers.'[22]

By the 1660s the Nine Men's assertion that 'privileges and exemptions' would be the 'mother of population' and prosperity was borne out by the success of New Amsterdam. The city's population had swollen to 2,500 as increasing numbers of settlers made the eight week voyage from the United Provinces. The dock bustled with activity as grain and furs came down the from upriver for loading aboard vessels bound for Holland with tobacco from Virginia and Maryland.[23] New Amsterdam's merchant leaders could scarcely contain their satisfaction at the progress of their 'capital' city whose 'many fine houses' were the envy of their English neighbors and which 'surpassed nearly every other place in these parts of North America.' The three militia companies ensured that the town was 'properly fortified' and 'formidable to evil-minded neighbors and savages.'

Dutch Legacy
For the post-conquest fate of this 'Dutch' civic order a quick sketch will suffice. The English conquerors were military men charged with the command of the largest English garrison in the North American colonies. They spent much of their time focused on the French and Indian threat to the north west and relied on the city's business leaders to administer local trade, collect taxes, and provision the soldiers in the newly-renamed Fort James. In return, New York's leading merchants and farmers secured continued recognition of the city's municipal administration and commercial privileges, enabling a well-positioned few to supplement the diminishing fur trade with a profitable business exporting primary

products and importing supplies and trade goods. Initially at least, city tradesmen and their families seemed content to submit to the new imperial authorities which confirmed, and in some cases extended, rights and trade privileges secured during the Dutch era. The respect shown by the conquerors for the municipal government's regulatory regime, trade privileges, and Dutch legal practices seemed to many to affirm the no despotic nature of English rule and to fulfill the undertakings given in the Articles of Capitulation.

Unfortunately, the pursuit of privileges and profits by a group of Dutch and English merchants failed to sponsor the general welfare of the town and the residential unity in the face of conquest in 1664 was ultimately shattered in what proved to be a protracted and divisive transition to English rule. Following the brief reconquest of the colony by the Dutch in 1672-74, the administrations of Edmund Andros and Thomas Dongan introduced commercial and governmental reforms that fell particularly hard on middling residents: new taxes to pay for improvements in the city's infrastructure and trade regulations and monopolies intended to promote commercial efficiency but which appeared to favor the interests of selected merchants at the expense of the population at large. Civic and commercial regulations that had once stood as guarantees of individual and community freedoms were increasingly despised as partial and therefore suspicious orders intended to advance the interests of a few at the cost of the many. In the late 1680s discontent amongst the city's tradesmen became bound up with anti-popery sentiments whipped up by Calvinist zealots and, forty years after the campaign against the West India Company, New Yorkers once again feared that they had fallen under the sway of an arbitrary and tyrannical government. In 1689, when news of the Glorious Revolution and the accession of William and Mary reached New York, city tradesmen rose up to defend their privileges and liberty from a perceived pro-Stuart and papist plot to deliver the city into the hands of its French and Indian enemies.

Conclusion

In conclusion, once we accept the fact that appeals to Dutch practices need not necessarily correlate to a former place of residence it is sensible to look for what *else* is being claimed by those who invoke the name of 'Amsterdam' and the practice of the fatherland. Neglecting the claim put forward by the colonists, the wic and Stuyvesant learned a lesson that would be suffered by other colonial authorities in New York and the other American colonies: regardless of vice regal paper authority holding and exercising power depended on maintaining a workable relationship with the colonists. The doggedness with which each pursued their respective vision suggests that these claims were intimately bound up with the efforts of colonizing powers, local administrators, and settlers to transform New World strangeness into familiarity and to fix authority on one form of colonial community to the exclusion of others.[24]

It is in these terms that we understand the connection between Old and New Amsterdam and why it continued to figure mightily in the hearts and minds of the colonists – Dutch and crypto-Dutch alike – following the English takeover. Every move the settlers made – the capitulation, signing of articles, squabbles over loyalties, collaboration – bespoke a desire to maintain the urban order they had made and which provided a measure of comfort and security in an uncertain world. When Andros and Dongan undermined this civic order they threatened not simply livelihoods and abstract liberties but brought real and present danger to the colonists and this perception provided the bedrock of discontent from which Leisler's Rebellion issued forth.

Notes

1 Gabriëlle Dorren, *Eenheid en verscheidenheid. De burgers van Haarlem in de Gouden Eeuw* (Amsterdam: Samenwerkende Uitgeverijen Prometheus/Bert Bakker, 2001).

2 Joyce D. Goodfriend, 'Writing/Righting Dutch Colonial History,' *New York History* 80 (January 1998): 5-28.

3 Alice P. Kenny, *Stubborn For Liberty: The Dutch in New York* (Syracuse, NY: Syracuse University Press, 1975), 69. For overviews of the recent flourishing of studies on Dutch New York see Joyce Goodfriend, 'The Historiography of the Dutch in Colonial America,' in Eric Nooter and Patricia U. Bonomi, eds., *Colonial Dutch Studies: An Interdisciplinary Approach* (New York: New York University Press, 1988), 6-32; Nancy Anne McClure Zeller, ed., *A Beautiful and Fruitful Place: Selected Rennsselaerswijck Seminar Papers* (Albany, NY: New Netherland Publishing, 1991); Wayne Bodle, 'Themes and Directions in Middle Colonies Historiography, 1980-1994,' *William and Mary Quarterly* 51 (July 1994): 357-358.

4 David S. Cohen, 'How Dutch were the Dutch of New Netherland ?' *New York History* 62 (1981): 43-60.

5 A.G. Roeber, "'The Origin of Whatever is Not English among Us': The Dutch-speaking and the German Speaking Peoples of Colonial British America,' in Bernard Bailyn and Philip D. Morgan, eds., *Strangers Within the Realm: Cultural Margins of the First British Empire* (Chapel Hill: University of North Carolina Press, 1991), 224; Dennis J. Maika, 'Commerce and Community: Manhattan Merchants in the Seventeenth Century' (Ph.D. dissertation, New York University, 1995), part one; Randall H. Balmer, *A Perfect Babel of Confusion: Dutch Religion and English Culture in the Middle Colonies* (New York: Oxford University Press, 1989).

6 Joyce D. Goodfriend, 'The Historiography of the Dutch in Colonial America,' in Nooter and Bonomi, eds., *Colonial Dutch Studies*, 15.

7 Oliver A. Rink, *Holland on the Hudson: An Economic and Social History of Dutch New York* (Ithaca: Syracuse University Press, 1986); Maika, 'Commerce and Community, part one; Donna Merwick, *Possessing Albany: The Dutch and English Experiences* (New York: Cambridge University Press, 1990), 3. *Burgerlijk* served as the New Amsterdammers' 'central cultural metaphor' and 'organizing principle of personal space, of social class, of events and actions, [and] of cultural time.'

8 A.J.F. Van Laer, trans. and ed., *Documents Relating to New Netherland, 1624-1626* (San Marino, CA: The Henry E. Huntington Library and Art Gallery, 1926), 2-17, 39, 113-114, 117; J.H. Wessels, *History of Roman Dutch Law* (South Africa, 1908), and R.W. Lee, *An Introduction to Roman Dutch Law* (Oxford: The Clarendon Press, 1953); John Romeyn Brodhead, *History of the State of New York. First period, 1609-1664* (New York 1859), 134-136; Martha D. Shattuck, 'A Civil Society: Court and Community in Beverwijck, New Netherland, 1652-1664,' (Ph.D. Dissertation, Boston University, 1993), 26-29.

9 E.B. O'Callaghan and B. Fernow (trans. and ed.), *Documents Relative to the Colonial History of the State of New York*. 15 vols. (Albany: Weed, Parsons and Company, 1853-1883) (hereafter abbreviated as *DRCHNY*), 1: 110-115; E.B. O'Callaghan, *The History of New Netherland*. 2 vols. (New York, 1845-48), 1: 392-93; Philip L. White, 'Municipal government comes to Manhattan', *New-York Historical Society Quarterly* 37 (1953), 146-157; Albert E. Mckinley, 'The English and Dutch Towns of New Netherland,' *American Historical Review* 6 (October 1900): 1-18.

10 New York Historical Society, *Collections* 18 (New York 1885), 1-4; Berthold Fernow (trans. and ed.), *The Records of New Amsterdam from 1653 to 1674 anno domini*. 7 vols. (New York: Knickerbocker Press, 1897, repr. Baltimore: Genealogical Publishing Company, 1976) (hereafter abbreviated as *RNA*) 1: 1-108. H.C. Syrett, 'Private Enterprise in New Amsterdam,' in *William and Mary Quarterly* 11 (1954): 536-550. As an alternative the Amsterdam chamber recommended that itinerant traders should keep an open store, thereby qualifying for tax payments, in the town. E. B. O'Callaghan, ed., *Laws and Ordinances of New Netherland, 1638-1674* (Albany 1868), 148-50. For the Company's arguments against restrictions on independent fur traders, *DRCHNY*, 14: 84, 194, 208; *Laws and Ordinances*, 149-50.

11 I thank this reference and the translation to Jaap Jacobs. See also Charles T. Gehring, trans. and ed., *Correspondence 1654-1658*. New Netherland Documents Series, vol. 12 (Syracuse, NY: Syracuse University Press, 2003), 5.

12 For example the 1654 disagreement between Stuyvesant and the burgomasters regarding the disciplining of unruly servants during Shrove-Tide festivities *RNA* 1: 172-73.

13 See the ordinance against retailing by brewers, 12 July 1648 in Charles Gehring, trans. and edit., *Laws and Writs of Appeal, 1647-1663* (Syracuse, NY: Syracuse University Press, 1991), 12; on city porters see *RNA*, 7: 145-147, and E.B. O'Callaghan ed., *Calendar of historical manuscripts in the office of the Secretary of State, Albany, N.Y. Part I. Dutch manuscripts, 1630-1664* (Albany 1865, reprint Ridgewood, 1968), 185. 'Letter from the Directors to Stuyvesant, March 1654' in *DRCHNY*, 14: 251-253.

14 *DRCHNY*, 1: 312-13.

15 'Petition of the Commonalty of New Netherland &c to Director Stuyvesant,' in *DRCHNY*, 1: 550-555.

16 *Laws and Ordinances*, 75-76; *DRCHNY* 1: 307, 315; *DRCHNY* 14: 218-219.

17 *DRCHNY* 1: 639; Allen W. Trelease, *Indian Affairs in Colonial New York: the Seventeenth Century* (Ithaca: Cornell University Press, 1960), 109, 138; *Calender of Dutch Manuscripts*, 158-59, 178; I.N. Phelps Stokes, *The iconography of Manhattan Island 1498-1909* 6 vols. (New York: Dodd, 1915-1928), 2: 165.

18 Merwick, *Possessing Albany*, introduction, 103-127; *Heere Gracht, Manual* (1862), 513; Class Maereschalk to repair the glass *RNA* 4: 57.

19 Lessor burghers were defined as all native-born residents and anybody who had lived in the town for a year and six weeks, or married 'native born daughters of Burghers,' or paid twenty guilders. The ordinance of 1657 was reissued by Stuyvesant his council in 1660 and by the burgomasters and schepens in 1660 and 1661 in, New York Historical Society, *Collections* (1885), 12-36.

20 Guild proposal, *RNA* 2: 410; 'daily household commodities,' *RNA* 1: 40-42; Baking regulations, *RNA*, 1: 43, 46-48.

21 Kammen, *Colonial New York*, 55; Roeber, ''The Origin of Whatever is Not English among Us'', 224.

22 Kenneth Scott, 'New Amsterdam's Taverns and Tavern Keepers,' part 1, *De Halve Maen* 39 (April 1964): 9, 10, 15; *RNA* 1: 263-64; *RNA* 7: 145-47, 258-259; *Calender of Dutch Manuscripts*, 203. *DRCHNY* 14: 155; *RNA* 1: 263-64; *RNA* 7: 145-47, 258-259.

23 In 1664 the magistrates estimated the male population of New York at fifteen hundred male residents, excluding women and slaves, almost sixty percent of whom had arrived in colony within previous ten years. O'Callaghan, *History of New Netherland*, 1: 540; *RNA*, 6: 110; Joyce D. Goodfriend, *Before the Melting Pot: Society and Culture in Colonial New York City, 1664-1730* (Princeton: Princeton University Press, 1991), 15. Evarts B. Greene and Virginia D. Harrington, *American Population Before the Federal Census of 1790* (New York: Columbia University Press, 1932; reprinted, 1966), 93; J.J. McCusker and R.R. Menard, *The Economy of British America, 1607-1789* (Chapel Hill: University of North Carolina Press, 1985), 188-200.

24 For this process in other colonial contexts see David Grayson Allen, *In English Ways: The Movement of Societies and the Transferal of English Local Law and Custom to Massachusetts Bay in the Seventeenth Century* (Chapel Hill: University of North Carolina Press, 1981); Patricia Seed, *Ceremonies of Possession in Europe's conquest of the New World, 1492-1640* (Cambridge: Cambridge University Press, 1995); James T. Lemon, 'Spatial Order: Households in Local Communities and Regions,' in J.P. Greene and J.R. Pole, eds., *Colonial British America: Essays in the New History of the Early Modern Era* (Baltimore: Johns Hopkins University Press, 1984), 86-122.

Claudia Schnurmann

ANGLO-DUTCH RELATIONS IN AND AROUND SEVENTEENTH-CENTURY NEW AMSTERDAM/NEW YORK

From its early beginnings, New Netherland, the Dutch colony on the Hudson, and its entrepot New Amsterdam was perceived as a stunning, to some even horrifyingly mixed society. While most European rulers tried to establish uniformity and conformity to support their control of and grip on their subjects, New Netherland must have been something like a nightmare to the typical Old World prince who was attuned to strong convictions about the importance of one faith, one language and one race for the maintenance and support of good government. In open contrast to all those dearly cherished notions, New Netherland was inhabited by people who hailed from nearly every religion, ethnicity, culture, nation and region of the Old as well as New Worlds: Settlers not only from the mother-country, the Netherlands, but as well as from the Spanish Netherlands which would become Belgium in 1830, from German territories in general and imperial cities in particular, from England, Scotland, France, or Scandinavian countries met Afro-Americans or Native Americans. Euro-American Protestants of every denomination and nationality (for example Lutherans, Calvinists, Huguenots, Quakers, Anglicans and members of the Dutch Reformed Church) met Catholics and Jews. It seemed that Europe had produced something like an appendix of itself on the other side of the big pond. But true to James Harrington that 'men, like flowers…being transplanted take after the soil wherein they grow',[1] those transplanted people not only recreated Old World troubles but changed them, gave them their very own regional touch or created developments of their own account with consequences for the Atlantic world that space allows me to mention only briefly.

While some historians celebrated this multicultural society as clear evidence of Dutch tolerance and free spirit, Dutch contemporaries of the seventeenth century felt rather disgusted by this 'melting pot' and criticized the colony mercilessly as a modern version of Babylon.[2] Although during the 1620s the Dutch West India Company had intensified her interest in the American colony and had tried very hard for a long time to keep control over her only main land American property, credit must be given to the colonies' merchants, who slowly, notwithstanding Governor Pieter Stuyvesant's strong regiment, finally succeeded in imposing their will on the cities' and the colonies' whereabouts. They, and not the Dutch West India Company, were the ones who really managed the colony, although it is true that the Dutch West India company back home had founded the colony as a product of her determination to run the colony so that it would serve the purposes of the Amsterdam chamber, the metropolis on the river Amstel and the province of Holland. For some time it had seemed that the company would reach that goal. But economic setbacks and financial needs forced her to give in. Slowly the company lost her grip and was forced to loosen those ties that had been obstacles to colonial trade. This loosening of control served the interests of the colonists of course. Municipal rights that were granted during the 1650s, further evoked hopes for urban progress and fostered mercantile expectations for profit and civil self-government in accordance with cherished traditions in patria. Well-to-do merchants developed their commercial networks notwithstanding the fading and weakening of the company's demands till 1664 and after an English interlude again from 1673 to 1674; the majority of them stayed on when in 1674 New Amsterdam and New Netherland mutated into English New York, that was named after her new owner, the English king's brother James, Duke of York.

In my essay I will emphasize those commercial behaviors and activities which demonstrate that trade and relationships could not then nor now be confined to closed national systems, created by European legal codes or mother countries' selfish notions of imperial supremacy. I want to turn your attention to the different commercial attitudes and patterns that early colonial merchants were able to develop. Merchants on the Hudson became crucial to the early modern colonial world, to its trade, its power structure and its budding political self-perceptions. These were much disliked on the other side of the big pond by merchants and politicians.

Different patterns and relationships emerged during the seventeenth century, which I can sketch here only broadly. First, the intercolonial trade relations of merchants from New Amsterdam/New York with English colonies on the mainland, and secondly, the New York merchants' transatlantic trade towards the Dutch Caribbean and Europe.

Intercolonial Trade in North America
The intercolonial trade in North America followed two models: on the one hand strong commercial ties between New England and New Amsterdam/New York since New Amsterdam's beginnings came into existence and were supported by diplomatic agreements like the Hartford Convention of 1650. The treaty concluded in Hartford/Connecticut on September 29, 1650, between the Dutch colony New Netherland and the Confederation of the United Colonies of New England, a confederation founded in 1643 by Massachusetts, New Plymouth, Connecticut and New Haven, is a striking example of early colonial efforts to achieve independence from English claims. Whereas the Dutch colony's leader Pieter Stuyvesant acted in accordance with the Dutch West India Company founding charter, when he took up diplomatic negotiations with his neighbors in New England, his counterparts could face hardships back home. By claiming the right to organize their own foreign policy, the New England colonies challenged London's dominance and authority. They not only challenged the mother country's perception of prestige and power, even worse – they broke the law and attacked the English notion of a working imperial system: by taking up diplomatic tools, propagating a foreign policy that mainly served colonial interests. Colonies had to serve metropolitan interests alone; colonists had to obey their mother country like servants, or – in English eyes – they were hardly more than slaves to work for the profit, the welfare, and the interest of the English state and lobbies. Given the geographical closeness of the participating colonies, the treaties' central articles concerned

problems caused by boundary disputes between Euro-Americans over rivers, territorial claims and infrastructure while all rivals with a European background were only too ready to ignore much older claims by the indigenous inhabitants, different Indian peoples. The colonists were brave enough to tackle problems that – to some extent – seemed unsolvable to Europe. In contrast to vague formulations of charters the crown had granted to English companies before, the colonists in their desire to make living easier were able to agree on drawing up a line between Dutch and New English territories. Long Island should be divided into a Western part that belonged to New Netherland; the Eastern parts should go to New England. On the main land a line ten miles east of the Hudson or the Noordt Rivier should separate Dutch and New English settlements, however, there are traces of future conflicts and recent hesitations to solve all problems once and for all : The negotiating parties could not agree where the line should end in the Northern hinterland of New Netherland and New England, a very sensitive zone in regard to French Canada and Indian peoples who were torn between the Europeans and their different offer of goods.

Besides topics of such crucial importance both parties managed to agree on problems arising from the daily colonial routine: intercolonial migrants like criminals, run-away indentured servants, escaped debtors, or deserters could prove to be a burden. They not only hurt individual interests: an escaped indentured servant did damage to his master, who lost his outlay and the servant's labor; a debtor did harm to moral and legal rules, damaging the colony's economic power. Deserters and criminals undermined the colony's legal competence; intercolonial migration of that type challenged the colony's internal stability by undermining its legal structure, social tissue, the authority of the colonial administration and its military strength on the one hand; on the other hand intercolonial migration could put a risk to intercolonial cooperation. Accepting emigrants who had left behind a mess in another colony, even more so when both colonies did not belong to one mother country, could disturb the subtle balance and burden it with stress that authorities did not really need; people could use gaps and holes in legal nets to increase tensions and conflicts between colonies.

To minimize those dangers which put at risk all colonies notwithstanding which nation they belonged to and could make them an easy prey to common enemies, Catholic French from La Nouvelle-France or Indian people alike, the negotiators in Hartford discussed the idea of concluding a treaty 'of a nearer union of friendship and amity betwixt [i.e. between] the English and Dutch nacon [nation] in these parts, especially against a common enimie [enemy].' The key term 'union' mentioned in this quotation tempts some scholars to put the Hartford convention in close context with negotiations performed by London at the same time towards the Netherlands.

To get hold of Dutch economic and commercial predominance and sea power, Oliver Cromwell had tried eagerly to sweet-talk the Dutch Republic into a union with the Protestant England Republic, emphasizing common faith and traditional friendship between both states. The Hague, especially Amsterdam, however, despised the murderer of King Charles I (1625-1649), although Dutch burghers had had their own way of dealing with princes and of getting rid of them. Quite aware of Cromwell's' efforts to subdue the Dutch Republic by declarations of friendship and to take over the Dutch role as a global player, the States Generals declined Cromwell's hypocritical approaches. Whereas in Europe plans of union favored by England aimed to destroy or at least control Dutch commercial and maritime power, in America the idea of a union between New Netherland and New England served Dutch/or rather New Netherland's as well as New English interests. During the negotiations it had become evident that the confederates within New England had their very own fishes to fry – they were far away of forming a confederation overflowing with harmony, love, and understanding – trouble, border disputes and territorial conflicts between English colonies were the order of a colonial day. Division between New England's colonies, however, favoured New Netherland. Whereas New Netherland and Connecticut had had their troubles over border disputes and territory, strong Massachusetts tried to keep Connecticut at bay by supporting New Netherland.

In 1650, however, the wish for intercolonial coexistence still grew strong and made the Hartford convention possible. That exclusively colonial interests were at stake did not go unnoticed by the mother countries. True to the Dutch West India Company charter from 1621 and influenced by New Netherlands' strong desire for local government, the West India Company and the States-Generals finally gave way: forced to grant more liberty and urban rule and strengthened by the Dutch conquest of New Sweden on the Delaware in 1655, the Dutch Republic finally accepted that piece of foreign policy achieved by settlers in 1656. England, however, neither the Commonwealth, the Lord protector Cromwell nor the restored Stuart monarchy paid any attention to agreements achieved by colonial settlers. Officially London ignored the colonial agreement – to go one step further and ratify the Hartford convention would have meant a loss to the credibility of London's political position . First it had meant to accept colonial policy as equal to the mother country; secondly it had meant to accept the existence of a Dutch colony on the Hudson, a fact which was far from English ways of seeing American realities.[3]

On the other hand, to merchants from New Amsterdam/New York their exchange with the English colonies and planter-merchants of the Chesapeake Bay i.e. Maryland and Virginia became equally important; these contacts were created and supported by lively migration and communication on public and private levels. Communication and cooperation not only worked on informal levels, between planters, planter-merchants and traders. They worked on the official level too. Commercial relations caused agreements of friendship and mutual trade. Favoured again by Dutch governor Pieter Stuyvesant first Virginia, then Maryland spread its wings and learned some lessons in foreign policy. In May 1653, while the mother countries England and the Netherlands were involved in a bloody and needless military conflict, Nieuw Amsterdam and Jamestown managed to live in peace and understanding. Dutch ambassadors came to Jamestown and discussed plans of 'alliance, correspondence, and commerce'. Although those negotiations failed in the end, they constituted the fact of high treason- collaborating with the enemy. Like Virginia, Maryland and New Netherland developed strong commercial ties. In open contrast to the acts of trade and navigation large amounts of tobacco were traded with Dutch merchants and skippers instead of going to England, and thanks to customs, filling English coffers. In 1659 Augustine Hermans was sent by Stuyvesant on an embassy to Maryland to negotiate another treaty improving correspondence and confederation for reciprocal trade and intercourse.

Although in the end both parties could not agree on written versions, communication between both settlements flourished: Hermans moved to Maryland for good and became the Lord of Bohemia Manor while his son stayed behind in New Netherland to become an influential long-distance merchant, which like his father he had visited several times; rumors were boiling in New Netherland that 'the governor of Maryland should come to New Amstel (till then always a point of conflict between territorial disputes of Maryland and New Netherland) ...to establish the trade in Tobacco then.' At the same time communications between New Netherland and Virginia was at their best: merchants and ships sailed back and forth, even the passage over land came into fashion and Virginia asked New Netherland if they needed any provisions because Virginia felt able to supply them.[4]

Commercial networks created and mostly maintained by merchants from New Amsterdam enabled the inhabitants of English colonies to steer their very own political course, which irritated and infuriated English authorities and London-based merchants. It is interesting to note that the changing political fortunes – wars (three Dutch-English wars 1652-1654, 1665-1667, 1672-1674) and informal conflicts – in the mother countries had no impact on the much strained metropolitan-colonial relations nor on the thriving Dutch-Anglo colonial relations. The troubles between colony and mother country continued irrespective of who was in the driving seat in London. King James I, King Charles I, and Lord Protector Oliver Cromwell obviously strongly differed in their political attitudes and beliefs – nevertheless they all used the same methods in dealing with their colonial opponents; they fought over the same problems with those hardy colonists who lived on the far-flung and difficult to control shores and rivers of the Chesapeake Bay as well as on the equally uncontrollable New England coast or on the West Indian islands like the sugar planters of Barbados. They all were united in their opposition to English claims to control the colonial trade. Particularly the West Indian planters were in a position similar to that of the tobacco planters in the Chesapeake: Solid Dutch support in marketing their produce enabled them, too, to take their own economic and political stand against London and English merchants.

From the very beginning inhabitants from New Amsterdam eagerly cast their profit-seeking eyes on the English colonies in the Atlantic world. In his history of Plymouth Plantation, the Governor of New Plymouth, William Bradford, described how in the 1620s-1630s those interactions had become important for his tiny colony on the fringe of the English world: '...there was many passages betweene them both [Plymouth and New Amsterdam] and they had ...profitable commerce together for diverse years.'[5] John Winthrop senior said the same thing for Massachusetts in 1634: 'Our neighbors of Plymouth and we had oft[en] trade with the Dutch at Hudson's River, called by them New Netherlands...We had from them about forty sheep, and beaver and brass pieces, and sugar,...strong waters, [and] linen cloth.'[6]

The same became true for Virginia and Maryland where Dutch merchants and merchant-sailors soon began to play an important part in the society of tobacco planters. Dutch contacts – buyers and alternative markets – helped Governor William Berkeley and the colony of Virginia to take a stand against London's demands to obey the stipulations of the first Act of Trade and Navigation. After an unsuccessful embargo in 1650 against Virginia, Barbados, Antigua, and the Bermudas, the mother country in 1652 resorted to stronger measures. Berkeley and his brothers in spirit in the Chesapeake as well as in Barbados were punished when Cromwell's fleet threatened to invade the planters' harbors and creeks; faced with brutal force in March 1652 Virginians were forced to accept Oliver Cromwell's Articles of Surrender.

New England was not particularly happy about English efforts to improve English control over her colonies in the New World. Another reason for Massachusetts to favour a strong New Netherland that was unmolested by its neighbor Connecticut was its economic interest: Massachusetts merchants especially from Boston had established strong relationships to merchants, money, and commercial know-how in the Netherlands and the Hudson colony, – they needed strong ties to Dutchmen and Dutch women around the Big Pond to support their notion of a free state, that was independent from English claims and control. Between 1650 and 1654 Cromwell changed his policy. He switched from cooperation to first declaring an embargo (1650), then in 1651 proclaiming the act of trade and navigation, and finally in 1652 to declaring war against the Netherlands. In 1654 he dispatched a fleet to New England to conquer New Netherland and thus close the – to metropolitan eyes disturbing – gap between Connecticut and Maryland in England's colonial world. Massachusetts reacted according to its own interests – each inch the self-conscious free state it tried to be. Destroying New Netherland and cutting the close-knit Dutch network would have been a heavy setback to Bostonian zeal for self-government. Instead of demonstrating national solidarity with England and demonstrating obedience to the mother nation, Massachusetts and New Plymouth refused any participation in the military actions ordered by Cromwell against New Netherland; Connecticut, Rhode Island and New Haven on the other hand happily jumped to the chance of getting rid of the Dutch rival for land, rivers and resources. Saved by Cromwell's empire building, these three colonies in New England tried to live up to the occasion and acquire new territory by expanding towards the Delaware, the Connecticut and into Long Island. On the other hand Massachusetts even took the New Netherlands' side. Whereas long-term border conflicts with New Netherland and hunger for land induced the inhabitants of Connecticut to eagerly follow Cromwell's order to destroy New Netherland, the hardy Puritans in Massachusetts had their very own fish to fry and strong reasons for refusing to obey Cromwell's orders. They refused to join efforts to conquer New Amsterdam, for Bostonians that would have meant to submit to that very person that tried to destroy their influence and cut the branch of the tree on which the majority of Massachusetts' merchants were happily sitting. New England was not one monolithic complex with one mind and judgment. On the contrary, the New England colonies followed very different attitudes towards English demands, colonial needs, and interests; their different policy toward New Netherland provides a perfect example for this.

Notwithstanding political and territorial interests English colonists all over the Americas did trade with inhabitants of New Netherland; they used those contacts to extend their commercial networks via New Amsterdam to the Netherlands; much to the disgust of Georgian England English, in later times colonial merchants started to trade directly with Amsterdam, Rotterdam and other Dutch port towns. In the growing rift between British North America and Great Britain in the late 18th century the Dutch connections of Bostonians and New Yorkers would increase in importance; they strengthened the conviction of British colonists in North American that economically they could do much better without British trade restrictions and obstacles to their trade and commerce.

Transatlantic Trade in North America
The close-knit networks established in New Amsterdam times lived on, survived the Eng-

lish takeover of New Netherland in 1674, and gradually evolved into what can be viewed as the centre piece of the transatlantic exchange system that had New York as its centre and stronghold. This takes us to the second part, to the important transatlantic network that merchants on the Hudson extended into different directions. After the Dutch takeover in 1667, one connected New York, Boston, Newport/RI and later Philadelphia with colonies in the Dutch Caribbean world – mainly Curacao and Suriname. In the 1690s and in the early 18th century North American connections enabled Suriname's planters to oppose Dutch control and get away with it for quite a while.

These North American activities in the Caribbean were kept hidden from British eyes, as were New Yorkers' European interactions. Archival evidence does, however, show that merchants from New York had their stake in world politics; in doing so they were connecting the former New Amsterdam/New York and its multi-ethnic society to the Atlantic world and thus combined crucial European developments with their colonial views of the world.

These networks that covered the Atlantic and whose routes merged particularly in the Netherlands and on the Hudson River, grew and bloomed notwithstanding all the efforts of officials and merchants in London to destroy them by law, by illegal attacks, by wars, and finally by diplomatic moves. They survived the English takeover of New Amsterdam in peacetime in 1664, because all honorable merchants of Manhattan were only too ready to follow their new political master and sign the fairly favorable articles of surrender. It was sensible to come to terms with the powers to be instead of trying to remain stubbornly loyal to a company that had neither raised emotions, nor evoked or appealed to non-existing national feelings in the multinational society of New York. The networks lived on and survived the Dutch retake in 1673 and the nicely tuned zigzags of the following years.

I can only draw a rough sketch of how freshly-baked New Yorkers used their contacts from former Dutch times by using double citizenship, working multinational connections and feeding the vanities of European authorities not only to stay in business but to expand their trade and keep in touch with relatives, friends and long-time partners in the Netherlands on the other side of the sea. New York merchants had to make the best of both worlds because they wanted to make profits, win power, and get ever more involved with Atlantic politics.

Let us take a short look at some of the key sectors of Atlantic trade: tobacco, furs, slaves and European goods. In all four sectors merchants who had begun business when New York was still New Netherland played an important part: I do not dare do estimate quantities. But just checking English port books from the 1670-1680s in the English Public Record Office allows me to suggest that the greater part of Chesapeake-tobacco as well as furs from up-state New York, from Canada and from the Great Lakes region, that were legally imported into Europe and South England, came through New York.[7] The same is true for most European goods used in New York households. I am thinking of foodstuff like cheese, luxury goods, tools, metal goods, weapons, maps, books, haberdasheries, textiles, and toys from Germany – you name it. In the seventeenth century, most of these dry goods and manufactures reached the American consumers through New York merchants and via Dutch entrepots like Amsterdam, a kind of showcase for European producers.

These Atlantic shipments were managed by New York-based merchants like Cornelius Steenwijk, Frederick Philipsse, Willem and Abraham De Peyster, Matthew Chitty, Jacob

Leisler and others. The trade started often in New York on the American side of the Atlantic. Ships owned or hired by New Yorkers went down to Chesapeake's Eastern shore. Busy New Yorker captains like John Cruchee, William Measure, or Jacob Moritz collected tobacco produced in the Chesapeake region, bought barrels at St Mary's, then sailed directly for Europe or took the hogsheads back to New York and proceeded from thence via Kingsale in Ireland to the English ports of Plymouth, Penryn, Falmouth or Dover, before they finally landed their American staple goods either in Amsterdam or in Rotterdam, where they were sold or passed on to other European ports.

Transatlantic or rather intercolonial trade with enslaved Africans represented another commercial option where New Yorkers in the 1670s tried very hard to get some footing. Enslaved Africans represented an important sector of the colonial labor force. In the late 1670s they attracted New Yorkers like the German Calvinist Jacob Leisler and his French-born brother in faith Gabriel Minvielle; both tried to win a stake in that trade. Rather cleverly they used their close connection to the former owner of New York, the Dutch West India Company. The company tried desperately to keep up appearances by pretending that it still controlled the monopoly of space, people and goods gained, or rather, declared in open opposition to older Spanish and Portuguese claims in 1621. In those days monopoly had covered a region from Africa down to the Cape of Good Hope and included both Americas and the Caribbean islands. For some time the Dutch West India Company had dominated transatlantic slave trade which as a distinct trade was just then slowly acquiring its distinct features. The young company first had opposed slave trade as something inhuman and not worth the trouble; the conquest of North Brazil and her sugar-producing plantations based on slavery and forced labor in 1630 had changed the *bewindhebbers'* notion of slavery and slave trade: the demand of labor force, the idea, that tropical plantations could only be managed by using enslaved Africans, and the convictions that slave trade produced profits, had changed their attitude. However, slave trade did not produce the long-term monetary profits the company had hoped for. The company went bankrupt; the newly founded second West India Company in 1673/74 tried very hard to reanimate past hopes and recreate a boom.[8]

In February 1676 Gabriel Minvielle sent a letter from New York to the Amsterdam Chamber of the West India Company. He asked for a license to send a ship from New York – he tactfully referred to it as 'Nieuw Nederland' – to Curacao loaded with provisions which he wanted to exchange for slaves, who because of physical handicaps or advanced age could not be sold to customers in Spanish America. Minvielle wanted the license to be extended to his soul mate, old pal and friend Jacob Leisler. It took nearly six months before the Amsterdam Chamber made up its mind. Proud to be asked and thus acknowledged as a power that still mattered, the Amsterdam branch of the West India Company granted the requested permission:

> Present De Heeren Pellicorne; Prest, van Beeck, van Erpecum, van Heuvel, Godin, Wickevoort, De Vicq, Noiret ...Den Heer Van Beeck, heefft de Vergadering gecommuniceert seekere Missive aen Zyn E: geschreeven uyt Nieuw Jorck; by eenem Gabriel Minvelle, en gedateert den 16 february Jongstleeden, versockende te Moogen hebben paspoort, om van daer een Schip te Zenden, met Vivres, naer Curacao, ende vant zelve Eylandt eenige Macquerons Slaaven affte halen, waerop omvraage gedaen weesend is

goetgevonden ende verstaan, t voorsz versoek te stellen in handen van hem Heer van Beeck en verdere commissarissen tot de Zaaken van America omme te Examineeren ende de Vergaderingh desweegen te dienen van haare consideratien en advis:[9]

...Ter Vergadering zynde gehoort het Rapport vanden Heere Van Beeck en verdere commissarissen, tot de zaake vand America, ingevolge ende tot voldoening der Resolutie commissionael vanden 2: des voorleedens maant Juny, hebbende geexamineert t versoek van eenem Gabriel Minvielle, woonende tot Nieuw Jorck, tendeerende omme te hebben paspoort, om van daer een schip te senden met vivres na Curacao ende vant zelve Eylandt eenige Slaaven affte halen; zoo is naer voorgaende Deliberatie goetgevonden ende verstaen, in het voorn schip mits desen te consenteeren, ende dat over sulx aanden gemelte Gabriel Minvelle de gerequireerde paspoort zal werden gedepesheert ende verwaerdigt; by welke Occagie in Deliberatie zeynde gelyt is goetgevonden ende verstaen, op het Versoek uyt den Name ende van Weegens Jacob Lycela [Leisler] coopman tot Nieuw Jorck voorn: gedaen, aendenzelven, mede toe te Staen, ende te consenteeren; gelyk hem toegestaen ende geconsenteert wert mits deesen de noodige paspoort omme van daer een schip met vivres en coopmanschapen te senden naer Curacao, ende vant zelve Eylandt Slaaven affte halen, inwegen als hier voorn: staet vermelt;[10]

...Wyders hat u [Jan Doncker, director on Curacao] E uyt de hier nevensgaende resolutie vande opgemelte vergaderinge der Thienen [chamber Amsterdam] konnen verstaen, hoe dat deselve heeft goet gevonden opt Eylant Curacao te stabilieeren een open-marcket van Slaven,...Wy sein te gemoet, dat met der tyt wel een goeden handel soude konnen gedreven werden met de Ingesetenen van Nieuwjorck, die sich wel genegen thonen omme van daer schepen te senden naer Curacao, met allerhande soorten van waren en coopmanschappen bysonder pelteryen, gelyck dan oock daer tou paspoort verleent hebben aen eenen Gabriel Minvelle, mitsgaders aen eenen Jacob Lycela [Leisler], te weten, omme, mits betalende/fol. 14 de geregtigheden en de recognitien vande Comp, aent' selve Eylant te komen, ende aldaer Slaven inte handelen. In welken gevalle wy u gerecommandeert willen hebben, dat op de [ar...eemitnge] van de goederen, die door de twe voorn en andere sodanige handelaers sullen werden aengebragt, behoorlycken mach werden gelet, ende dat sulch geschieden met goede kenisse en distinctie soo van de Bevers die wel gewassen syn, otters, possen, Beeren, Mincken, hispans ander Bontwerck, als mede vanden Tabacq in bladeren en gesponnen....[11]

The New Yorkers used their traditional Amsterdam relations and invoked the colonies' Dutch origins in order to get permission from the failing Dutch slave trading company to acquire a share in the Atlantic slave trade. They were quite eager to change their nationality when it served their economic purposes. For economic profits they pretended to obey the Acts of Trade and Navigation; but at the same time they smuggled enumerated goods whenever they could; on the other hand they used the West India Company's vanity with their insinuation that the West India Company still owned New York and that it still enjoyed the slave trade monopoly.

Yet this is not all: Merchants from New York and Boston played an active part in crucial European events; they used European events to manipulate colonial power relations. One word will illuminate my meaning: the Glorious Revolution (1688-1689). I do not need to go into details about the impact of the Glorious Revolution on Dutch, English, British, or European history due to the change from King James II to his nephew and son-in-law William III, prince of Orange. Whig historiography has for a long time told a story that belittled the Dutch role in these momentous events. Now British, Dutch, and even German scholars have provided us with exciting new insights into the importance of the Glorious Revolution.[12]

Let me just point out some of those that changed our notion about what happened in New York and New England. Thanks to David W. Voorhees and our work on the Jacob Leisler papers we can prove that during summer, fall and winter of 1688-1689 leading merchants in New York and Boston were excellently informed early on about what was going on in the Netherlands and in England. And of course they were willing to put that knowledge to good use. Already in December 1688 they knew of William of Orange's invasion of England and of his plans to claim the English throne as a means to rescue the dangerously threatened Netherlands from her arch-enemy Louis XIV, the French king.

Let me repeat: These merchants within two to three months of the event in Europe knew of these momentous happenings; even better, they were determined to contribute their share in bringing England under the Prince of Orange's control. The notarial records of the Municipal Archives of Rotterdam yield clear and striking evidence of New York-ers' and Bostonians' participation in the sophisticated arrangements in late summer 1688 to get William's fleet ready for the invasion of England. The long-time agent of Leisler's son-in-law John Milborne in Rotterdam, Samuel Tucker, Leisler's New York colleague and later follower Samuel Edsall, and members of the Fanueil family from Boston actively co-operated in the hiring of ships that joined William's invasion fleet in the summer of 1688. Perhaps Milborne even saw the fleet set sail; if so he would have been able to tell Leisler of its departure when he returned to New York in early December 1688.[13]

It is now becoming clear that the Glorious Revolution in New York and the leading role in 1689 Jacob Leisler played in it was not just the product and result of regional problems or just a copy of European events or an expression of Leisler's belief in William. It certainly was not a spontaneous reaction of Leisler to news from Europe that slowly spread from one colony to the next. Leisler had had time, information, and alternatives enough to make up his mind. The New York merchant, ex-militiaman, and devout Calvinist had strong connections to the continent, to Amsterdam and her merchant citizens. He had partners and colleagues in the Old World who knew perfectly well what was going on in the States General and might even have been a part of those financial webs that supported William's of Orange military efforts.

Although there is still a lack of evidence of Leisler's personal convictions, his attitudes and behavior during his power-play within New York 1689-1691 strongly suggest that he understood those military and political events in Europe to be essential for a working Atlantic tradingsystem with New York in a specially strong position. Of course he used the events in Europe, too, for solving some of the problems like the infamous *Dominion of New England* (1686-1689) with Edmund Andros and Francis Nicholson as henchmen of King James. And yes, Leisler, too, took up William's cause because he feared that Protestant

New York would be threatened by Catholic France in cooperation with Indian tribes from the Great Lakes and in the backwoods of New York, Connecticut, and Massachusetts.

But let me insist that Leisler's rebellion was also primarilyan expression of his appreciation of the importance of an Atlantic perspective of the world and of New York's as well as Dutch cities like Amsterdam's or Rotterdam's position in it. It was no mere coincidence that merchants from North America who had spent some time of their professional life in Holland and had become well connected there promoted the Dutch invasion fleet, and that merchants and transatlantic orientated cities like Boston, New York, and St. Mary's staged their rebellions against King James and in favour of William in early summer 1689. On the other hand, lesser maritime cities in the hinterland did not pay much attention to political events in the Atlantic world as long as they did not affect their interests. These colonial merchants who had linked their economic wellbeing to international commerce, communication, and cooperation had a vision: With their actions (later they were styled rebellions) they meant to prepare the way for an unlimited Atlantic free trade within the colonies, free trade with the West Indian British Isles and with the European continent, undisturbed by national restrictions like the Acts of Trade and Navigation or other nationalistic demands. The military alliance between England and the Netherlands personified by William III, prince of Orange, should have, so New York's merchants hoped, be combined with commercial cooperation between Dutch and English colonies all over the American-Atlantic space. With their actions in favour of the Dutch Stadholder and English King William III (1688-1691), these merchants meant to support an Atlantic trading network; the Glorious Revolutions in America were Atlantic events that connected American colonists and Europeans.

Conclusions

First, New Amsterdam/New York should not be viewed as an enclosed and isolated settlement but on the contrary as being rather firmly set in its Atlantic context, that takes into account American as well as European constellations.

Second, as early as the seventeenth century, people on the Hudson and on the Amstel provide us with marvelous proof that globalization is nothing new. They already practiced what many think so startlingly new (fight it or love it): They traded without paying any attention to national boundaries, national laws, national rules or just plain nationality.

Third, to understand the chances and possibilities of early modern Atlantic history properly, we are forced to look beyond nationally defined claims and rules of individual nations. Instead of being taken in by state affairs and high policy, we need to concentrate on those individuals who by their actions produced and shaped historical events; and in doing so, we will find that they simply do not fit the nationalistic pattern of traditional historiography. Our approach to Atlantic history in the twenty-first century will put the nineteenth-century concept of national history where it belongs: onto the shelf of historiography.

Notes

1   See J.G.A.Pocock, ed., James Harrington, *The Commonwealth of Oceana and a system of Politics* (Cambridge: Cambridge University Press, 1992), 16.

2   See Joyce Goodfriend, *Before the Melting Pot: Society and Culture in colonial New York City, 1664-1730* (Princeton, NJ: Princeton University Press, 1992); Randall Balmer, *A Perfect Babel of Confusion: Dutch religion and English Culture in the Middle Colonies* (New York: Oxford University Press, 1989).

3   See Jaap Jacobs, 'The Hartford Treaty: A European perspective on a New World Conflict,' *De Halve Maen* 68.4 (1995): 74-79. I want to thank Jaap Jacobs for giving me a copy of his fine article; Claudia Schnurmann, *Atlantische Welten. Engländer und Niederländer im amerikanisch-atlantischen Raum, 1648-1713* (Cologne: Böhlau, 1998), 86ff; Ronald D. Cohen, 'The Hartford Treaty of 1650. Anglo-Dutch Cooperation in the seventeenth Century,' *The New-York Historical Society Quarterly* 53 (1969): 311-332; Oliver A. Rink, *Holland on the Hudson: An Economic and Social History of Dutch New York* (Ithaca, NY: Cornell University Press, 1986), 246-249; Max Savelle, *The Origins of American Diplomacy: The International History of Anglo-America, 1492-1763* (2nd ed., New York: Macmillan, 1968), 159-164.

4   See Schnurmann, *Atlantische Welten*, passim.

5   William T. Davis, ed., *Bradford's History of Plymouth Plantation* 1606-1646 (New York: C. Scribner's sons, 1908), 226f; see Schnurmann, *Atlantische Welten*, 149.

6   James Kendall Hosmer, ed., *Winthrop's Journal: History of New England, 1630-1649*, 2 vols. (New York: C. Scribner's sons, 1908), 1:.130f.

7   See Schnurmann, *Atlantische Welten*, passim.

8   Norbert H. Schneeloch, *Aktionäre der Westindischen Compagnie von 1674. Die Verschmelzung der alten Kapitalgebergruppen zu einer neuen Aktiengesellschaft.* Beiträge zur Wirtschaftsgeschichte, 12. (Stuttgart: Klett-Cotta, 1982); Henk den Heijer, *De Geschiedenis van de WIC* (Zutphen: Walburg Pers, 1994); Johannes Menne Postma, *The Dutch in the Atlantic Slave Trade 1600-1815* (Cambridge: Cambridge University Press, 1990); Albert Wirz, *Sklaverei und kapitalistisches Weltsystem* (Frankfurt/Main: Suhrkamp, 1984).

9   2 June 1676, Kamer Amsterdam, minutes Nationaal Archief Den Haag (= NADH) 1.05.01.02 331 fol. 181-183.

10 7 July 1676, Kamer Amsterdam, minutes NADH 1.05.01.02 331 fol. 203-204r. fol. 203: 'Present De Heeren De Vicq, Prest, van Beeck, Godin, Broen, Nys, Pellicorne, Wickevoort.'

11 [11 July 1676] West India Company/Kamer Amsterdam to the Director of Curaçao, Jan Doncker, 11 July 1676 NADH 1.05.01.02 Tweede Westindische Compagnie 467 fol. 12r-14r.

12 See the fine articles compiled in Jonathan Israel, ed., *The Anglo-Dutch Moment: Essays on the Glorious Revolution and its world impact* (Cambridge: Cambridge University Press, 1991); Claudia Schnurmann, 'Die Rekonstruktion eines atlantischen Netzwerkes – das Beispiel Jakob Leisler, 1660-1691. Ein Editionsprojekt,' *Jahrbuch für Europäische Überseegeschichte* 2 (2002): 19-39.

13 See Andrew Russell Papers, National Archives of Scotland, Edinburgh.

Joyce D. Goodfriend

THE LIMITS OF RELIGIOUS PLURALISM IN
EIGHTEENTH-CENTURY NEW YORK CITY

New York City's religious pluralism was impressive by eighteenth-century standards. By 1771, with its population nearing 22,000, the city could boast eighteen congregations representing thirteen different religious persuasions.[1] These included a variety of Protestants – Dutch Reformed, Lutheran, Huguenot (French Reformed), Quakers. Anglicans, Presbyterians, Baptists, Moravians, German Lutheran, German Reformed, (Scottish) Seceder Presbyterians, and Methodists – as well as Jews. Worship was not compulsory and people were not required to belong to a particular church. No single church had a monopoly on churchgoers and no preacher could take his audience for granted. Individuals could alter their denominational affiliation at will and many seized the opportunity, leading one Reformed domine to decry the fact that 'people run from one church to another.'[2] Eighteenth-century New York City's panorama of faiths, the peaceful coexistence of people of different backgrounds and beliefs, and the range of choices residents enjoyed with respect to doctrine, ecclesiastical organization, forms of spirituality, and clergy seemed noteworthy to contemporaries and have continued to impress scholars, who hail the city's religious variety as a precursor of modern American religious pluralism.

Yet the version of religious pluralism that existed in the pre-revolutionary city had its limitations, limitations that call into question Jon Butler's claim that 'Britain's eighteenth-century mainland American colonies [and Butler uses New York City as one of his prime examples] displayed a religious pluralism that dwarfed the mild diversity found in any early modern European nation.'[3] One can, as well, dispute Butler's contention that no place in Europe exhibited more than 'mild diversity' on the grounds that it fails to take into account the variety of religions practiced in Amsterdam in the seventeenth and eighteenth centuries. Contemporary visitors and historians have offered ample evidence of the fact that Protestants of all sorts, Jews, and Catholics assembled for worship in the city. Most Protestants, as well as Jews, could attend services in public, while Catholics and some Protestant groups were compelled to gather in *schuilkerken* or hidden churches, whose existence was widely known.[4] Not all of these congregations enjoyed total religious freedom, but the system of accommodation worked out by Amsterdam's civil authorities ensured that their religious life could proceed without interference. Notwithstanding the restrictions that bounded Amsterdam's religious order in the years prior to 1795, when church and state were separated in the Netherlands, there is ample evidence to show that the scope of religious diversity in the city was far more extensive than Butler would have it.[5]

The purpose of this essay, however, is to challenge Butler's generalization from the American side, by placing the case of New York City under the microscope. Specifically, I contend that three features of New York City's religious pluralism mark it as far from modern and compel us to reconsider the exceptionality of religious life in the city that began as New Amsterdam.

First, despite its amplitude, New York's religious spectrum, was far from comprehensive, since it encompassed only Protestants and Jews. As a Dutch domine succinctly put it in 1741, 'there is here perfect freedom of conscience for all, except Papists.'[6] Immigrants raised as Roman Catholics in Ireland – mostly soldiers and indentured servants – were denied any forum for public worship in the city and New Yorkers of African descent, whether slave or free, were also barred from assembling in public to express their traditional beliefs. While some Africans cast their lot with Christian congregations, others, especially newcomers, were cut off from collective spiritual practice.

Second, those who were perceived as diverging too far from Protestant orthodoxy were vulnerable to attack from the pulpit, criticism in the press, and even official sanctions. During the course of the eighteenth-century, alarms were raised not only about Moravians but also about alleged Deists, whose controversial positions on certain issues unsettled the city's religious life.

Third, New York City's churches did not stand on an equal footing. The Church of England had the force of the state behind it because British governors interpreted the controversial Ministry Act of 1693 to mean that the Anglican church was 'established' in New York City. The Dutch Reformed church had obtained a charter that secured its legal status and set it apart from the rest of the city's religious institutions. The denial of charters to the Presbyterians and other congregations relegated them to an inferior position in New York City's religiously diverse society.

By proscribing Catholicism, policing Protestantism, and privileging Anglicanism, those in power in eighteenth-century New York City created a variant of religious pluralism that was more attuned to the values of the *ancien regime* than to modern standards. Sustaining this system entailed procuring the assent of the city's men and women to the exclusions and preferences incorporated in it. Yet New Yorkers were not of one mind on the priorities that defined their religious system. Most seem to have subscribed to the anti-Catholic prejudices that underlay official policy, but more than a few were reluctant to support sanctions against Moravians and suspected Deists. By far the greatest source of division in the community was the perpetuation of Anglican privilege. Presbyterians and others classified as Dissenters in England questioned the legitimacy of the Church of England's establishment in New York City, and after mid-century, mobilized to contest Anglican claims to special power. In the process of making the case for Dissenter rights, they adumbrated a more inclusive conception of religious pluralism.

Dissenters were not the only New Yorkers to recognize the shortcomings of the city's religious arrangements, but they were the only ones to have a voice. African Americans and Catholics stood to benefit from the introduction of a more encompassing form of pluralism, but they had to depend on others to make the case for broadening religious rights in New York.

To fully understand eighteenth-century New York City's religious patterns, then, it is essential to explore not only the genesis of the limits placed on religious pluralism in eighteenth-century New York, but also the reception of these qualifications by the populace.

Cultural Pluralism and Religious Pluralism

New York City originated as the Dutch settlement of New Amsterdam. Established in the 1620s as a trading post by the Dutch West India Company, by the 1660s it had gained a municipal charter and become a flourishing Atlantic port.[7] From its earliest days, the city boasted a heterogeneous mix of peoples, including Dutch, Germans, French, English and other Europeans, as well as Africans, many of whom were enslaved by the West India Company. In 1646, a visiting Jesuit, struck by the diversity of the population, recorded that New Netherland's Director-General had told him that 'there were men of eighteen different languages' on Manhattan Island.[8] But New Amsterdam's cultural pluralism did not readily translate into religious pluralism. The only officially sanctioned church in the city was the Reformed church, and here all residents were welcome to worship, marry and have their children baptized. 'No religion is publicly exercised but the Calvinist,' the Jesuit asserted, but immediately qualified his statement by saying that people of other religious persuasions were present in the colony.[9] This is not surprising, given the fact that liberty of conscience was a foundational principle of the Dutch Republic. Nevertheless, though New Amsterdam's inhabitants were guaranteed freedom of conscience, in practice, religious uniformity was the rule.

In the 1650s, the monopoly of the Reformed church was directly challenged. The growing number of Lutherans began to press for permission to worship in public, refugee Jews sought to practice their faith, and Quaker missionaries attempted to spread their message in the city and its environs. Director-General Petrus Stuyvesant, an ardent Calvinist, staunchly defended the existing policy of religious exclusiveness and, with the support of the local clergy, worked to ensure that the Reformed church remained New Amsterdam's only church. He did so because he feared that the open practice of faiths other than the Reformed would not only imperil communal order, but also incur God's displeasure. 'If the Lutherans should be indulged in the exercise of their (public) worship,' the city's Reformed ministers explained, 'the Papist, Mennonites and others, would soon make similar claims. Thus we would soon become a Babel of confusion, instead of remaining a united and peaceful people.'[10]

Stuyvesant's uncompromising stance on religious toleration, manifested in efforts to bar Lutherans, Jews and Quakers from openly expressing their faith in the city, was rejected by his superiors in Amsterdam, who mandated concessions and compromises designed to accommodate these religious minorities along the lines of practice in the Netherlands. In the end, however, he did succeed in preventing rival religions from gaining a foothold in New Amsterdam. Quakers never established a presence in the city and the small Jewish community disbanded after a few years. The Lutherans, who, because of their sizeable numbers and activism, posed the most formidable threat to Stuyvesant's ideal of a religiously unified society, were essentially driven underground. Yet, during their struggle for formal recognition, believers in the Augsburg Confession cemented bonds with each other and developed a sense of common purpose. Though some succumbed to the pressures exerted by Stuyvesant and drifted away, a substantial nucleus – estimated at 100 in December 1664 – remained to gather for public worship in English New York City.[11]

The incipient religious pluralism of New Amsterdam only came to fruition under the governance of the English. Almost immediately after the transfer of sovereignty, the new English Governor granted the Lutherans permission to worship openly.[12] The city's Lutherans expressed their joy at the turn of events, noting that 'we have been spurred on by prominent persons of the English nation, yes, have even been furnished pens and hands, to carry on this Christian work.'[13] While the colony remained under the control of the Duke of York (later James II), Protestants of many varieties, as well as Catholics, were free to assemble for worship. For motives of his own, the Catholic Duke of York inaugurated a policy of religious toleration in his colony.[14] In 1687, the Catholic Governor, Thomas Dongan, described the variety of religions practiced in New York. In addition to those belonging to the Church of England, there were Dutch Calvinists, French Calvinists, and Dutch Lutherans, as well as 'few Roman Catholics; abundance of Quakers preachers men [and] Women especially; Singing Quakers, Ranting Quakers; Sabbatarians; Antisabbatarians; Some Anabaptists Some Independents; some Jews; in short of all sorts of opinions there are some, and the most part of none at all.'[15]

Not all New Yorkers saw eye to eye with the Duke and Governor Dongan on the range of toleration. In 1685, city leaders rebuffed an initiative to allow Jews the same religious freedom as their Christian counterparts. 'The Jews Petition to the Governor for Liberty to Exercise their Religion, Being by him Recommended to the Mayor and aldermen was read in Common Councell, and they Returned their opinions thereupon That noe publique Worship is Tolerated by act of assembly, but to those that professe faith in Christ, and therefore the Jews Worship not to be allowed.'[16] The city's few Jews had to remain content to meet in private.

William Byrd, a Virginian who visited New York City in 1685, may not have appreciated the irony when he commented that 'they have as many sects of Religion there as at Amsterdam, all tolerated.'[17] It had taken the priorities of the Catholic Duke of York to turn the small urban center at the tip of Manhattan Island into a mirror image of its namesake. The religious pluralism that emerged in the city took shape not under the Dutch, with their vaunted reputation for creating the most tolerant society in seventeenth-century Europe, but under the aegis of the English.

Catholics

The particular form that religious pluralism assumed in eighteenth-century New York City was directly related to the English vision of religion and national identity that emerged in the aftermath of the Glorious Revolution. 'The drive to create a truly Protestant nation,' identified by scholars as the defining theme of government policy in Georgian England, lay behind the legal repression of Catholics.[18] Catholics were prohibited from owning land, holding office or graduating from university, and periodically were harassed, but, in practice, the government's anti-Catholic policy was usually mitigated by local officials who were reluctant to enforce the harsh penalties stipulated in the penal laws.[19] Catholics could gather for mass in the private chapels of recusant gentry or the chapels of foreign embassies and not be molested. This is not to discount the significance of the deep reservoir of anti-Catholic sentiment in eighteenth-century England – Catholics remained in a vulnerable position throughout the eighteenth century – but rather to emphasize the importance of loopholes that permitted clandestine Roman Catholic worship in London and elsewhere in England.[20] In New York, by contrast, the strict enforcement of statutes proscribing Catholic preaching effectively kept Catholics from practicing their faith.

Why were New York City's relatively few Catholics – primarily Irish soldiers stationed in the fort and Irish servants indentured to artisans and merchants – forced to remain concealed while English Catholics were allowed to attend Mass at private chapels and Catholics in the neighboring colony of Pennsylvania could worship openly at the Roman Catholic chapel that had been built in Philadelphia by the early 1730s?[21] New York's official anti-Catholic policy may have been inspired by England's legal sanctions against Catholics, but it built upon a legacy of ill feeling toward Catholics dating from the 1680s, when Governor Thomas Dongan, an Irish Catholic appointed by the Duke of York, offered preferment to several Catholics, allowed Jesuits to operate a New York City school to teach Latin, and built a chapel in the Fort in which Father Thomas Harvey, a Jesuit, presided.[22] In 1683, Dutch Reformed merchant Oloff Stevenszen van Cortlandt apprised his daughter Maria that 'It is said that the Beeltsnyder is making an altar – they intend to build a popish church over it.'[23] The 'Images erected by Col. Thomas Dongan in the fort' were mentioned in a 1689 deposition.[24] The timing of Dongan's pro-Catholic initiatives did not sit well with New York's largely Calvinist population, whose numbers were augmented in the 1680s by Huguenots who streamed into the city with fresh recollections of persecution at the hands of French Catholic officials.

A groundswell of anti-Catholic sentiment among these Reformed Protestants was unleashed during Leisler's Rebellion, the popular movement that erupted in New York following the Glorious Revolution.[25] Soon after he took control of the city, Leisler declared his intent to 'have some papists disarmed & also those Idolls destroyed which we heare our dailly still worshipped.'[26] New York's militia, overjoyed at 'our deliverance from Tyranny, popery and slavery,' assailed the local 'papists, who had... subverted our ancient priviledges making us in effect slaves to their will contrary to the laws of England.'[27] Jacob Leisler's efforts to preserve the Protestant religion by rooting out Papists were applauded by large numbers of New Yorkers, whose hostility toward Catholics was only further inflamed by reports of the depredations of the Catholic French and their Indian allies on the colony's northern frontier.[28]

Provincial officials tapped into this powerful current of anti-Catholicism as events in England unfolded. In 1696, following an attempt on the life of William III, Association oaths were signed by hundreds of New Yorkers to demonstrate their loyalty to the Protestant King.[29] Only recently the beneficiaries of official favoritism, Catholics were now singled out for retribution. 'Roman Catholicks, and reputed Papists in New Yorke... are all disarmed and obliged to give bond with surety for their good behaviour or be confined in prison' reported Governor Benjamin Fletcher in 1696.[30] Ordered by the Governor and Council to prepare a list 'of all the Roman Catholicks or such as are reputed Papists within the City of New Yorke,' the Mayor named ten Catholic men.[31] It was in this climate that New York's penal laws were devised. In 1691, a provincial law guaranteeing liberty of conscience for New Yorkers stipulated that 'noething herein mentioned... shall extend to give Liberty for any persons of the Romish religion to exercise their manor of worship' and in 1700, 'An act against Jesuits & popish preists' banished 'all and every Jesuit and Seminary Preist missionary or Ecclesiasticall person made or ordained by any Authority... derived... from the Pope or See of Rome' from the colony.[32]

New York authorities placed a premium on keeping the community solidly anti-Catholic, periodically requesting residents to visibly reaffirm their loyalty to the Protestant succession and to reject Catholicism by taking an oath. Holding office in New York was contingent on forswearing Catholicism. In 1705, New York City's Justices, Aldermen and Assistants signed a Protestant declaration that repudiated transubstantiation and characterized other Catholic beliefs as superstitious and idolatrous.[33] The city's constables and other officials signed the same oath in 1714.[34] In 1715, when fears of the uprising in behalf of the Catholic Pretender were at their height, the Governor, Council, Mayor, Principal Men, and Ministers signed an Oath for King George I and against the Pretender, and a host of foreign born-Protestants took the oath of abjuration.[35]

New Yorkers of all sorts – officeholders, well-to-do merchants, foreign-born artisans – signed oaths similar to these, and also oaths of allegiance, periodically until the 1770s.[36] Even those at the fringes of the religious continuum – the Jews – jumped on the anti-Catholic bandwagon to demonstrate their commitment to the Protestant community and its values. Abigail Franks, a Jew who prided herself on her friendships with members of the city's Protestant elite, gave evidence that she had absorbed their negative views of Catholics in a self-deprecating comment. 'I don't think religeon Consist in Idle Cerimonies & works of Supperoregations Wich if they Send people to heaven wee & the papist have the Greatest title too.'[37] In April 1741, 21 naturalized Jews, presumably suspected of having sympathy for the Catholic Jacobites, signed a loyalty oath to George II in which 'they pledged to abjure 'that damnable Doctrine & position, that princes excommunicated or deprived by the pope, or any authority of the see of Rome, may be deposed or murthered by their Subjects'' and affirmed the Protestant succession.[38] Such public rituals were critical in defining the bounds of community in a society composed of disparate peoples. To disavow Catholicism was to claim a place among the protected majority.

Forswearing Catholicism was not just a means of assuring immunity from reprisal. It was a way of reinforcing sentiments that were widely shared in New York City. When Yale-educated lawyer William Livingston spoke glibly of 'the superstitious rites and fantastic trumperies of popery'[39] or future Revolutionary leader John Jay characterized Catholicism as 'a religion fraught with sanguinary and impious tenets,'[40] they were voicing what amounted to clichés in a culture saturated with anti-Catholic messages. New Yorkers were routinely alerted to the doctrinal errors and political dangers associated with Catholicism through sermons, literature, and public celebrations. Ministers used their pulpits to point out mistakes in Catholic beliefs as well as to issue more general denunciations of the faith. Louis Rou, of the French Reformed church, for example, included comments critical of the Roman Catholic church in a number of his sermons.[41]

Familiarity with the genre of anti-Catholic literature also colored New Yorkers' views of Catholics. In 1725, local printer John Peter Zenger issued a volume purportedly written by a Protestant gardener titled *The French Convert. Being a True Relation of the Happy Conversion of a Noble French Lady, From the Errors and Superstitions of Popery to the Reformed Religion.* This book, which had been published in Boston in 1708 and went through many editions, overflowed with lurid details of the sexual depravity and greed of Catholic priests.[42] In all likelihood, other publications in this vein were imported from England or Boston and were read by city residents. Newspapers were an additional source of anti-Catholic material. In 1726, the *New-York Gazette* printed a lengthy account of an *auto-da-fe* in Lisbon and the burning at the stake of a priest.[43]

The institutionalization of the Protestant calendar in New York City fostered consciousness of the chasm that separated Protestants and Catholics in the eighteenth-century British world.[44] Commemorations of the birthdays and coronations of Protestant monarchs were occasions for instilling not only patriotic pride but also religious prejudice. One holiday – Guy Fawkes Day – became the focal point for inciting passions against Catholics. Almanacs included Guy Fawkes Day in their list of significant dates and, at least as early as 1737, New York authorities sponsored a celebration of the November 5 anniversary of 'that horrid and Treasonable Popish Gun-Powder plot.'[45]

When rumors circulated in 1741 that Catholic soldiers and servants had conspired with Africans to burn New York City and indiscriminately murder white people, both governmental officeholders and ordinary inhabitants were quick to cast about for villains. Judge Daniel Horsmanden, who suspected that 'there had of late been Popish Priests lurking about the Town' interpreted this 'Scheme w[hi]ch must have been brooded in a Conclave of Devils, & hatcht in the Cabinet of Hell' as a Catholic conspiracy.[46] During the trial of John Ury, a teacher alleged to be a Roman Catholic priest and a key figure in the conspiracy, New York's Attorney General, Richard Bradley, unleashed a scathing attack on Roman Catholicism, calling it a 'hocus pocus bloody religion' and heaping scorn on the 'pretended pardons and indulgences of that crafty and deceitful church, and their masses to pray souls out of purgatory, which they quote (or rather wrest) scripture for, when no such thing is to be found there' and 'their doctrine of transubstantiation, which is so big with absurdities that is shocking to the common sense and reason of mankind.'[47] Bradley's diatribe was calculated to harden popular anti-Catholicism. When a Spanish Negro who had been convicted as one of the conspirators in the alleged plot was brought to the place of execution, 'he made a long Prayer in the Spanish Tongue, making use of his Beads, with a Crucifix in his Hand, which he often Kissed, and Crossed himself, after the Manner of the Roman Catholicks'[48] This spectacle could only have increased New Yorkers' loathing for Catholics.

New Yorkers' anti-Catholic prejudices were soon stoked again by news of the Jacobite rebellion in Britain. Governor Clinton proclaimed February 26, 1746 a day of fasting and prayer in light of the rebellion in Scotland for the 'Popish Pretender.'[49] Success against the rebels in Scotland prompted the Governor to declare July 31, 1746 a day of Thanksgiving.[50] On that day, Presbyterian minister Ebenezer Pemberton exhorted his congregation to 'return thanks to our heavenly Father, for his goodness in defending our King and Nation, from the attempts of a Popish Pretender, when we were threatened with the loss of everything, that is dear to us, either as Men or Christians, as Englishmen or Protestants.'[51]

If New Yorkers thirsted to read about the Protestant victory over the Popish Pretender, they could turn to several products of the local press. In addition to printing Pemberton's sermon, James Parker brought out editions of two English accounts of the Jacobite rebellion, John Marchant's *The History of the Late Rebellion, in Great-Britain* and James Ray's *The Acts of the Rebels*. [52] Catherine Zenger issued John Anderson's *The Book of the Chronicles of His Royal Highness, William Duke of Cumberland: Being an Account of the Rise and Progress of the Present Rebellion*.[53] The anti-Catholic sentiments that pulsed in New York City at mid-century even found visual expression in two silver beakers engraved by

Joseph Leddel. Jr. with anti-Catholic, anti-Jacobite motifs and mottoes.[54] The three couplets on the 1754 beaker read 'I wish they were all hang'd in a rope/ The Pretender Devil and the Pope;' 'Three mortal enemies remember./ The Devil Pope and the Pretender;' and 'Most Wicked damnable and Evil./ The Pope Pretend[e]r and the Devil.'[55]

Animosity toward Catholics did not abate in the aftermath of the Jacobite scare, but instead was fueled by the ongoing conflict with the French. Popular outrage that the British government had prematurely ended King George's War in 1748 intensified hatred of French Catholics, leading commoners to refashion the Guy Fawkes' holiday.[56] According to a newspaper report, 'a grand Procession, being the first of the Kind in these Parts, was carried thro' the Principal streets of this City, and many Windows were broke by the populace.'[57] By 1755, the celebration of what had come to be called Pope Day had evolved into a 'mock ceremonial.' Onlookers of all ranks witnessed 'The 'Devil Pope and Pretender' [being] carried about the city on a bier at night, 'hideously formed, and as humorously contrived, the Devil standing close behind the Pope, seemingly paying his compliments to him, with a three prong'd Pitchfork in one Hand, with which at Times he was made to thrust his Holiness on the Back, and a Lanthorn in the other, the young Pretender standing before the Pope, waiting his Commands.'[58] As long as anti-Catholic ideology was powerful enough to bridge the city's social divide, there was little likelihood that Catholics would be allowed to worship openly in New York.

Though most New Yorkers of European descent seem to have embraced the anti-Catholicism codified in New York's statutes, there was less unanimity on the appropriate stance toward those who were perceived as espousing views that were at odds with fundamental Protestant values. Preserving orthodoxy was integral to government policy in New York, as it was in England, during the eighteenth century. Local ministers, unnerved by their congregants' flirtations with novel creeds and irregular preachers in the years after 1740, invested considerable energy in warding off challenges to the status quo. Devout lay people were no less vigilant than their pastors when it came to detecting groups that imperiled orthodoxy, members of the Scotch Presbyterian Society warning in 1754 that New Yorkers were 'exposed to an inundation of Deism, Atheism, Moravianism, Quakerism & Superstition.'[59]

Though strict Presbyterians may have seen threats to Protestant principles emanating from all corners of the religious map, the primary sites of concern were at opposite poles of the religious spectrum. The Moravians, a pietistic sect whose members held antinomian ideas, indulged in exotic practices such as love feasts and washing of the feet, and were unwilling to take oaths were prime candidates for censure. After Moravian leaders visited New York City in the early 1740s, local sympathizers began regular meetings in private homes. Moravianism soon became a topic of wider interest. In 1742, Presbyterian preacher Gilbert Tennent came to New York to deliver a series of powerful sermons criticizing 'the erronious [sic] Notions, of a pernicious new sect of People, called *Moravian Brethren*... who have lately come into this Country.' 'I cannot stand as an unconcern'd spectator, to behold the *Moravian* tragedy,' Tennent intoned from the pulpit. '[M]y Heart bleeds within me to see the precious Truths of Christ opposed, slighted and trodden under foot by our new Reformers; and that under a Pretext of extraordinary Sanctity, Love and Meekness!' [60] When these sermons were published the following year with an 'Appendix relating to Errors lately Vented by some Moravians in those parts,' Tennent, eager to enlist New York's

Reformed Dutch in the anti-Moravian coalition, included a translated excerpt from a letter sent to local merchant George Brinkerhoff by a correspondent in Amsterdam who called attention to pastoral letters and tracts written by Dutch Reformed clergy hostile to the Moravians.[61]

Moravians

By then, the city's Reformed church had been warned by the Classis of Amsterdam 'to be on our guard against the Herrenhutters [Moravians]' and had received 'a Pastoral Letter cautioning us against that pernicious sect' as well as a book on the subject by Mr. Kulenkamp.[62] When the venerable minister, Gualterus Du Bois, replied to the Classis in May 1741, he told them that he had 'taken a stand against the Herrenhutters.' Noting that he had already received 'a copy of the Pastoral Letter from Holland about them,' he assured the Classis that 'it had been published everywhere in my congregation.'[63]

Though his tone was more moderate than that of Gilbert Tennent, New York City's own Presbyterian minister, Ebenezer Pemberton, did not conceal his antipathy toward the Moravians when he responded in 1743 to a clerical colleague in England who had expressed a 'charitable opinion' of them. '[W]ith us they [the Moravians] are evidently endeavouring to draw off the affections of the people from the soundest and most zealous ministers in these parts.'[64] In 1744, New Yorkers were alerted to the publication of a critical volume compiled from Moravian writings purporting to show that 'they are not of that Church of the Antient United Moravian and Bohemian Brethren.' The book contained observations by local painter Gerardus Duycking.[65]

By that time, New York's Governor Clinton and his Council, concerned that Moravian missionaries in Dutchess county were encouraging the Indians to side with the French against British interests in the war that had just broken out, ordered them to the city for interrogation. The refusal of these Moravians and some of their colleagues to take the oath of allegiance to King George left them in a vulnerable position. In this charged atmosphere, the fear of Catholic preachers infiltrating New York was so intense that the Moravian missionaries were even suspected of being Papists. At the Governor's urging, the New York Assembly enacted a temporary law in 1744 that provided that 'no Vagrant Preacher, Moravian or Disguised Papist, shall Preach or Teach Either in Publick or Private without first takeing the Oaths appointed by this Act.'[66] Since the Moravians scrupled to take any oaths, this law became a pretext for expelling them from the province.

British authorities frowned on the excessive zeal the New York government exhibited against the Moravians and the Board of Trade demanded to know the reasoning behind the 1744 law. A statement drawn up by Council chairman Daniel Horsmanden makes clear that this law, which was designed to expire in a year, was conceived in an atmosphere of apprehension by men who had recently expressed their 'Abhorrence [of] the base Designs of his Majesty's Enemies, to invade his Kingdoms, and excite Revolts and Disturbances among his Subjects in Favour of a Popish Pretender,' who were dealing with a war with the French Catholics on their borders, and who believed that they had just narrowly averted a catastrophic uprising of slaves and Catholics in their midst.[67]

The Moravian missionaries' mistreatment was, at least in part, grounded in the perception that the Moravian faith went beyond acceptable Protestant practice, a view nurtured by local clergymen and no doubt endorsed by many of the laity. Nonetheless, more than a few respectable New Yorkers found the sect's teachings appealing. Women seem to have been particularly attracted to the group. William Smith, Jr., who noted that the Moravians' service was in the English tongue, claimed that the membership 'consist[ed] principally of female proselytes from other societies.'[68] The detailed memoir of a woman raised in the Dutch Reformed church who turned to the Moravians when her spiritual needs went unfulfilled makes clear the difficulties converts had to overcome in New York City's hostile climate. Sarah van Vleck Grube noted that in 1744 'I went to a Brethren's meeting for the first time, but I was very scared that one of my relatives or friends would see me because at that time the Brethren were much despised, especially by the Reformed pastors.' Over a decade later, when she finally decided to join the Moravians, she had to satisfy both her two eldest brothers and the Reformed minister, who 'came himself and testified to his pain that I wanted to leave his church.'[69]

Merchant Thomas Noble, a Presbyterian, was an early and influential supporter of the Moravians in the city. He and his wife opened their home for meetings of the fledgling group. Noble's slave, Andrew the Moor, who later recalled the pious atmosphere in the Noble home, became a Moravian convert.[70] David Van Horne, a prominent New York merchant and Presbyterian lay leader, was also drawn to the Moravians, though he never formally affiliated with them. '[O]ne reason for my Esteem for [th]em here,' Van Horne explained, 'is the simplicity of their Worship and Freedom from Ceremonys.'[71] In 1748, a Moravian congregation was organized in New York City and by 1752 the members had erected a church building.[72] According to Lutheran minister Henry Muhlenberg, writing in 1753, 'the Zinzendorfers [Moravians] were attracting a large following in New York.'[73]

Yet New York's ministers continued to vilify the sect, even after the British Parliament had passed an Act in 1749 that recognized the Moravian Church as 'an antient Protestant Episcopal Church' and granted it concessions with respect to military service and oath-talking.[74] The continuing diatribes of the Dutch Reformed and Presbyterian clergy against the Moravians led William Livingston to craft an essay defending the sect. The publication of 'A Vindication of the MORAVIANS, against the Aspersions of their Enemies' in 1753 unleashed a torrent of criticism against Livingston, less for his advocacy of a conciliatory posture toward the Moravians than for his condemnation of the dogmatic pronouncements that he saw issuing from New York City pulpits.[75] When the pillars of religious orthodoxy 'branded [him] with the opprobrious language of Rascal, Scoundrel, Atheist, Deist, [and] Mocker of Things Sacred,' they were, in effect, accusing him of transgressing the bounds of acceptable religious belief in another way.[76]

Non-Trinitarians

Britain's definition of itself as a nation of Protestant Christians was built on a foundation of Trinitarianism. This put anyone who questioned belief in the Trinity – whether Arian, Socinian, Deist or atheist – beyond the purview of religious respectability. Though governmental authorities made plain that they would not stand by and allow freethinkers to undermine the fundamental tenets of Christianity, in practice, non-Trinitarians enjoyed considerable latitude to express their views in England. Nevertheless, they had to exercise caution for much of the eighteenth century and the same was true in New York.

The public expression of ideas challenging the Christian scheme of salvation was condemned as sacrilegious by both civic and clerical leaders in mid-eighteenth-century New

York. In the late 1730s, the consistory of the city's Reformed church alerted ministers 'to be on their guard, and oppose the artful misleadings of one Peter Venema, a crafty free-thinker of Groningen, who had previously been a Reader and Schoolmaster just outside that city.' Domine Du Bois was quick to heed this advice. 'I, therefore, determinedly set myself against him. Under God's blessing, my efforts accomplished much good, although some still adhere to him. Among these is one Jacob Goelet, who, with his conventicles, endeavors to do all possible harm to our Church.'[77] Goelet, a bookseller, had arranged for the printing of a mathematical text by Venema in 1730.[78] It is unclear, however, what sort of ideas Venema might have been advancing. Du Bois implausibly asserted that some Herrenhutters who had arrived from Philadelphia 'have as yet but little influence, except among the followers of Venema, and some Independents.'[79] All heterodox notions seemingly were of a piece to the aged cleric.

Deism was a more clear-cut target. Pronouncing it 'melancholy to hear of the extensive progress of Deism in the European world,' Presbyterian minister Ebenezer Pemberton heaped praise on an English colleague for his efforts to 'maintain the divine authority of the Gospel against the impetuous attacks of its adversaries.'[80] In 1745, Henry De Foreest reprinted a work called 'A Short and Easie Method with the Deists wherein the Certainty of the Religion is Demonstrated... .' and in 1753 *The New-York Mercury* published an anti-Deist letter purporting to give 'a faithful picture of a Modern free-thinker.'[81]

Educated young men of New York's elite were most likely to be familiar with writings on rational religion and there is evidence that some had begun to flirt with the heterodox notions propounded by British intellectuals. Presbyterian layman William Smith discovered, to his dismay, that several New Yorkers favored 'a Modern Scheme in Divinity.'[82] In April 1754, Obadiah Wells informed Joseph Bellamy, an evangelical minister from Connecticut who had just preached in New York City, that 'Last night a clubb of yonge Deists or rather Atheists met, who it seems had all of them heard your fore noon sermon yester day; it happened that the toppick of their Conversation turned upon your discourse & one in partickuler made a Banter & Ridicule of it, on which another of them Rose up and debated the point with him in a very Engaiged maner & then solemnly Reproved him & all the rest of them.'[83] Samuel Loudon extolled Bellamy for the salutary effect his preaching had had on unbelievers in the city, noting that 'some Deistical persons... have been convinced under your preaching.'[84] Quaker Lindley Murray, who came of age in the 1760s, considered himself fortunate that 'my principles were never disturbed by infidelity or scepticism... . Some of my acquaintances were either deists or sceptics: but I always found replies to their reasonings, which perfectly satisfied my own mind.'[85]

That deism was seen as akin to atheism in New York was revealed in a *cause celebre* of 1752. Printer James Parker, urged by apothecary Patrick Carryl, had published an article in *The New-York Post-Boy* widely viewed as endorsing deistic theology.[86] Henry Barclay, the Rector of Trinity Church, labeled it a 'Scandalous Piece' and noted that 'the English and Dutch ministers preached against it in all the churches.'[87] Parker and Carryl were subsequently 'indicted in the Supreme Court for publishing 'a Writing containing scandalous Reflections against the Christian religion.''[88] Parker protested the indictment as a violation of English liberty and the case was not carried forward, most likely due to the intercession of Benjamin Franklin.[89] Nevertheless, according to Lutheran minister Henry Muhlenberg 'there was much unrest in the city and this matter was the subject of many conversations.'[90] Though never legitimated in any religious forum, deistic ideas indirectly threatened New York's religious status quo. Those who cast doubt on the claims of revealed religion were held in check by the power of public opinion rather than government sanctions. Thus, Protestant orthodoxy in New York City was elastic enough to incorporate Moravianism, solid enough to withstand the verbal jabs of exponents of rational religion, and cohesive enough to present a united front against Catholicism.

Anglicans

Eighteenth-century New York City may have been a Protestant citadel, but its foundation was not nearly as firmly anchored as its Anglican defenders pretended. The structure rested on the legal inequality of the city's churches and, more specifically, the elevation of the Church of England to a position above all other religious bodies. Since Anglicans never enjoyed overwhelming numerical superiority in the city, civil and ecclesiastical leaders had to find ways to garner support for the Church of England as well as to negate the influence of non-Anglicans.[91] Most significant was a concession to the large and influential Dutch Reformed church, the grant in 1696 of a charter that placed it on a solid legal foundation and ensured that church property acquired through gifts and inheritance was safe. While the transaction was lubricated by a timely gift of silver plate from the consistory of the Dutch Reformed church, the primary concern of Governor Benjamin Fletcher was to persuade the Dutch Reformed to agree with an interpretation of the ambiguous Ministry Act of 1693 that 'established' the Church of England in New York City.[92] Though it took decades to fill the pews of Trinity Church, newly founded in 1697, the preeminent position of New York's Anglican church had been assured by a political maneuver that defined the Dutch Reformed church as a national church.

Aggressive promotion of Anglicanism also bolstered the church's ranks. Agents of the Society for the Propagation of the Gospel in Foreign Parts (SPG), a missionary organization devoted to disseminating Anglican doctrines, used Trinity Church's charity school as a vehicle for bringing poor children and presumably their families into the Anglican fold, and the Negro school for inculcating Anglican views in the city's blacks.[93]

Despite securing the acquiescence of the Dutch Reformed in their design of reproducing England's church-state arrangements in New York City, and using educators funded by the SPG to proselytize among the poor and enslaved, backers of the Church of England did not have a monopoly on religion in the city, nor were they capable of silencing their critics, especially after 1740, when the ranks of Dissenters began to swell as evangelical preachers spread their message to New Yorkers.

Dissenters were highly dissatisfied with the church-state linkage that had been forged in New York City to elevate Anglicans to a position of supremacy. In the 1750s, they seized the occasion of the public debate over the denominational identity of the city's proposed college (King's College) to contest Anglican pretensions to power and influence.[94] Officials envisioned an Anglican college, but they were opposed by Presbyterian William Livingston who contended that 'a Public academy is, or ought to be a mere civil Institution, and cannot with any tolerable Propriety be monopolized by any religious Sect.'[95] The paper war between polemicists defending the Dissenter and Anglican positions exposed the ambiguities and imperfections in New York's version of religious pluralism and destabilized official and popular understandings of church-state relations. Livingston generalized that 'in a new Country as ours, it is inconsistent with good Policy, to give any religious Profession the Ascendancy over others.'[96] From this point on, religion and politics were interwoven in New York City as shown in the texts produced by clergymen and laymen on both sides of the Anglican-Dissenter divide during the mid 1760s' controversy over the appointment of an American Bishop.[97] This elite discourse centering on church-state issues furnished middling people with intellectual armament to challenge the religious status quo.

Anglicans were adamant about retaining the upper hand for the Church of England (or, in modern parlance, to keep the playing field uneven) in New York City. In their way of thinking, 'a balancing of sects was impossible [and] 'a preference then, must of necessity be given to some one denomination among us.''[98] Anglicans' determination to prevent other churches from attaining a measure of legal equality is best illustrated by the active role they took in lobbying for the rejection of petitions for charters from several city congregations – Presbyterians, Dutch Lutherans, Huguenots (French Protestants), and Baptists. The lack of a charter constituted a major impediment to a congregation's corporate identity and financial security and consigned it to an inferior position vis a vis the Dutch Reformed or the Anglicans. The case of the Presbyterians was the most egregious, since their requests were turned down on four separate occasions.[99] Trinity Church's Rector, Samuel Auchmuty, worked assiduously to ensure that the Presbyterians were denied a charter, boasting in 1767 that 'I have left no stone unturned... to render abortive the pernicious Scheme' and exulting in 1768, 'when the proposed charter was 'knocked on the head' by the Board of Trade.'[100]

The inordinate lengths to which Auchmuty went to preserve the restrictions on Presbyterians was a measure of Anglicans' recognition of their church's vulnerability in a voluntaristic religious system. Far from being invincible, the Anglican Church was involved in a fierce competition for adherents with other churches by the third quarter of the eighteenth century. To put the city's Presbyterian congregation on a sounder footing with a charter would have been to empower the Anglicans' major rivals.

Despite the edge they enjoyed in New York, Anglicans could not be shielded from competing in what was becoming a religious marketplace. In 1764, the Vestrymen of Trinity Church stated bluntly that Anglicans were 'under a necessity of Building a third church at their own expence to accommodate [the increased number of worshippers] lest our Adversary's for want of room with us should gain an advantage over us.'[101] The Dissenters' plan of placing every Protestant church on the same legal foundation would, in essence, have accelerated a process of competition that was already underway.

The issues raised in the campaign for Dissenter rights had broader implications for the ordering of a religiously diverse society. When Dissenters sought the elimination of Anglican privilege and the creation of parity among the city's churches, they were, in essence, re-visioning the axioms of New York City's religious pluralism. But William Livingston's proposal for a more equitable religious system was hedged with a qualification that most colonial New Yorkers would have endorsed. 'I should always for political Reasons, exclude the *Papists* from the common and equal Benefits of Society.'[102]

Only when the freedom of choice that is the touchstone of religious pluralism was coupled with the legal equality of all religious institutions, including Catholic churches, would the residents of New York City finally enjoy the fruits of the religious diversity that had existed on Manhattan Island ever since the Dutch had first settled there. This did not occur until the New York state Constitution was written in 1777.[103]

Notes

1   In 1771, New York City's population measured 21,863 (18,726 whites and 3,137 blacks).
2   Reply of the Consistory of New York, Johannes Ritzema, New York, 9 May 1769, Edward T. Corwin, ed. *Ecclesiastical Records of the State of New York* [hereafter *Ecc. Rec.*] 7 vols. (Albany: J.B. Lyon, 1901-16), 6:4159.
3   Jon Butler, *Becoming America: The Revolution Before 1776* (Cambridge, MA: Harvard University Press, 2000), 2.
4   On the function of *schuilkerken*, see Benjamin J. Kaplan, 'Fictions of Privacy: House Chapels and the Spatial Accommodation of Religious Dissent in Early Modern Europe,' *American Historical Review* 107 (2002): 1031-1064.
5   To appreciate the complexities of Amsterdam's religious order in the early modern era, see R. Po-Chia Hsia and Henk van Nierop, eds., *Calvinism and Religious Toleration in the Dutch Golden Age* (Cambridge: Cambridge University Press, 2002); Willem Frijhoff, *Embodied Belief: Ten Essays on Religious Culture in Dutch History* (Hilversum: Verloren, 2002); and Wayne te Brake, 'Religious Identities and the Boundaries of Citizenship in the Dutch Republic' in James E. Bradley and Dale K. Van Kley, eds., *Religion and Politics in Enlightenment Europe* (Notre Dame, IN: University of Notre Dame Press, 2001), 254-293.
6   Rev. Gualterus Du Bois to the Classis of Amsterdam, New York, 14 May 1741, *Ecc. Rec.*, 4: 2756.
7   For an overview of the history of New Amsterdam, see Russell Shorto, *The Island at the Center of the World: The Epic Story of Dutch Manhattan and the Forgotten Colony that Shaped America* (New York: Doubleday, 2004).
8   'Novum Belgium by Father Isaac Jogues, 1646,' in J. Franklin Jameson, ed., *Narratives of New Netherland 1609-1664* (New York: Charles Scribner's Sons, 1967; originally published 1909), 259.
9   'Novum Belgium by Father Isaac Jogues, 1646,' 260.
10 Petition of the Revs. Megapolensis and Drisius to the Burgomasters, Etc., Against Tolerating the Lutherans,' 6 July 1657, *Ecc. Rec.*, I, 387-388.
11 In December 1664, Lutheran leaders estimated the group's size as 'about one hundred persons.' 'Letter from the Lutherans at New York to the Amsterdam Consistory,' 8/18 December 1664, Arnold J. H. van Laer, trans., *The Lutheran Church in New York, 1649-1772: Records in the Lutheran Church Archives at Amsterdam, Holland* (New York: New York Public Library, 1946), 50.
12 On 6 December 1664, Governor Richard Nicolls consented to the Lutherans' request for 'Liberty to send for one Minister or more of their Religion, and that they may freely and publiquely exercise Divine worship, according to their consciences.' Peter R. Christoph and Florence A. Christoph, eds., *New York Historical Manuscripts English. Books of General Entries of the Colony of New York 1664-1673. Orders, Warrants, Letters, Commissions, Passes, Licenses Issued by Governors Nicolls and Francis Lovelace* (Baltimore: Genealogical Pub. Co., 1982), 67.
13 'Letter from the Lutherans at New York to the Amsterdam Consistory,' 8/18 December 1664, Van Laer, *The Lutheran Church in New York, 1649-1772*, 50.
14 The English background to the emergence of religious pluralism in New York is discussed in Evan Haefeli, 'The Creation of American Religious Pluralism: Churches, Colonialism, and Conquest in the Mid-Atlantic 1628-1688,' (Ph.D. dissertation, Princeton University, 2000),

182-262.

15 'Governor Dongan's Report on the Province of New-York, 1687,' E.B. O'Callaghan, ed., *The Documentary History of the State of New York*, 4 vols. (Albany: Weed, Parsons & Co, 1850-1851), 1:186.

16 Herbert L. Osgood, ed., *Minutes of the Common Council of the City of New York, 1675-1776*, 8 vols. (New York: Dodd, Mead, 1905), 1:169. On this point, see also Haefeli, 'The Creation of American Religious Pluralism,' 261-262.

17 Quoted in Joyce D. Goodfriend, *Before the Melting Pot: Society and Culture in Colonial New York City, 1664-1730* (Princeton, Princeton University Press, 1992), 218.

18 Tony Claydon and Ian McBride, 'The trials of the chosen peoples: recent interpretations of protestantism and national identity in Britain and Ireland,' in Tony Claydon and Ian McBride, eds., *Protestantism and National Identity: Britain and Ireland, c. 1650 – c. 1850* (Cambridge: Cambridge University Press, 1998), 28.

19 On the situation of Catholics in eighteenth-century England, see Colin Haydon, *Anti-Catholicism in Eighteenth-century England, c. 1714-1780: A Political and Social Study* (Manchester: Manchester University Press and St. Martin's Press, 1993) and Colin Haydon, "I love my King and my Country, but a Roman Catholic I hate': Anti-Catholicism, Xenophobia and National Identity in Eighteenth-century England,' in Claydon and Ian McBride, eds., *Protestantism and National Identity*, 33-52.

20 For an interpretation of the significance of clandestine worship, see Kaplan, 'Fictions of Privacy.'

21 New York City's Catholics are discussed in Joyce D. Goodfriend, "Upon a Bunch of Straw': The Irish in Colonial New York City,' in Ronald H. Bayor and Timothy J. Meagher, eds., *The New York Irish* (Baltimore: John Hopkins University press, 1996), 43-44. On Catholics in Philadelphia, see Sally Schwartz, '*A Mixed Multitude': The Struggle for Toleration in Colonial Pennsylvania* (New York: New York University Press, 1987), 104 and Patricia U. Bonomi, *Under the Cope of Heaven: Religion, Society, and Politics in Colonial America* (New York: Oxford University Press, 1986), 230, note 54.

22 David William Voorhees, "In behalf of the true Protestants religion': The Glorious Revolution in New York,' (Ph.D. dissertation, New York University, 1988); Peter Christoph, 'The Time and Place of Jan van Loon: A Roman Catholic in Colonial Albany: Part II,' *De Halve Maen* 60 (1987): 9-12.

23 Oloff Stevensen van Cortlandt to Maria van Rensselaer, [New York], 16 January 1683, A. J. F. van Laer, ed., *Correspondence of Maria Van Rensselaer 1669-1689* (Albany: University of the State of New York, 1935), 83.

24 Deposition of Andries & Jan Meyer, 26 September 1689, E.B. O'Callaghan, ed., *The Documentary History of the State of New York* [hereafter *DHNY*], 4 vols. (Albany: Weed, Parsons & Co., 1850-51), 2:17.

25 On Leisler's Rebellion, see Voorhees, "In behalf of the true Protestants religion," David S. Lovejoy, *The Glorious Revolution in America* (New York: Harper & Row, 1972), and John M. Murrin, 'The Menacing Shadow of Louis XIV and the Rage of Jacob Leisler: The Constitutional Ordeal of Seventeenth-Century New York,' in Stephen L. Schechter and Richard B. Bernstein, eds., *New York and the Union: Contributions to the American Constitutional Experience* (Albany: New York State Commission on the Bicentennial of the United States Constitution, 1990), 29-71.

26 [Jacob Leisler] to William Jones in Newhaven, New York, 10 July 1689, *DHNY*, 2:6.

27 Address of the Militia of New-York to William and Mary, June 1689, Edmund. B. O'Callaghan, Berthold Fernow, John Romeyn Brodhead, eds., *Documents Relative to the Colonial History of the State of New York* [hereafter *Doc. Rel.*] 15 vols. (Albany: AMS Press, 1853-1885), 3:583.

28 For the meshing of anti-Catholic and anti-French rhetoric in British American discourse, see

David S. Shields, *Oracles of Empire: Poetry, Politics, and Commerce in British America,* 1690-1750 (Chicago: University of Chicago Press, 1990), 195-220.

29 Benjamin Fletcher to Mr. Blathwayt, 13 July 1696, *Doc. Rel.,* 3:165. See also Wallace Gandy, ed., *The Association Oath Rolls of the British Plantations (New York, Virginia, etc.) A.D. 1696: Being a Contribution to Political History* (London: n.p., 1922).

30 Benjamin Fletcher to the Lords of Trade, 10 June 1696, *Doc. Rel.,* 4:160. Additional evidence of anti-Catholicism in late seventeenth-century New York can be found in Jason Kennedy Duncan, "A Most Democratic Class': New York Catholics and the Early American Republic,' (Ph.D. dissertation, University of Iowa, 1999).

31 Names of the Roman Catholics in the City of New-York; June 1696, *Doc. Rel.,* 4:166. Governor Fletcher stated that 'we have not ten Papists in [New York] and those of no ranke or fortune.' Benjamin Fletcher to Mr. Blathwayte, New York, 30 May 1696, *Doc. Rel.,* 4:157.

32 'An Act declareing what are the Rights and Priviledges of their Majesties Subjects inhabiting within their Province of New York,' passed 12 May 1691; 'An act against Jesuits & popish preists,' passed 9 August 1700, *The Colonial Laws of New York from the Year 1664 to the Revolution.* 5 vols. (Albany: J.B. Lyon, 1894), 1:244-248; 428-430.

33 I.N. Phelps Stokes, *The Iconography of Manhattan Island 1498-1909.* 6 vols. (New York, 1915-1928), 4:452.

34 Stokes, *Iconography,* 4:481-482.

35 Herbert L. Osgood, ed., *Minutes of the Common Council of the City of New York 1675-1776.* 8 vols. (New York: Dodd, Mead, 1905), 3:107; Stokes, *Iconography,* 4:484.

36 Several of these oath rolls are in the Manuscript collection of the New-York Historical Society.

37 Abigail Franks to Naphtali Franks, New York, 17 October 1739, in Leo Hershkowitz and Isidore S. Meyer, eds., *Letters of the Franks Family (1733-1748)* (Waltham, MA.: American Jewish Historical Society, 1968), 66.

38 David L. Barquist, *Myer Myers: Jewish Silversmith in Colonial New York* (New Haven, CT: Yale University Press, 2001), 250. The original manuscript of the oath is in the New-York Historical Society.

39 Quoted in Arthur J. Riley, *Catholicism in New England to* 1788 (Washington, DC: The Catholic University of America, 1936), 212. According to Livingston's biographer, 'Livingston's writings abound in hostile references to 'romish' priests and Catholicism.' Milton M. Klein, *The American Whig: William Livingston* (New York: Garland, 1990), 256, note 31.

40 Quoted in Patricia U. Bonomi, 'John Jay, Religion, and the State,' *New York History* 81 (2000): 12-13.

41 An analysis of Rou's sermons can be found in Paula Wheeler Carlo, 'Anglican conformity and nonconformity among the Huguenots of colonial New York,' in Randolph Vigne and Charles Littleton, eds., *From Strangers to Citizens: The Integration of Immigrant Communities in Britain, Ireland and Colonial America, 1550-1750* (Brighton: Sussex Academic Press, 2001), 317-318, 321, note 18. See also John A. F. Maynard, *The Huguenot Church of New York: A History of the French Church of Saint Esprit* (New York: n.p., 1938), 125.

42 *The French Convert. Being a True Relation of the Happy Conversion of a Noble French Lady, From the Errors and Superstitions of Popery to the Reformed Religion* (New York, 1725). Linda Markson Kruger, 'The New York City Book Trade, 1725-1750,' (D.L.S. thesis, Columbia University, 1980), 79. New York printer William Bradford may also have published an edition of this book in 1724. The book's plot and characters are analyzed in Francis D. Cogliano, *No King, No Popery: Anti-Catholicism in Revolutionary New England* (Westport, CT: Greenwood Press, 1995), 10-11. The book's printing history is discussed in Thomas S. Kidd's forthcoming article, 'Recovering *The French Convert:* Views of the French and the Uses of Anti-Catholicism in Early America.' I am grateful to Professor Kidd for allowing me to read his article in manuscript.

43 Charles E. Clark, *The Public Prints: The Newspaper in Anglo-American Culture, 1665-1740* (New York: Oxford University Press, 1994), 241. On anti-Catholic news printed in colonial newspapers, see David A. Copeland, *Colonial American Newspapers: Character and Content* (Newark, DE: University of Delaware Press, 1997), 205-208. For an analysis of anti-Catholic content in Boston newspapers, see Thomas S. Kidd, ''Let Hell and Rome Do Their Worst': World News, Anti-Catholicism, and International Protestantism in Early-Eighteenth-Century Boston,' *New England Quarterly* 76 (2003): 265-290.

44 On the Protestant calendar, see David Cressy, *Bonfires and Bells: National Memory and the Protestant Calendar in Elizabethan and Stuart England* (London: Weidenfeld and Nicolson, 1989).

45 *New York Gazette*, 7 November 1737, quoted in Stokes, *Iconography*, 4:554.

46 Quote from Horsmanden's journal in Stokes, *Iconography*, 4:569, and quote from 7 August 1741 letter of Horsmanden to Cadwallader Colden in Stokes, *Iconography*, 4:570.

47 Daniel Horsmanden, Thomas J. Davis, ed., *The New York Conspiracy* (Boston: Beacon Press, 1971), 342-343.

48 *American Weekly Mercury*, Philadelphia, 13-20 August 1741. On 1 October 1733, Jacobus van Cortlandt advertised for a runaway slave named Andrew Saxon who 'professeth himself to be a Roman Catholic.' Graham Russell Hodges and Alan Edward Brown, eds., *'Pretends to be Free': Runaway Slave Advertisements from Colonial and Revolutionary New York and New Jersey* (New York: Garland Publishing, 1994), 9.

49 Stokes, *Iconography*, 4:594.

50 Stokes, *Iconography*, 4:598.

51 E. Pemberton, *A Sermon Delivered at the Presbyterian Church in New-York July 31, 1746. Being a Day of solemn Thanksgiving to Almighty God for the late Victory obtained by his Majesty's Arms, under the conduct of His Royal Highness the Duke of Cumberland, over the Rebels in North Britain* (New York: printed by James Parker, 1746), 15.

52 Pemberton, *A Sermon Delivered at the Presbyterian Church in New-York July 31, 1746*; John Marchant, *The History of the Late Rebellion in Great Britain* (New York: printed by J. Parker, 1747); James Ray, *The Acts of the Rebels: being an abstract of the journal of Mr. James Ray of Whitehaven, volunteer under His Royal Highness the Duke of Cumberland* (New York, 1747).

53 John Anderson, *The Book of the Chronicles of His Royal Highness, William Duke of Cumberland: Being an Account of the Rise and Progress of the Present Rebellion* (New York, 1746). This book had been published in Edinburgh in 1746.

54 The beaker engraved in 1750 is pictured in Jerry E. Patterson, *The City of New York: A History Illustrated from the Collections of The Museum of the City of New York* (New York: H. N. Abrams, 1978), 53. There are four views of the 1754 beaker in Ian M. G. Quimby, *American Silver at Winterthur* (Winterthur: University Press of Virginia, 1995), 232-233. See also Janine E. Skerry and Jeanne Sloane, 'Images of Politics and Religion on Silver Engraved by Joseph Leddell,' *Antiques* 141 (March 1992): 490-499.

55 Quimby, *American Silver at Winterthur*, 232.

56 On this connection and, more generally, on the evolution of New York's Pope Day celebrations, see Paul Gilje, *The Road to Mobocracy: Popular Disorder in New York City, 1763-1834* (Chapel Hill: University of North Carolina Press, 1987), 25-30.

57 *New-York Post Boy*, 7 November 1748, quoted in Stokes, *Iconography*, 4:612.

58 Quoted in Stokes, *Iconography*, 4:673.

59 Quoted in Joyce Goodfriend, 'Scots and Schism: The New York City Presbyterian Church in the 1750s,' in Ned C. Landsman, ed., *Nation and Province in the first British Empire: Scotland and the Americas, 1600-1800* (Lewisburg, PA: Bucknell University Press, 2001), 227.

60 Gilbert Tennent, *The Necessity of holding fast the truth represented in three sermons on Rev. iii.3. Preached at New-York, April 1742. With and Appendix Relating to Errors lately vented by some Moravians in those Parts* (New York: S. Kneeland and T. Green, 1743). For Gilbert

Tennent's views on the Moravians, see David S. Lovejoy, *Religious Enthusiasm in the New World: Heresy to Revolution* (Cambridge, MA: Harvard University Press, 1985), 208-209.

61 *Ibid.*, 75-76.

62 Rev. Gualterus Du Bois to the Classis of Amsterdam, New York, 14 May 1741, *Ecc. Rec.*, 4: 2755-2756.

63 Rev. Gualterus Du Bois to the Classis of Amsterdam, New York, 14 May 1741, *Ecc. Rec.*, 4: 2756.

64 E. Pemberton to [Philip Doddridge], New York, 16 December 1743, in John Doddridge Humphrey, ed,. *The Correspondence and Diary of Philip Doddridge D.D.* 5 vols. (London: Henry Colburn and Richard Bentley, 1829-1831), 4:300.

65 Gerardus Duyckinck, *A Short though True Account of the Establishment and Rise of the Church so called Moravian Brethren... . The Same is Taken out of their own Writings, and Some Observations on it.* (New York, [1744]). Advertisements for this book appeared in *The New-York Gazette* on 25 June 1744 and 13 August 1744. In the 13 August advertisement, the book's title was amended to read 'Observations on it by G. Duycking.'

66 'An Act for Securing of his Majesties Government of New York,' passed 21 September 1744, *The Colonial Laws of New York*, 2:424-429.

67 Horsmanden's defense of the law is in *Ecc. Rec.*, 4:2906-2908. The quotation is from an address of New York's Council and General Assembly to Governor George Clinton, 25 April 1744, included in *Journal of the votes and proceedings of the General Assembly of the colony of New York... .* 2 vols. (New York: J. Buel, 1764-1766), 2:16.

68 William Smith, Jr. Michael Kammen, ed., *The History of the Province of New-York.* 2 vols. (Cambridge, MA: The Belknap Press of Harvard University Press, 1972), vol 1, 208. Names of females who affiliated with the Moravians in New York City can be found in Harry Emilius Stocker, *A History of the Moravian Church in New York City* (New York: n.p., 1922).

69 'Memoir of Sarah Grube, nee van Fleck,' in Katherine M. Faull, transl. and ed., *Moravian Women's Memoirs: Their Related Lives, 1750-1820* (Syracuse, NY: Syracuse University Press, 1997), 40, 41. This volume includes material on the experiences of other New York City Moravians. Female Moravians traveled from New York to visit the Moravian community at Bethlehem, Pennsylvania in 1744. Kenneth G. Hamilton, transl. and ed., *The Bethlehem Diary, Volume I, 1742-1744* (Bethlehem, PA: Archives of the Moravian Church, 1971), 196, 197, 202, 204.

70 On Thomas Noble and his wife, see Stocker, *History of the Moravian Church in New York City.* On Andrew the Moor, see Daniel B. Thorp, 'Chattel With A Soul: The Autobiography of a Moravian Slave,' *Pennsylvania Magazine of History and Biography* 112 (1988): 433-451.

71 [David Van Horne to B. Brandon], New York, August 1753, Letter Book of an Elder of the New York Presbyterian Church, Mss., Presbyterian Historical Society, Philadelphia. Van Horne's views on the Moravians can be traced in this Letter Book.

72 Stocker, *History of the Moravian Church in New York City*, 76.

73 Theodore G. Tappert and John W. Doberstein, transls., *The Journals of Henry Melchior Muhlenberg* 3 vols. (Philadelphia: Evangelical Lutheran Ministerium of Pennsylvania and Adjacent States, 1942), 1:361.

74 C.J. Podmore, *The Moravian Church in England, 1728-1760* (Oxford: Clarendon Press, 1998).

75 Milton M. Klein, ed., *The Independent Reflector or Weekly Essays on Sundry Important Subjects More particularly adapted to the Province of New-York by William Livingston and others* (Cambridge, MA: Harvard University Press, 1963). William Smith, Jr. also defended the Moravians. Klein, *The American Whig*, 252.

76 *Independent Reflector*, 129.

77 Rev. Gualterus Du Bois to the Classis of Amsterdam, New York, 14 May 1741, *Ecc. Rec.*, 4: 2756.

78 This book is listed in Hendrick Edelman, *Dutch-American Bibliography* 1693-1794 (Nieuwk-oop: De Graaf, 1974), #17. *ARITHMETICA OF Cyffer-Kinst, Volgens de Munten Maten en Gewigten, te NIEU-YORK, gebruykelyk Als Mede Een kort ontwerp van de Algebra,* Opgestelt door Pieter Venema, Mr. in de Mathesis en Schryf-Konst. NEU-YORK, Gedruckt voor Jacob Goelet, by de Oude-Slip, by J. Peter Zenger, MDCCXXX. According to Edelman, Venema had published an introduction to algebra in Groningen in 1714.

79 Rev. Gualterus Du Bois to the Classis of Amsterdam, New York, 14 May 1741, *Ecc. Rec.,* 4: 2756.

80 E. Pemberton to [Philip Doddridge], New York, 16 December 1743, in *The Correspondence and Diary of Philip Doddridge,* 4:301.

81 *New-York Evening Post,* 22 April 1745, 20 May 1745; *New York Mercury,* 9 July 1753.

82 William Smith [Sr.] to Rev. Anthony Stoddard... New York, 15 May 1754, Joseph Bellamy Papers, Mss., Hartford Seminary, Hartford, Connecticut.

83 Obadiah Wells to Rev. Joseph Bellamy, New York, 8 April 1754, Bellamy Papers.

84 Samuel Loudon to Rev. Joseph Bellamy, New York, 12 June 1754, Bellamy Papers.

85 Memoir of Lindley Murray printed in Stephen Allott, *Lindley Murray 1745-1826: Quaker Grammarian of New York and old York* (York: Sessions Book Trust, 1991), 10. On Murray's intellectual development, see Charles Monaghan, *The Murrays of Murray Hill* (Brooklyn, NY: Urban History Press, 1998), 23-42.

86 This episode is detailed in Alan F. Dyer, *A Biography of James Parker, Colonial Printer* (Troy, NY: Whitston Pub. Co, 1982), 27-29.

87 *Journals of Henry Melchior Muhlenberg,* 1:323-324.

88 Dyer, *James Parker,* 27.

89 See Benjamin Franklin to Cadwallader Colden, Philadelphia, 14 May 1752, *The Papers of Benjamin Franklin* ed. Leonard Labaree (New Haven, CT: Yale University Press, 1959-), 4: 310-312.

90 *Journals of Henry Melchior Muhlenberg,* 1:323.

91 For an analysis of early New York City's ethnic demography and its consequences for religious alignments, see Goodfriend, *Before the Melting Pot.*

92 Stokes, *Iconography,* 4:396. Lord Bellomont, Fletcher's successor as Governor, viewed the gift of silver plate as a bribe for the charter. *Ibid.,* 412, 413.

93 On these initiatives, see Goodfriend, *Before the Melting Pot.*

94 Extended accounts of the King's College controversy can be found in David C. Humphrey, *From King's College to Columbia 1746-1800* (New York: Columbia University Press, 1976) and Donald F.M. Gerardi, 'The King's College Controversy 1753-1756 and the Ideological Roots of Toryism in New York,' *Perspectives in American History* 11 (1977-1978): 145-196.

95 *Independent Reflector,* 182.

96 *Independent Reflector,* 183.

97 For background on New York politics in this era, see Patricia U. Bonomi, *A Factious People: Politics and Society in Colonial New York* (New York: Columbia University Press, 1971) and Alan Tully, *Forming American Politics: Ideals, Interests and Institutions in Colonial New York and Pennsylvania* (Baltimore: John Hopkins University Press, 1994). A useful guide to the literature on the controversy over an American Bishop is Frederick V. Mills, Sr., 'The Colonial Anglican Episcopate: A Historiographical Review,' *Anglican and Episcopal History* 61 (1992): 325-345.

98 Joseph Ellis, *The New England Mind in Transition: Samuel Johnson of Connecticut, 1696-1772* (New Haven, CT: Yale University Press, 1973), 186.

99 The issue of charters is discussed in Richard W. Pointer, *Protestant Pluralism and the New York Experience: A Study of Eighteenth-Century Religious Diversity* (Bloomington, IN: Indiana University Press, 1988), 61-62.

100 Auchmuty's 1767 letter is quoted in Pointer, *Protestant Pluralism* 61 and Auchmuty's 1768

letter is quoted in Clifford K. Shipton, *New England Life in the Eighteenth Century: Representative Biographies from Sibley's Harvard Graduates* (Cambridge, MA: Belknap Press of Harvard University, 1963), 475. For the Anglican campaign against the Presbyterian petition for a charter, see Klein, *American Whig*, 479.

101 Church Wardens and Vestry of Trinity church to the Society for the Propagation of the Gospel in Foreign Parts [SPG], New York, 22 September 1764, SPG Letter Books B, 2:f. 181 (Microfilm).

102 *Independent Reflector*, 183.

103 For an overview of church-state relations in New York, see John Webb Pratt, *Religion, Politics and Diversity: The Church-State Theme in New York History* (Ithaca, NY: Cornell University Press, 1967).

Dirk Mouw

RECRUITING MINISTERS: AMSTERDAM, NEW YORK, AND THE DUTCH OF BRITISH NORTH AMERICA, 1700-1772

Through much of the eighteenth century, the Dutch Reformed congregation in New York City, like its sister congregations in the North American colonies, had its feet planted firmly in two very different worlds. Politically, members of these churches were the subjects of an English sovereign. Ecclesiastically, however, the churches were, for at least most of the century, subordinate to the Classis of Amsterdam. Inhabiting these two worlds presented serious challenges but also opportunities. The best that the New York church and its American sisters could generally hope for from British officials was indifference. The New York City church, however, played a pivotal role ecclesiastically in the colonies, and usually enjoyed a special status among American churches in its relationship with the Classis of Amsterdam, which recognized it as the church of 'the chief town in the Province.'[1]

The recruiting and calling of ministers in particular presented challenges, but also opportunities for ecclesiastical creativity. Calling a minister was central to the life of a Reformed church, and getting a good minister was very important to the Dutch Reformed laity. They would listen to him expound for many hours; he would have a part in some of the most important occasions in their lives; their children would often be taught by him; he would sometimes serve as liaison and arbiter for the community; and he would lead the consistory in exercising church discipline. An incompetent, lazy, or ill-tempered minister, or one otherwise not compatible with the congregation to which he was called, could be disastrous for the congregation and the community, and under Dutch Reformed church order this was not a situation always easily remedied.

Dutch Reformed Church Order in New York City
Dutch Reformed church order accorded to the consistories[2] of congregations a great deal of control over the process by which ministers were chosen and called. The New York City church and its American sisters, however, had not always been able to exercise this power. Prior to the English conquest of 1664, the Classis[3] of Amsterdam and its subcommittee for colonial churches generally played the role of both consistory *and* classis by canvassing for men available and willing to serve as ministers in the colonies, choosing among them, anointing them with classical approbation, issuing the instrument or letter of call, and then installing or ordaining them in a classical meeting. The Directors of the Dutch West India Company played the role of magistrate when their approval of the

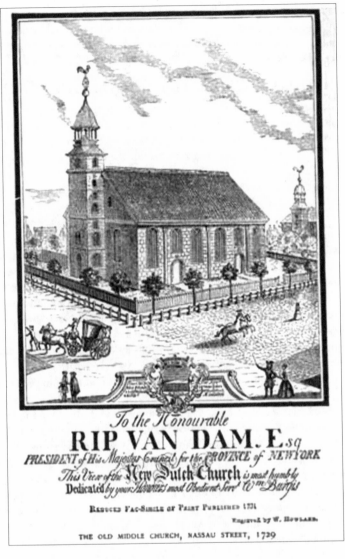

To the Honourable

RIP VAN DAM, Esq

PRESIDENT of His Majesty Council for the PROVINCE of NEWYORK
This View of the New Dutch Church is most humbly
Dedicated by your Honours most Obedient Sert Wm Burgis

REDUCED FAC-SIMILE OF PRINT PUBLISHED 1731

Engraved by W. Howland.

THE OLD MIDDLE CHURCH, NASSAU STREET, 1729

1. Nassau Street/New/Middle Church in New York City, ca. 1730
E.T. Corwin, *Manual of the Reformed Church in America.*

call was then sought.[4] In this sense, at least, the charge that members of the Classis of Amsterdam behaved like 'episcopal' or 'bishop-like' ministers (*Bischoplyke predicanten*) is understandable. [5] Despite periodic strains in the relationship such as those indicated by words like these, however, the relationship between the classis and the North American congregations was an important one: the role of the classis as ally, judge, advocate, and the principal point of contact for these congregations with the mother church remained important to the colonists well into the period of the American Revolution. Nevertheless, one could argue that the Classis of Amsterdam was acting, albeit as a committee, more like a bishop than a Dutch Reformed classis in its relations with the North American churches, perhaps especially in the control it exercised over the ministerial selection, ordination, and promotion processes.

Ironically, the English conquest in 1664 had given the Dutch churches in the American colonies the chance to experiment with techniques that afforded them much more control over the ministerial recruitment process, permitting them to behave in a manner more closely in keeping with Dutch Reformed church order and with practice in the Reformed Churches in the fatherland, without directly threatening their relationship with the Old-World classis. Thus, through these means the colonial congregations could be faithful to two components of their Dutch-Reformed identity: their commitment to following the church order of the mother church, and to maintaining a vital ecclesiastical connection to the fatherland. It is not surprising, therefore, that these techniques, introduced in the late seventeenth century – in many cases by the New York City church – became common practice throughout the Dutch Reformed Churches of the American Middle Colonies as those churches grew and became more numerous during the eighteenth century.

Why, exactly, the North American congregations did not unite to form a full classis, is a subject deserving a lengthy discussion of its own. The evidence suggests that Dutch colonists and ministers in various regions of the globe attempted to form assemblies with classical powers, but were opposed by synods and classes in the fatherland. The same was true in New York. The so-called Coetus-Conferentie schism divided the American congregations into bitterly antagonistic factions for decades. One of the groups, the Coetus, openly defied the Classis of Amsterdam and the Synod of North Holland from 1757 to 1772, claiming for itself the right to examine, promote, and ordain men to the ministry.[6]

Short of referring themselves to an American ecclesiastical body claiming classical powers, however, North American churches could do much to influence the ministerial selection process. Examining the eighteenth-century calls issued by one of these congregations, the Dutch church of New York City, one can see nearly every technique used by the churches of the American colonies to gain control over the process of selecting ministers, and we can thereby gain insight into a number of aspects of the experiences of the Dutch Reformed of the Middle Colonies and their connections to the Dutch fatherland and the mother church – perhaps most importantly as these connections were manifested in the colonists' relationship to the Classis of Amsterdam.

The first new Dutch Reformed minister in the eighteenth century to ascend a pulpit in New York City was Gualterus Du Bois.[7] DuBois' arrival was the result of a multistage process initiated by the consistory of the New York City church. In a document sent to the Classis of Amsterdam, the church formally called 'the Reverend, Pious and Very Learned Domine Hieronymus Verdieren' then minister 'in the Classis of Ziericksee.' They reported to the Classis of Amsterdam that they had heard excellent things of him, and simultaneously sent him word of their decision as they sent the instrument of call to the Classis of Amsterdam for execution.[8] That Verdieren declined the call should probably not surprise us. One of the problems facing churches like that of New York City was that they were so far away from the vast majority of men eligible to accept a call from a Dutch Reformed congregation, a 'disadvantage' the New York City consistory lamented.[9] How they learned of Verdieren or his qualifications is unclear, but it would have been difficult for them to ascertain whether he was open to receiving a call. The vast expanse of ocean between New York and the Netherlands undoubtedly made getting good information on specific ministers difficult – and New York City's sister churches in America apparently had similar problems. Of the calls I have been able to document that were issued or authorized by Dutch Reformed churches in the Middle Colonies between 1700 and the founding of an American ecclesiastical assembly with classical powers in 1772, only a few of those sent to Europe mention a prospective individual by name.[10]

The consistory of New York City anticipated that Verdieren might not accept their call and they had a backup plan. In the letter calling Verdieren, they wrote that if he 'has died, or has removed away, or is not inclined to come over here ... then full power and authority are given to the Classis of Amsterdam after consulting with ... Livinus van Schaick and Willem Banckers, natives of this place, and merchants in Amsterdam.'[11] The merchants Van Schaick and Bancker, former inhabitants of the colony now living in Amsterdam, were unusually well positioned to assist in the process. They undoubtedly could offer the classis information useful for making a good choice for the New York church, and in this instance also pressed the matter with the classis, in an effort to make sure the matter was attended to promptly. The classis did consult with the merchants, who had found a former tailor whom they nominated for the position. The classis, however, acting in the place of the New York consistory, rejected the tailor, members of the classis themselves made nominations from among 'those who had offered themselves [to the classis] for service in foreign lands,' and the classis elected Gualterus Du Bois minister of the New York City church.[12]

Agents

Men formally commissioned as agents by colonial consistories could play a variety of roles. In most calls sent to the fatherland a layperson served at least as a financial conduit, someone authorized to pay the significant classical, transportation, and miscellaneous costs associated with procuring a minister, on behalf of the congregation. Their roles, however, were often greater, serving as advisors, sources of information, and advocates for the church, as they did in the call to Du Bois. They could even be empowered to act on behalf of the consistory through letters that have the character of a 'power of attorney' letter. In 1715, for example, the consistory of New York City conferred on three ministers in Amsterdam 'all needful power, right and authority, acting unanimously or by a majority, to make out a complete Call ... as our representatives.'[13]

Documents regarding the commission sent by the New York City church to agents nearly three decades later offer an unusual glimpse into how the agents were chosen. Having decided that the need and resources were sufficient for a third minister for the congregation, the consistory decided to draft a document empowering two ministers and two merchants in the Netherlands to make the call on their behalf.[14] The two ministers already serving the congregation were each allowed to pick one minister, and the laymen on the consistory together chose the two merchants.[15] One minister chose his *neef* (cousin or nephew), the other chose a minister whose grandfather had lived and died in New Netherland and whose father had visited the colony. The merchants were apparently men well known to some New Yorkers, and people whom the consistory members could address as 'friends.'[16]

The New York City church continued to use agents or commissioners to find them ministers throughout the eighteenth century. When after much deliberation they decided to call a minister in 1763 to preach in English, they issued a 'blank call' empowering two ministers to find and call a minister. As ministers of Anglophonic Reformed churches in Amsterdam, these clergy were well qualified to find an appropriate person.[17] And (since the New York City Church remained bilingual until 1803, holding services in each language), this practice proved useful even after the period under consideration here. Such was the case, when in 1785 the New York City consistory decided to call a minister to preach in Dutch; they commissioned a professor at Utrecht who had instructed one of the other New York City ministers.[18] In this way congregations unable to 'hear the gifts' of the candidates themselves could at least put the power to do so in the hands of the people they thought best suited to act in their interests. Undoubtedly it is for this reason that the practice of empowering agents to call a minister on behalf of the consistory became quite common among colonial consistories between 1700 and 1772, accounting for one quarter of the calls I have been able to document.[19]

Calling Familiar Ministers
According to the reports of clergy in the American colonies in the eighteenth century, members of congregations did not like sending calls to the Netherlands for at least two reasons: first, they did not know who they were going to get; and second, the process involved classical meetings and transportation which cost a great deal of money.[20] One way they could avoid the costs and get a person whom they had heard or at least had received substantial reports about was to call a man who was, for one reason or another, already in America. This was the case when, in 1749, Eggo Tonkens van Hoevenberg stopped in New York City on his way from Surinam to the fatherland, having had difficulties with the governor in that colony. Van Hoevenberg was prevailed upon to preach, and the congregation was 'greatly pleased' with his gifts. Subsequently, the consistory seized the opportunity presented by the presence of a minister in their city available for call, and with whom the congregation was acquainted and pleased, presenting van Hoevenberg with a letter of call.[21] Likewise in 1750, when Rev. Lambertus de Ronde left Surinam for New York because he believed the climate of Surinam was bad for his health, the consistory of New York issued him a call.[22]

Seizing upon unusual circumstances was not, however, the only way a congregation could make a call to a minister with whom they were familiar. Indeed, the ministers of neighboring congregations could also become the recipients of a call. Shortly after Rev. Haeghoort arrived in America, having received a call to three churches in New Jersey, the New York City consistory invited him to preach there twice to see whether they wanted to call him. When the consistory was satisfied that most of the congregation was pleased with him and that there were sufficient financial resources available to support him, they issued him a call.[23] Even more than commissioning agents to find a suitable minister for a congregation, the calling of a minister already in the Middle Colonies presented colonial consistories with the opportunity to find a minister who was a good fit with the congregation. The letters of call almost always specified the basis of their knowledge of the person: 'having heard the laudable gifts of' the minister or having 'heard of' his learning and godly life. Furthermore, they enabled the consistories to act in a way even more closely in keeping with Dutch church order and the common practice in the fatherland. It comes, therefore, as no surprise that among the calls examined in this essay, calling a minister from a sister congregation in the North American colonies was more common than any other single method of procuring a minister.[24] When one adds to this the calls made to men in the region who had not yet been ordained as ministers, and who, after receiving a call, were sent to one ecclesiastical body or another for examinations and ordination, more than half of the calls made by the colonial churches are accounted for.[25]

Given the advantages Dutch Reformed consistories could see in making calls using agents, or calling men already in the American colonies, it is hardly surprising that there are very few instances between 1700 and 1772 of churches turning their consistorial powers over to the Classis of Amsterdam without restriction – indeed there were only seven such cases.[26] But problems could arise with these methods of ministerial recruitment as well, especially with the use of agents.

Potential Problems

One instance which exemplifies this potential for problems, as well as the important role of the agents commissioned by the colonial consistories and the intense desire of congregations to exercise control over the ministerial recruitment process, occurred after Rev. Dellius was forced to leave New York City's smaller sibling up the Hudson, Albany, and return to Europe. The consistory of the Albany church wrote to the fatherland and asked that Dellius, Willem Bancker, and Livinus van Schaik, in conjunction with the Classis of Amsterdam, select and call another minister for their church, if it became clear that Dellius would not be able to return. The problems began when one of these agents, Bancker, did not conceive of his commission in the same way as the others. According to one report, Bancker had been unwilling to come to the meeting of the agents with the classis, 'saying that two [agents] were enough to attend to this business... .' In that meeting it 'came to the knowledge of Classis' that Rev. Johannes Lydius, 'was willing to make a change and go over to Albany,' if Dellius could be called to the church in the Netherlands Lydius was then serving. The men agreed, and Lydius accepted the call to Albany. In the meanwhile, however, Willem Bancker had written to his brother Evert in Albany, asking that he not be restricted to working with the Classis of Amsterdam in his search for a minister; to this they consented. Evert reported to the consistory that Willem had found 'a certain and proper person' when he had been asked to assist in finding a minister for New York City, but the classis had rejected Willem's selection.[27]

The 'certain and proper person' Bancker had found was Bernardus Freeman. Freeman was a Dutch pietist, influenced by many of the same theological forces that had shaped Guillam Bertholf, and was later a close personal friend of Theodorus Jacobus Frelinghuysen.[28] Bancker proceeded to issue an instrument of call to Freeman. Bancker found it 'necessary' to work with the Classis of Lingen in Westphalia 'to execute this holy design....'[29]

The Classis of Amsterdam soon heard about what had happened and discovered that Bancker had 'quietly put on board ship' without the knowledge of the Amsterdam classis or his two fellow agents. The Amsterdam classis quickly put Lydius aboard another ship and wrote a letter to the Albany church for him to carry. They expressed surprise at Bancker's actions and assured the Albany church that Lydius had been called in accordance

BERNARDUS FREEMAN, BEDIENAAR
des Godlyken Woords tot Midwouw &c. in Nieuw-Jork.

B. de Broen Sculps.   *J. Roman Excudit*

2. Bernardus Freeman. Holland Society, New York.

with the request and with the authorization granted them by the church, and with the 'entire approbation and satisfaction' of the other two agents. Since, the classis concluded, the Albany church had always expressed their trust in and appreciation for the classis, Bancker must have 'acted in bad faith' and must have told the Albany church 'things which exceeded the truth.' The classis barely contained their rage against Bancker in their letter to the Albany church: 'We cannot understand how such a frightful undertaking can be entered upon by a member of the church, such as Banckert professes to be.' The classis declared Freeman's call illegal and asked Albany to receive Lydius and send Freeman, the 'patch-cutter,' back to the Netherlands.[30]

Despite Bancker's quiet speed, Lydius' ship arrived in New York on July 20, 1700. Freeman's arrived July 23. Lydius remained in New York City for a few days before proceeding up the river to Albany. By the time he was ready to leave, Freeman had arrived, and the two boarded the same vessel bound for Albany.[31] They arrived late in the day on a Saturday and were both received well by civil and ecclesiastical officials. They turned over their paperwork, and the consistory was called into private session to consider the matter. Apparently they did not mind being presented with a choice of ministers. Since the consistory judged it was 'already too late' in the day to look over the papers, 'they asked each [minister] to favor the congregation the next day with a sermon... .'[32]

On Monday, the consistory called another session. Many members of the congregation were apparently inclined to accept both ministers (though sufficient funds to pay both could not be raised), others favored Lydius, and fewer, Freeman. But the discovery which came to light in the consistory meeting that Monday morning made the decision somewhat easier for the elders and deacons, as they assessed the legality of the calls to the two men. As the consistory members examined the documents, they realized that Bancker had altered one document to make it appear that he had been given authority to act alone. When this discovery was made, everyone in the room, current and past consistory members, 'to the number of thirty persons, flew to the table to look,' and when they perceived the deception, 'looked long at them, and [were] silent.'[33]

After the consistory concluded that the deception was Bancker's alone and Freeman was innocent, the decision had to be made about how to proceed. Observing that the nearby Schenectady church was without a minister as well, they solved the problem by suggesting that if Freeman were 'disposed to locate at Schenectady' and if 'that church had a liking for him and would call him,' Freeman would not have to be sent back to Europe, an act that 'could not be approved of, when there was so great [a] need of ministers' in the colonies.[34] Freeman was later called to Schenectady.[35] Thus two churches in the colonies seized upon opportunities to welcome ministers whom they had had the chance to hear for themselves before they had finalized the call. Although the episode underscores the voluntary nature of the relationship between churches of an English province and one particular Dutch classis, Amsterdam, it underscores the deep desire of the colonial congregations to play their proper roles under Dutch Reformed church order, despite considerable geographic and even political obstacles.

Conclusion

Likewise, the stories about the ways in which the New York City Dutch Reformed church and its American counterparts recruited their ministers illuminate several important aspects of the lives of the Dutch in British North America and their relationships with the Dutch fatherland and mother church. First, it enabled some American churches to recruit ministers with theological styles different from those generally preferred by the Classis of Amsterdam. It is interesting to note, in this regard, that Willem Bancker himself was a commissioner in the calls of the pietist-leaning Cornelius van Santvoort and Theodorus Jacobus Frelinghuysen in addition to Freeman.[36] Second, these efforts to gain greater control over the ministerial selection process cast additional light on the desire of some Dutch Reformed, particularly in the second half of the eighteenth century, to have an American ecclesiastical assembly with at least some classical powers in which their own consistories would be represented. And finally, the pattern demonstrates a desire among colonial consistories to behave in a manner consistent with Dutch Reformed church order and the practice of their counterparts in the fatherland. Even as their counterparts in Amsterdam and elsewhere in the Netherlands were struggling to maintain consistorial powers against incursions from civil authorities, the consistories of the British colonies in North America – frequently following the lead of the consistory of the church of New York City – were pursuing ways to increase their own authority over the selection of ministers, and thereby bring themselves more closely into line with Dutch Reformed practice and principle in the Netherlands, while maintaining strong ties to their longtime ally, the Classis of Amsterdam.

Notes

1 Edward T. Corwin and Hugh Hastings, eds., *Ecclesiastical Records: State of New York*, 7 vols. (Albany: James B. Lyon, 1901-1916), 6:3803. Hereafter *ERNY*.

2 The consistory was the ruling body of a Dutch Reformed congregation, composed of elders and deacons. These men were members of the congregation who held office for a fixed term, typically two years. As terms ended, the consistory elected replacements. Ministers, when present, served as president of consistory.

3 In Dutch Reformed church order, the classis was a 'broader assembly' composed of delegates from the congregations within its geographical boundaries. Classes attended to issues of import and issues which affected all the regional churches in common. Classes, in turn, sent delegates to provincial synods.

4 There were, of course, exceptions to this pattern, but the Classis of Amsterdam guarded its role jealously, especially against incursions from the directors of the Dutch West India Company.

5 Ibid., 3:1956.

6 See Gerald F. De Jong, *The Dutch Reformed Church in the American Colonies* (Grand Rapids, MI: Eerdmans, 1978), 188-210. My dissertation, forthcoming, also devotes a chapter to this schism.

7 Admittedly, I might be stretching the eighteenth century a bit. DuBois may have preached his first sermon in late 1699, but the earliest evidence of his having arrived in New York is found in a letter of March 1700 from deputies of the Classis of Amsterdam. *ERNY* 2:1344. Du Bois was not, of course, the first new Dutch Reformed Minister to begin serving the New York City Dutch Reformed Church since the conquest of 1664. Five ministers served that congregation between 1664 and the start of Du Bois' tenure.

8 Ibid., 2:1195-6.

9 Ibid.

10 Evidence of these calls is found in ibid., 4:2805, 6:3821-22, 3827, 4145-47. The first of the 92 calls examined here was authorized by the consistory of the Albany church in 1699, but not executed by their commissioners until 1700.

11 Ibid., 2:1196.

12 Ibid., 1297-98, 1304-05, 1356-57.

13 Ibid., 3:2077-81, 2088-91. Quote is from 2078.

14 Ibid., 4:2770, 2771-72.

15 Ibid., 2772-73.

16 Ibid., 2849, 2806, 2833.

17 Ibid., 6:3854-6, 3859-61. They also asked these two agents to consult with a third minister in Amsterdam, and specifically asked them to consider two men about whom the consistory had received reports. From Laidlie's arrival until at least until the mid 1770s, it appears that about 500 worshippers regularly attended the English services in the New York City church. Daniel James Meeter, *'Bless the Lord, O My Soul': The New-York Liturgy of the Dutch Reformed Church, 1767*. Drew Studies in Liturgy, eds. Kenneth E. Rowe and Robin A. Leaver, no. 6 (Lanham, MD.: Scarecrow Press, 1998), 77-78. For a recent and helpful discussion of the English language controversy in the New York City Dutch Reformed Church see Joyce D. Goodfriend, 'Archibald Laidlie and the Transformation of the Dutch Reformed Church in Eighteenth-Century New York City,' *Journal of Presbyterian History* 81 (2003): 149-62.

18 'The Rev. Gerardus Arense Kuypers, D.D.,' *Year Book of the (Collegiate) Reformed Protestant Dutch Church of the City of New York*, 10 (1889): 79-81. This article incorrectly states that the call was issued in 1786. Kuypers continued to preach in Dutch in New York City until 1803. Outside of New York City, English language preaching came much later, and Dutch preaching persisted longer. The last regular Dutch language service was probably conducted in 1835. See De Jong, *Dutch Reformed*, 211-227.

19 Evidence for the 23 calls in this category can be found (in approximately chronological order) in *ERNY* 2:1341-45 (on this call, see note 10 above); 3:1843-44, 2077-81, 2088-90, 2044-46, 2119, 2121; 4:2331, 2330, 2475; Churchville, Pa. Consistory (Csty.) to David Knibbe and Johannes Wilhelmius, 3 May 1730, Churchville, Pa., Church Papers, 1704-1870, vol. 1, 3b, Presbyterian Historical Society, Philadelphia, Pa.; *ERNY* 4:2506-13, 2520, 2599, 2497-2502; Fishkill, NY Csty. to Herman van de Wal, Hageles, Beels, and Reitsma, [20 April, 1734], 'Kerkboek van de Visch Kill,' First Reformed (Ref.) Church (Ch.), Fishkill, NY; New Brunswick, NJ Csty. to G. Schuilenborg and Jan Stockers, 19 April [1737], New Brunswick Ref. Ch. Records, 1717-1794, Special Collections, Rutgers University Library, New Brunswick, NJ (RUSC); *ERNY* 4:2771-73; Fishkill, NY Csty. to Joannes Clemans, 20 September 1742, 'Kerkboek van de Visch Kill'; *ERNY* 4:2869-70; 6:3832-33, 3896; Schoharie, NY Csty. to Daniel Gerdes and Michael Hertling, March 1762, in Royden Woodward Vosburgh, ed. [and trans.], *Records of the High and Low Dutch Reformed Congregation at Schoharie now the Reformed Church in the Town of Schoharie, Schoharie County*, NY ([New York: New York Genealogical and Biographical Society], 1917), vol. 1, 391-94; *ERNY* 6: 3952, 4021-22, 4051, 3853-56; Brookville, NY Csty. to Ulpianus van Sinderen, Johannes Rubel, Johannes Ritzema, and Lambertus de Ronde, 4 November 1763 in Henry A. Stoutenburgh, ed., *A Documentary History of the Dutch Congregation of Oyster Bay, Queens County, Island of Nassau (Now Long Island)* (N.p.: author, 1902-1907), vol. 1:78-79. Many of the letters cited throughout this essay were issued by the consistories of more than one congregation; for brevity, I have noted as author only the consistory of the congregation in whose records the correspondence was found. Many congregations and communities have been known by various names over time; throughout I have used the nomenclature (except when quoted in the titles of document) as given in Russell L. Gasero, *Historical Directory of the Reformed Church in America, 1628-1992* (Grand Rapids, MI: Eerdmans, 1992).

20 *ERNY* 6:3932, 4008; see also 5:3351, 3493, 3499.

21 Ibid., 4:3090-91. The call was subsequently revoked because he was unwilling to join the Coetus (ibid., 3092, 3097).

22 Ibid., 3122, 3123, 3127.

23 Ibid., 2577-79. The fact that Haeghoort remained in New Jersey suggests that he declined the call.

24 *ERNY* 3:1522-26, 2056; 6:3935; Schoharie, NY Csty. to George Michael Weiss, 12 November

1731, *Records of Schoharie*, 366-70; *ERNY* 4:2600-1; Katskill, NY Csty. to Weiss, 8 February
1732, in Royden Woodward Vosburgh, ed. [and trans.], *Records of the Reformed Dutch
Church of Catskill in the town of Catskill, Greene County, N.Y.*, (New York: [New York Genealogical and Biographical Society], 1919), 206-207; Kingston, NY Csty. to Mancius, 16 May
1732, 'Consistory Minutes of the Old Dutch Church, Kingston, N.Y.,' vol. 2, p. 92v, Old
Dutch Ch., Kingston, NY; *ERNY* 4:2577-79, 2674; Belleville, NJ Csty. to Gerardus Haeghoort,
20 February 1735, 'Kerkelijk Protocol der Gemeinte Jesü tot Second-River in Provintii van
Nieuw Jerseij,' transcription, RUSC; *ERNY* 6:3935; Passaic, NJ Csty. to Johannes van Dries-
sen, 1735, 'Kerkelijk Protocol der Gemeinte J. Xti tot Akquegnonk &c in de Provintie van
Nieuw-Jerseij in Noord-America,' (microfilm, Passaic, NJ, Acquackanonk Ch. Records,
RUSC); *ERNY* 4:2703, 6:3935; 4:2755; Csty. minute, 13 January 1742, 'Kerckenboek van de
Gemeynte van Smithfield, begonnen met den Predickdienst van Joh: Casparus Fryenmuth,'
Smithfield, Pa. Ref. Ch. Records, 1741-1814, Historical Society of Pennsylvania, Philadelphia, Pa.; Fishkill, NY Csty. to Johannes Casparus Fryenmoet, 20 September 1742, 'Kerkboek van de Visch Kill'; *ERNY* 4:3028; Churchville, Pa. Csty. to John Henry Goetschius,
[ca. 1748,] Churchville, Pa., Ch. Papers, vol. 1, 18a; *ERNY* 5:3302, 3489-90, 3559; Schraalenburgh, NJ Csty. to Johannes Schuyler, 17 May 1756, Bergenfield, NJ South Presbyterian
Ch. Records, vol. 2, 'Het Doop Boek van Hackensack en Schraalenburgh voor de Gemeente
van Do: Joh: Schuijler,' RUSC; Claverack, NY Csty. to Fryenmoet, 1 June 1756, 'Records of
the Reformed Church at Claverack, New York,' vol. 1, 249-252 (New York State Library, Albany, NY, photostat; microfilm [of photostat], Salt Lake City: Genealogical Society of Utah,
1968); Brookville, NY Csty. to Eggo Tonkens van Hovenbergh, 1 January 1757 in Stoutenburgh, 62-64; *ERNY* 5:3732-33; New Paltz, NY Csty. to Johannes Mauritius Goetschius, 18
January 1760, trans. B. Fernow, in Edmund Elting papers, New York Genealogical Society,
New York, NY (microfilm, Salt Lake City: Genealogical Society of Utah, 1941), 50; *ERNY*
3950-51; *ERNY* 6:3823; Csty. minutes 29 December 1767 and 18 March 1768, 'Baptismal
Register of the Ref. Prot. Dutch Church Raritan, N.J. Commencing in the year 1699 March
8 and extending to Dec 29, 1839,' United Ref. Ch., Somerville, NJ; Schodack, NY Csty. to
Fryenmoet, 24 April 1770, 'Kerkenboek van de Gemeynte Sch[odack]... .' Archives of the
Reformed Church in America, New Brunswick, NJ

25 Evidence for the 23 calls in this category can be found (in approximately chronological
order) in *ERNY* 4:2580-81, 2673-74; 2743-45, 2801-03 (Although Fryenmoet had been previously called as a minister, his earlier ordination was judged irregular. This call should
therefore be considered a call on a licensed candidate); *ERNY* 4:3028, 2935-2938, 3085;
Churchville, Pa. Csty. to Jonathan Du Bois, 21 September 1749, Churchville, Pa., Ch. Papers, vol. 1, 23a; *ERNY* 5:3148; 4:3133; Passaic, NJ Csty. to David Marinus, 12 November
1750, 'Kerkelijk Protocol der Gemeinte J. Xti tot Akquegnonk'; *ERNY* 5:3199-3200, 3169,
3304-3306, 3555, 3445-46, 3710, 3721, 3719; 6:3827; Fishkill, NY Csty. to Henricus Schoon-
maker, [1763], 'Kerkboek van de Visch Kill.'

26 *ERNY* 3:1560-62, 4:2662, 2761, 6:3949-51, 4036, 4076-77, 4109. Five others include requests
to the classis that they make the call after consulting with someone or after considering a
potential candidate (3:1544-8, 1803-4; 4:2803-5; 6:3853-56, 4145-47).

27 *ERNY* 2:1336-37, 1342-43.

28 For more on Freeman's theology and relationship with Frelinghuysen, see James Tanis,
*Dutch Calvinistic Pietism in the Middle Colonies: A Study in the Life and Theology of Theodorus
Jacobus Frelinghuysen* (The Hague: Martinus Nijhoff, 1967), *passim*, esp. pp. 48, 108, 113.

29 *ERNY* 2:1340-41, 1343, 1349.

30 Ibid., 1341-45. See also 1348-49.

31 Ibid., 1371.

32 Ibid., 1371-72, 1423.

33 Ibid., 1372-73, 1389, 1423-4. For Bancker's defense, see 1359-60.

34 Ibid., 1424-25, 1387.
35 Ibid., 1425, 1373.
36 Ibid., 2:2119, 2120.

Robin A. Leaver

DUTCH SECULAR AND RELIGIOUS SINGING IN EIGHTEENTH-CENTURY NEW YORK

Dutch colonists, like other immigrants to North America, brought with them their own cultural contexts for everyday life which they reconstructed as close as possible to those of the home country. For these Dutch Protestants the rhymed versions of the Biblical Psalms were essential. They sang them every day on the ships that brought them to the New World, and they continued to sing them in public and in private as they founded new towns and established the colony that they named New Netherland: in their homes the day began and ended with the singing of a psalm, and every occasion of public worship had its complement of sung psalms.

New Netherland and New Amsterdam

New Netherland, comprising the largely coastal area from Delaware to Connecticut, and inland along the Hudson Valley, was nominally founded in 1614. Then in 1626 the island of Manhattan was purchased and the settlement at the southern tip was named New Amsterdam (later New York). The spiritual lives of the Dutch settlers on the island were first served by a *ziekentrooster* in 1624, with another appointed in 1626. In the absence of ordained clergy these lay leaders were also responsible for worship and each would also have acted as *voorlezer*, leading the singing of the psalms.[1] In 1628 a Dutch Reformed church in New Amsterdam was formally constituted with a newly-appointed Dominee, Jonas Michaelius, who had arrived on 11 August that year.[2]

The first Dutch church in New Amsterdam was a converted barn, which was replaced by a stone-built church in 1642 in the Old Fort (now Battery Park). This eventually ceased to be used for public worship, being replaced in 1693 by what was to become known as the Old Dutch Church, Garden Street (later known as Exchange Place). As the Dutch population of New Amsterdam and the surrounding area increased throughout the remainder of the seventeenth century new churches were founded. Many more followed in the eighteenth century, with two more being added in Manhattan, now named New York.

Dutch Reformed Psalmody

The worship of these Dutch Reformed churches had a more distinct liturgical form than was customary in English-speaking Calvinist churches, though its structure was nevertheless simple.[3] The singing of metrical psalms was fundamental for these Dutch congregations. They were regularly sung at the beginning and end of the service, before and after sermons, and during the Lord's Supper when it was administered. The psalm singing was lead by the *voorlezer* (or *voorzanger*), who read each stanza before it was sung. The sermons were long, around one and a half hours, but were generally divided into two parts, with a stanza of a Psalm being sung in between the two halves, the stanza being announced by the preacher in the pulpit and led in the customary manner by the *voorlezer*.[4] The singing in the Netherlands was extremely slow,[5] around one half-note per second – or slower! – and there is no reason to believe that the Psalms were sung at a quicker tempo in New Netherland. Thus one stanza of Psalm 42, for example, would have taken between around two-minutes to sing, and if they sang the whole psalm it would have taken them around fifteen minutes or more! The singing was unaccompanied; the first organ to be introduced into a Dutch Reformed church in the colony was in New York in the 1720s. Organs came much later, if at all during this period, in the churches of the rural areas of the colony.

Psalmody was closely associated with teaching the Heidelberg Catechism. The local *voorlezer* was frequently the teacher of the associated school and was required to teach the catechism in the context of psalmody. On 4 November 1661 it was decreed that the schoolmaster, Evert Pietersen, 'before school closes... shall let the pupils sing some verses of a Psalm.'[6] Similarly, in the early 1660s the *voorlezer*, Engelbert Steenhuysen, of the Bergen church, which was then served by New Amsterdam clergy, opened and closed both morning and afternoon school sessions with the singing of a Psalm.[7] In 1679-1680 Jasper Danckaerts visited New Netherlands with the view of finding a home for Dutch Labadists who wanted to emigrate to north America. In his journal, under the date of 5 October 1679, Danckaerts gives the following account of the catechization he observed in the New York Dutch Reformed congregation:

> I... found a company of about twenty-five persons, male and female, but mostly young people. It looked like a school, as indeed it was, more than an assembly of persons who were seeking after true godliness... They sang some verses from the Psalms, made a prayer, and questions from the catechism, at the conclusion of which they prayed and sang some verses from the Psalms again...[8]

Almost twenty years later the situation was somewhat different in that there were sixty-five young people of the New York congregation, aged between seven and fourteen, who, according to the report of the Dominee to the Amsterdam Classis, dated 14 September 1698, 'had learned and repeated... publicly, freely and without missing [not only the Catechism, but also] all the [metrical] Psalms, hymns, and prayers in rhyme, in the presence of my Consistory and of many church members.'[9] Every catechized young person had to commit to memory all the items of the Dutch psalter. Thus on the afternoons of Easter Monday, Ascension Day, and Pentecost Monday in 1698 the sixty-five catechumens took turns to recite the complete psalter from memory.[10]

Some seventy or so years later Dutch psalmody and catechizing were the subject of correspondence in the newspaper, *The New York Journal*, published in New York City. Alexander McDougal, a Scottish privateer soldier and ardent opponent of British rule in the colony – later a major general in the Continental Army during the Revolutionary War – had been jailed for libel in New York. In March 1770 it was reported that '45 virgins of this city, went in procession to pay their respects to a patriot [McDougal], now unjustly confined in the common jail... [and they sang] the 2d part of the 45th psalm, according to Tate and Brady's version, having first undergone some slight alterations.'[11] The charge was that they had altered the text of the Psalm for political ends. A week later the newspaper carried a response in order to put the matter straight. The facts as stated by the previous correspondent were incorrect: the date, the number of young ladies involved, the language, and the psalm that was sung were all wrong! 'Whereas the truth is,' wrote the new correspondent, 'that on Monday the 12th instant 28 virgins belonging to the Dutch Church, went from their catechizing, to pay Mr. M'Dougal a visit, and after tea was served, some of the company proposed the singing a psalm and fixed on the 128th of the Dutch translation which was accordingly done...'[12]

The Metrical Psalter of Petrus Dathenus
The Dutch psalms in universal use in these colonial Dutch Reformed churches were those of Petrus Dathenus, first published in Heidelberg in 1566, and reprinted numerous times – more than 300 editions were issued by 1700,[13] and probably as many or more were published in the eighteenth century. Seventeenth century editions followed the corrected and emended text authorized by the Synod of Dordrecht, 1618-19. Editions of the Dathenus psalter were continuously imported into the Dutch and English colonies, as can be seen in the succession of advertisements that general importers placed in New York and other newspapers. For example, in the immediate decades before the Revolution importers such as Peter T. Curtenius, Lodewick Bamper and Peter Low took out advertisements in New York newspapers in the weeks following the arrival of merchant ships.[14] For example, in January 1762 the following appeared:

> Peter T. Curtenius, at the sign of the Golden Anvil and Hammer... has just imported in the Ship 'Grace,' and in other vessels from Bristol, London, and Amsterdam, the following fresh and complete assortment of ironmongery, cutlery, and braziery ware, which he will sell on the lowest terms, either wholesale or retail... [then follows a long list of goods.] Also, Dutch bibles, testaments, and sundry sorts of small school books, coffee pots and mills, scates [ice-skates], slates, violins and strings... white-wash, paint, shoe, and hearth brushes, &c.&c.[15]

Here the reference to Psalm books is indirect; only Bibles and New Testaments in Dutch are mentioned, but these usually included the Dathenus psalter bound-in as an appendix. Although these volumes were essentially Bibles or New Testaments bound with the Psalms, they were almost universally called 'Psalm Boeken.' Other advertisements were more specific, declaring that 'Psalm-Books, and sundry sorts of Dutch books,'[16] or 'Testamentum, en Psalm Boeken, in quarto en octavo,'[17] or 'Dutch... psalm-books, in coarse and fine print,'[18] or 'psalm and other Dutch books as usual,'[19] or 'Low Dutch Psalm Books...,'[20] were also available for purchase. Most of these editions of the Dathenus Psalms were in duodecimo format and were usually bound with complete Bibles, or New Testaments, and always included the Heidelberg Catechism. There were numerous page-for-page Amsterdam reprints of such editions issued for more than a hundred years and continuously imported into the New Netherland.

1. Portrait of Gerrit van Wagenen (1697-1743) by an anonymous artist ca. 1735. Wunsch Collection of The Decorative Arts of New York 1700-1900. New York State Museum, Albany, New York. No. 76.255.1

It was customary for individuals to own their own copy of the Psalms. For example, there is the witness of the diary of Samuel Sewall, later a judge and precentor of Old South Church, Boston. Sewall visited New York in 1690 and attended the Dutch Reformed Church in the Fort on Sunday, 4 May. In his diary he records that part of Psalm 69 by Dathenus was sung in the Sunday service and that he had learnt it the night before by borrowing the Psalm book of his host: 'Went to the Dutch Church in the morn. Sung the 69th Ps. 2d Pause from the 24th v. to the end, which Capt. Lodowick [of one of the six militia companies, later mayor of New York] taught me the evening before, and lent me his [Psalm] Book, pointed to every syllable.'[21]

In the Wunsch Collection of The Decorative Arts of New York 1700-1900, which forms part of the New York State Museum, Albany, New York, there is an interesting portrait of a Dutch *voorlezer*, Gerrit van Wagenen (1697-1743), painted by an unknown artist around 1735 (see ill. 1).[22] Van Wagenen was born in Kingston, Ulster County, on the west bank of the Hudson River, about fifty or sixty miles to the north of New York City. He became the *voorlezer* of the Kingston Dutch Reformed Church (founded in 1659) and teacher of the local school. The painting, a typical example of eighteenth-century American 'Folk Art' portraiture, shows van Wagenen holding in his right hand the 'tool of his trade,' that is, one of the duodecimo editions of the Dathenus psalter (see table 1). The psalter is clearly an edition of the psalms of Petrus Dathenus, since the language is Dutch, the prose text of the Psalm appears in the margins, the number of the Psalm (Psalm 42 on the left-hand page) appears at the head of each page both in the center and in the outer margin, and every stanza of the text appears with musical notation – all characteristics of seventeenth and eighteenth-century editions of the Dathenus psalms.

Dathenus Revisions and Alternative Psalters
Following its authorization at the provincial Synod of Dordrecht in 1574 the Psalms of Dathenus were universally sung by Dutch Reformed congregations and families in subsequent generations – indeed they are still being sung in parts of the Netherlands today. But as well-loved as they became it did not mean that these psalms were accepted uncritically by all. The texts of these Psalms were revised from time to time, such as the revisions authorized by the Synod of Dordrecht, 1618-19, and the individually issued revised versions such as those of Jacobus Revius (Deventer, 1640) or Christian van Heule (Leiden, 1649). Many were offended by the plainness of the language and poetry and in almost every generation there were those who registered critical comments about the Dathenus psalms, suggesting that they needed to be replaced.[23] Among the most significant was that of the poet Constantijn Huygens (1596-1687), a comment that begins with a pun on Datheen's name.

Maar DAT EEN van DATHEEN dar is de wereldt zot na.
Hoe zo! 't is 't oudtste kindt, en daarom goedt en zoet.

Table. 1. Two 'American' songs written in the Netherlands in 1779

The Hague 1779	Amsterdam 1779
God save the Thirteen States!	God bless the Thirteen States,
Long rule th' United States!	And save for ev'r our fates,
God save our States!	From tyranny!
Make us victorious;	This is the joyful day,
Happy and glorious;	Whereon we glory may,
No tyrants over us;	We saw the glitt'ring ray,
God save our States!	Of Liberty.
[+ 9 stanzas]	[+ 3 stanzas]

De vromen zyn 'er meê te vreen in haar gemoedt
't Mag wezen; maar ik vrees, 't is al te vreên, op Godt na.[24]

The quest for an alternative versification of the Psalms continued throughout many generations, and various psalters were issued, such as the rhymed version of Philips van Marnix (Antwerp, 1580), Diderick Campenhuysen (Amsterdam, 1630), Cornelius Boey (Rotterdam, 1648), Jacob Clerkius (Amsterdam, 1664), Johannes Six (Amsterdam, 1674), Gerardus Borstius (Amsterdam, 1695), Abraham Trommius (Amsterdam, 1695), and Joannes Eusebius Voet ('s Gravenhage, 1763). But none of these psalm books were issued in any great numbers, and none displaced the popular Psalms of Dathenus.

There is no evidence that these alternative psalters were in use in New Amsterdam/New York, though it is possible that they were imported in small numbers and are to be counted among the general 'Psalm and other Dutch books' that were advertised in the newspapers. There was however another attempt to create a psalter that would hopefully replace the Dathenus Psalms, a psalter that was largely written in New Netherland but never issued in a published format.

Frederick Nagtglas was an antiquarian and member of the Zeeland Academy of Sciences, Middleburg, in the second half of the nineteenth century. He reported in his *Levensberichten van Zeeuwen* that in 1874 he 'bought at a book-stall in Middelburg a very neatly [hand-] written translation of the Psalms, with musical notes.'[25] The identity of the author is given simply as 'J. D.' on the title page: 'The 150 Psalms of David newly brought into Dutch and into Dutch rhyming verse by J. D. lover of poetry at Wieuwerd in Friesland.'[26] The identity of 'J.D.' is clarified by the preface that is signed '8 January [16]91, Jasper Danckaerts,' that is, the Jasper Danckaerts who in 1679-80 traveled to New Netherland on behalf of Labadists who wished to emigrate to the New World, and commented on the Psalm-singing at a catechism class in New Amsterdam (see above).[27] The Labadists formed a quietist off-shoot from Dutch Reformed orthodoxy yet nevertheless shared much with the older church body, including the tradition of psalmody.

Danckaerts begins his preface by drawing attention to the deficiencies of the Dathenus Psalms and of his intention to make an new attempt at translating the Psalms from French into Dutch, so that they could be sung to the familiar Genevan melodies.[28] He then explains how he was able fulfill his intention of preparing a new rhymed psalter:

[It was]... when I found myself called upon for the second time to make a journey to New Netherland in the year 1682-1683. And although such journeys by water and land seem to offer little good opportunity for composition... yet I began with a good will and by God's grace pursued and happily finished it... After returning home and revising and correcting it, it was thought advisable to submit it for further revision to the Juffrouw N.N., which was done, and after two years I received it back with corrections.[29]

Frederick Nagtglas's identification of the anonymous 'Juffrouw' as Anna Maria van Schuurman is compelling,[30] since she was both a known poet and a Labadist, but she cannot have been the revisor of these New Netherland Psalms because she died in 1678, the year before Danckaerts's first trans-Atlantic journey and four years before his second. Thus the identity of the young lady remains a mystery. What is clear, however, is that Danckaerts's rhymed version of the Psalms originated in New Netherland and that, by implication, they were first sung in the colony, since the only effective way to test such new Psalms is to sing them.

Danckaerts's original intention was for his Psalms, duly revised, to be published. But, as he explains towards the end of his preface, on the publication of Hendrick Ghysen's edition of the psalter in '1690' he abandoned his plan.[31] Ghysen's psalms, which were constructed out of the versions of seventeen different authors, including Dathenus, were in fact published some years earlier, in 1686,[32] which probably means that Danckaerts himself did not discover them until the year 1690.

An interesting feature of the Danckaerts' psalter is the simplified forms of the melodies. The melodies in the printed editions of the Dathenus Psalms retain the two note-values – whole-notes and half-notes – of the Genevan psalm tunes of the sixteenth century. In contrast Danckaerts notates all the tunes in equal whole-notes throughout. Almost a century later Daniel Zacharie Chatelain, in the preface to his *Psautier evangélique* (Amsterdam, 1781), explains that his psalm tunes are essentially notated in equal note-values. He wrote: 'Each stanza begins and ends with a whole note, while all the notes between are half notes. Our psalms have been sung thus for some years in various of our churches, if not in all.'[33] The evidence of Danckaerts's psalter demonstrates that the practice had originated much earlier, which, in his case, might have been influenced by English psalm-singing in the North American colony: most of the English psalm tunes in use at that time were sung in uniform equal note values.

Not all the Dutch colonists were confessionally Dutch Reformed. There was a Dutch Lutheran presence in New York dating from 1649, which in the same way that the New York Dutch Reformed church came under the jurisdiction of the Amsterdam Classis, the New York Lutheran congregation was supported by the Consistory of the Lutheran Church in Amsterdam. The New York Lutheran church remained small without regular clergy until the early eighteenth century, when Justus Falckner, a German pietist with Swedish Lutheran connections, became its pastor.[34] Falckner issued a small catechism on basic doctrine: *Grondlycke Onderricht* (New York: Bradford, 1708). According to bibliographical descriptions the volume contained 'prayers' at the end of the volume.[35] These 'prayers' turn out to be three, rather poor, Dutch translations of German hymns: Luther's credal hymn, the almost universal Lutheran pulpit hymn to be sung before the sermon, and a less familiar hymn to be sung 'before the children's sermon.'[36]

Later the New York Lutheran congregation sang from the Amsterdam Lutheran hymnal, *Nieuw verbetert psalm en geestelyke liederen en lofsangen*, edited by Jan van Duisberg, first issued in 1687 and continuously reissued well into the second half of the eighteenth century. The *Proctocol* of the New York City Lutheran Church records that 24 copies were purchased in 1728 and a further 3 in 1730.[37] The hymnal contained many German Lutheran hymns and psalms translated into Dutch that were set to their associated German tunes.

Secular Singing

While the religious singing of the Dutch colonists is relatively easy to evaluate their secular music-making is more difficult to describe with certainty. A hopeful starting point would be to investigate the newspaper advertisements in which are found from time to time references to 'Psalm and other Dutch books.' That there were secular collections of songs imported into New York is certain since there are such references to 'A merry collection of Low Dutch Songs...,'[38] and other similar descriptions in these advertisements, but they are non-specific as to detail. Some newspaper advertisements do give some titles but these are difficult to identify because the titles are so abbreviated and as often as not the names of their authors are frequently misspellt. Some can be identified, such as 'Uylenbroeks Gesangen,'[39] and 'Van Loo Gesangen,'[40] but in both cases the contents of these song books was religious rather than secular: the former is Hendrik Uylenbroek [or Uilenbroek], *Christelyke Gezangen*, which had already reached a fifth edition in Amsterdam by 1666, and continued to be reissued in Amsterdam and Utrecht well into the eighteenth century; the latter is Adrianus van Loo, *Geestelyke Gezangen* published in many editions in Amsterdam, Delft, Deventer, Groningen, Middelburg and Utrecht during the eighteenth century. There is also an advertisement in the *New York Weekly Journal* that gives the information that a Dutch spiritual song was published in New York towards the end of 1740:

> Just published, Een Geestelyk Lied, Bequaam om Gesongen te werden in alle Godvruchtige Vergaderingen, ofte Particuleere 't Samenkomsten [A Spiritual Song, suitable to be sung in all devout meetings or private assemblies]. Printed and sold by John Peter Zenger, or Jacob Goelet.[41]

No copy has survived and nothing further is known about it.

An example of an ambiguous title in these advertisements is 'Wits groote Lieden Boek.'[42] This could be *Boertigh, amoreus en aendachtigh Groot Lied-boeck*, first issued in Amsterdam in 1622. But the author of this collection was G.A. Brederode and not 'Wit.' Alternatively 'Wit' might be a misprint for ' Wilts Gesangen,'[43] which itself might be a misprint for the publisher Georg Wittig, who published *Een nieuw bundeltje uitgekipte Geestelyke Gezangen* (Dordrecht, 1750).

Although the evidence is somewhat frustrating, these newspaper advertisements do reveal other pieces of information that help to build the picture of secular music-making by the Dutch in New York. There are the adverts for runaway slaves, which comment on the slave's linguistic and music abilities. Here is a sampling dating between 1741 and 1761: 'Run away... from... New-Brunswick, in East-New-Jersey, a Negro man... speaks Dutch...

He is a fiddler, and took his fiddle with him, he uses the bow with his left hand'[44]; 'Run away... a mulatto... can talk good Dutch and English, and can play very well upon the fiddle'[45]; 'Runaway from... New-York... a Negro fellow named Jacob... speaks both Dutch and English... he is a great fiddler, and has a violin along with him.'[46] ; 'Long-Island... Run-away a Negro man... speaks very good English and low Dutch, plays on the violin... . [signed] Henderick Onderdonk'[47]; and 'Run away... a mulatto wench... can speak good Dutch and English, and sings a good song...'[48] The fact that these slaves in Dutch-speaking households had musical abilities underlines the importance of music among the Dutch colonists. The same inference is to be drawn from the advertisements in the newspapers listing goods for sale. Many of the adverts that mention Dutch books for sale also include among sundry other items various musical instruments, such as 'violins,' 'fiddles,' 'German flutes,' as well as 'fiddle strings' and 'guitar strings.' By all accounts fiddle music was an important feature of Dutch weddings in the colony.

There were also concerts from time to time which, to judge from the names of the people involved or the location of the concert, had strong Dutch connections. For example, in November 1761 the *New York Mercury* advertised the following:

A concert, of vocal and instrument musick, to be held at the new assembly room, to-morrow, at 6 o'clock. No person to be admitted without tickets, which are to be had at the house of Alexander Van Dienval, musick master near the New Dutch Church, and but two doors from Messrs. Haynes and Oudenard's store.[49]

In March 1767 the same newspaper carried the following:

To be sold very cheap, a beautiful clavecort, and organ joined together, that can be played with or without the organ, and is very proper for learners; the organ and clavecort can be both played at one time, with one sett of keys; it will be sold much under the value. For further particulars enquire of Peter Boufman, organist, of the Dutch-Church, in the street between the French and new Dutch-Churches.[50]

Undoubtedly the colonists would have sung and played Dutch folk songs that were available in various published collections, small oblong volumes that could easily fit into a pocket. The notable collection of such melodies was Adriaen Valerius, *Neder-landtsche gedenck-clanck: kortelick openbarende de voornaemste geschiedenissen van de Seventhien Nederlandsche provintien*, published in Harlem in 1626.[51] The songs in this collection are presented within an historical and political and framework and the melodies are not only Dutch but also French, Italian and English.[52] If these melodies were sung in New York City it means that the various language-groups heard each other singing different songs and in different languages but to the same familiar melodies. One of the songs that must have been sung among the Dutch colonists was the enormously popular *Wilhelmus van Nassaue*, celebrating the foundation of the modern Dutch state, that originally appeared 1581, and reprinted in Valerius's collection and in many other anthologies over the years, and, of course, it was also sung from memory.[53]

The same kind of political songs circulated around the time of the American War of Independence and the establishment of the new nation. In January 1780 *The Pennsylvania*

Packet, published in Philadelphia, reprinted two songs, both originating in the Netherlands, that were intended to be sung on 4 July. The first was 'Made by a Dutch Lady at the Hague, for the Sailors of the five American vessels at Amsterdam. June 1779'; the second was 'Made by a Dutch gentleman at Amsterdam, to be sung by the same, on the 4th of July.' Both texts were quoted in full and were contributed by 'The Steady Friend of America at the Hague.'[54] The songs are parodies of the British National Anthem and were intended to be sung to the familiar British melody (see fig. 3). Undoubtedly these songs would have been copied from the newspaper and sung in New York and elsewhere as well as in Philadelphia.

Another witness to the kind of folk songs sung by the Dutch in New York is Jacob van Eyck's *Der fluyten lust-hof*, first published in Amsterdam in between 1646 and 1649, with further editions in 1654 and 1655, though there is no known copy in the United States.[55] Van Eyck was the blind virtuoso recorder player of Utrecht who wrote a series of variations on popular folk songs that were known and sung by the Dutch, and therefore it represents a corpus of French, English, as well as Dutch and other folk songs on which the variations are based that provides a repertory of song that was likely to have been known and sung by the Dutch in New York and in the surrounding areas. Again, like the Valerius anthology, van Eyck's includes *Wilhelmus van Nassaue*.[56] But not all the melodies elaborated by van Eyck were secular in origin; a significant number were Genevan psalm tunes that were found in the Dathenus Psalter (see table 2).[57] The implication is that these were perhaps the most familiar of melodies of the Dutch psalter. There are also two other melodies in van Eyck's *Der fluyten lust-hof* that must have been known in New York, both associated with Christmas, and sung by Protestants and Catholics alike. *Een Kindeken is ons gebooren*, which has been described as the most popular Christmas song with a Dutch text throughout the sixteenth through to the eighteenth century.[58] *O heylich zaligh Bethlehem*

Table 2. Psalms Tunes, with Datheen's Associated Texts, in Jacobus van Eyck's Der fluyten lust hof

Psalm 1	*Die niet en gaat in der godlozen raad*	FLH II (1646)
Psalm 9	*Heer, ik wil U uit 's harten grond*	FLH II (1646)
Psalm 15	*Wie is 't, die zal wonen eenpaar*	FLH II (1646)
Psalm 33	*Weest nu verheugd, al gij oprechten*	FLH II (1646)
Psalm 68	*Sta op, Heer, toon U onversaagd*	FLH I (1649)
Psalm 101	*Van Gods goedheid en oordeel wil ik zingen*	FLH II (1646)
Psalm 103	*Mijn ziele, wil den Heer met lofzang prijzen*	FLH I (1649)
Psalm 116	*Ik heb den Heer lief, want Hij heeft verhoord*	FLH II (1646)
Psalm 118	*Danket den Heer zeer hoog geprezen*	FLH I (1649)
Psalm 119	*Gelukzalig is de mense die leeft*	FLH II (1646)
Psalm 133	*Ziet hoe fijn en lieflijk is 't alle stonden*	FLH II (1646)
Psalm 134	*Alle gij knechten des Heeren*	FLH II, 2nd ed (1654)
Psalm 140	*O mijn God, wil mij nu bevrijden*	FLH I (1649)
Psalm 150	*Laat nu God geprezen zijn*	FLH I (1649)
Onse Vader	*Onse vader in Hemelryck*	FLH I (1649) 1
Lof-zangh Marie	*Myn ziel maeckt groot der Heer*	FLH I (1649) 17

was another very popular Christmas song, second only to *Een Kindeken* in the seventeenth and eighteenth centuries.

The Transition from Dutch to English

Even though the English governed the colony from 1664, demographically English-speakers were in the minority: they only constituted about a third of the white population of New York City in 1700, compared with almost two-thirds of Dutch-speakers. Parity between the two populations was only reached around 1710-20, but Dutch language and culture continued to be strong in the city.[59] From the middle of the eighteenth century English began to dominate the life and culture of Manhattan, the result of an expansion of the English-speaking population, the use of English as the language of commerce, and the increasing inter-marriage between the English and the Dutch. In 1748 Dominee Gualterus Du Bois reported that 'the Dutch language is gradually, more and more being neglected,' especially by younger people, and therefore there was the necessity of 'calling a minister, after my death, to preach in the English language, but in accordance with our manner and doctrine.'[60] Not all agreed with the Dominee but eventually – fifteen years later in 1763 – the New York *Kerkenraad* called Archibald Laidlie, who had been the pastor of the Scottish Church in Vlissingen, to be the English 'Dutch' Dominee. There were two Dutch Reformed churches in New York City: the 'Nieuwe Kerk' (later known as the Middle Church) was built in 1729, which meant that the earlier church in Garden Street was thereafter known as the 'Oude Kerk.' But it was only in the Nieuwe Kerk that English was permitted, at least to begin with.[61] Laidlie commenced his English preaching in the Nieuwe Kerk on the afternoon of 15 April 1764, and more than a thousand people heard him.[62] Laidlie's preaching had a significant impact not only on the congregation of the Nieuwe Kerk but on the Dutch Reformed presence in the city as a whole: the Oude Kerk was rebuilt in 1766; the North Church, the largest of the three, was built in 1768-69; and a second English preacher was called in 1770. Even though the Psalms continued to be sung in Dutch in the Nieuwe Kerk, led by *voorzanger* Jacobus Van Antwerp,[63] plans to sing in English were in place even before Laidlie began his pastorate. A minute of the *Kerkenraad*, dated 5 July 1763, records that 'the draft of certain Psalms in English rhyme, according to our music [na onse zangtonen gestelt] was laid before the consistory, and so far approved.'[64] The *Kerkenraad* must have known of Triemer's English psalter, a version of the Psalms of Tate and Brady, issued in Amsterdam in 1753. But Triemer's Psalms were published for use among Anglicans in Amsterdam and did not employ all the familiar Genevan melodies. Thus rather than use the Triemer English Psalms the *Kerkenraad* decided to produce its own English psalter that would facilitate the possibility of the congregation of the Nieuwe Kerk singing the Psalms in both Dutch and English simultaneously. Just who was responsible for the draft English Psalms examined by the *Kerkenraad* in 1763 is uncertain but by the following year Francis Hopkinson of Philadelphia – musician and later signer of the Declaration of Independence – had been engaged to complete the English 'Dutch' psalter, though his name never appeared in the psalter when it was published.[65] A second edition of the Heidelberg Catechism in English was published by Holt for the Dutch Reformed Church in April 1767 and it included two of the English psalms. The advertisement placed in the *New York Journal*, 30 April, read:

Just published and to be sold at the printing-office at the Exchange, The Heidelberg Catechism... as... is taught in the Reformed churches and schools of Holland.... to which is added, two psalms of the new-version. Translated for the use of the reformed Protestant Dutch church, of the city of New-York.[66]

The complete edition of the 'new' Psalms was published eight months later, on 17 December 1767: *The Psalms of David... Translated from the Dutch: For Use of the Reformed Protestant Dutch Church in the City of New-York* (New York: Parker, 1767). Like its Dutch counterparts the new psalter was printed with musical notation for every stanza of each Psalm, printed with music type especially imported from Amsterdam.[67]

In the event these English Psalms were not 'new' and neither were they 'translated from the Dutch.' They were in fact mostly revisions of the Psalms of Tate and Brady[68] and their metres did not always match those of the Dutch Psalms. Thus the declared aim of having the Nieuwe Kerk congregation sing in both English *and* Dutch simultaneously was not realized as the *Kerkenraad* had intended: only 27 Psalms were set to the same melodies as their equivalents in the Dutch psalter; 23 Psalms were given abbreviated Genevan melodies, which rendered bi-lingual singing impossible; and the remainder were either assigned different (and sometimes modified) melodies than those used in the Dutch psalter. No less that 86 Genevan melodies found in the Dathenus psalter were omitted from this English psalter.[69] Thus for most Psalms the congregation could either sing in Dutch *or* English but not both at the same time.

An interesting, and to some degree a revolutionary, publication appeared in 1774: a musical supplement to the English Psalm book that was published seven years earlier: *A Collection of the Psalm and Hymn Tunes Used by the Reformed Protestant Dutch Church of the City of* New-York, *agreeable to their Psalm Book, published in English. In four Parts, Viz. Tenor, Bass, Treble, and Counter... . New-York: Printed by Hodge and Shober. M.DCC.LXXIV.*[70] Using the same music type that was imported from Amsterdam, this tune book set out the psalm tunes in four independent parts, with the tenor and bass on the left-hand page, and the treble and counter on the right. The 'Advertisement' on the preliminary pages begins with the following paragraph:

A collection of [Tenor,] Bass, Treble and Counter, was formerly made in France by *Claude de Goudemel*, in 1572, and printed at Leyden 1620, and afterwards reprinted with all the Psalms at Harlem, 1753. To this book the Editors are greatly indebted for the following collection.[71]

The immediate source for these four-part settings was *Davids psalmen en alle de Lof-Zang-en... obergeseet door P. Dathenum. Geheel op musyk-nooten met de IIII. Stemmen, als tenor, bassus, altus en discant. Alle op de C. Sleutel gesteld* [David's Psalms and all the hymns translated by P. Dathenus. Complete with musical notes in four voices, that is, tenor, bass, alto and discant. All given in the C clef] (Haarlem: Enschedé, 1753).[72] But this was a reissue of the four-part settings that were published by Goudimel in Geneva in 1565, *Les pseaumes mis en rime françoise... mis en musique*, that was later issued with the Psalms in Dutch in Leiden in 1620. The editors of the 1774 tune book are not named but Francis Hopkinson is not likely to have been among them because of the rough and inept way the harmonizations were fitted to the frequently truncated melodies of the English 'Dutch' Psalm Book of 1767.

These four-part settings of Goudimel were originally intended for domestic use and were so used in the sixteenth and seventeenth centuries, but in the eighteenth-century some Dutch churches began singing them within public worship. This is explained in the Consistory's 'Approbation,' dated 11 January 1774, which appears at the beginning of the tune book:

> Whereas a collection of the [Tenor,] Bass, Treble and Counter has been made to the Tunes used in the Reformed Protestant Dutch Church of the city of *New-York*, by a number of the members of the said Church, in order that the singing of Psalms, in all four parts of music, agreeable to the practice of many Churches in *Europe*, particularly those in *Holland* and *Germany*, may be rendered more easy and familiar, and the same has been laid before the Consistory, for their approbation: The said Consistory, desirous of promoting harmony and good order in every part of public worship, and of praising *God* with the voice, as a part of the believer's reasonable service, have, after an examination of the following Collection, approved of the same, and recommend the use thereof in their Church.[73]

The implication is that with the issuing of this four-part tune book for use in public worship, a group of singers, a choir, had been formed in the church, and that the hitherto monolithic practice of the unison singing of the Psalms was now augmented by vocal harmony. Thus the Nieuwe Kerk in New York City were keeping up with the practice of leading churches in cities and towns in the Netherlands, as well as reflecting the practice of some of the English churches in the colony by forming a choir. But whereas the English-speaking choirs tended to sing the recently-composed psalm-settings by Andrew Law, Francis Hopkinson, William Tansur, William Billings, among others, the settings sung in the Dutch church were Goudimel's sturdy diatonic harmonies of the sixteenth century.

How long the four-part singing of the Psalms continued is uncertain. The tune book was issued on the eve of the Declaration and War of Independence, during which time the New York Dutch Reformed Churches were badly damaged and it was quite some time before there were repaired and brought back into use.

In the towns and cites outside of Manhattan the move towards the use of English proceeded at a much slower pace and the Dutch Psalms of Petrus Dathenus continued to be sung in unison and led by *voorlezers*. For example, Catherina Van Driesen was a member of the Dutch Reformed Church in Albany, New York. She was probably related to Dominee Petrus Van Driesen who served the Albany congregation at that time, though I have not been able to locate her name in the registers of the church. Her Dutch New Testament, an undated Dordrecht edition, includes a bound-in 1699 Amsterdam imprint of the Dathenus' Psalms. On the flyleaf of the volume there is an inscription mostly in Dutch:[74] '1738 Den 15 August op Dinghdag is My een Doghter Gebore Genamt Cathrene [1738 The 15 August on Tuesday to me a daughter is born named Catherine].' To this is added, which may have been penned at a later date, in English: 'Cather[in]a Van Dr[i]esen har [sic] Psalm Book in Albany.' Similarly, Elizabeth Sickels, who was a member of the Bergen church – and probably a relative of Abraham Sickels, the church's *voorlezer* between 1761-1789 – once owned a Dutch New Testament, published in Dordrecht in 1778, which was bound with an undated Amsterdam imprint of Dathenus' Dutch Psalms. Her ownership inscription is dated 1787 and is entirely in English: 'Elizabeth Sickels Her Psalm Book Bought in the year of Our Lord 1787. 1787.' [75] This would indicate that Dutch was still being used for the Psalms sung in public worship, though English might have already begun to be employed at least on some occasions. For example, the Dutch church in Middletown, New Jersey, resolved in March 1785 'That if, for want of Dutch singers, it seem expedient the pastor, if he choose, may have English singing and preach in Dutch.'[76] But many of the Dutch Reformed churches in New Jersey and the Hudson Valley continued singing the Dutch Psalms into the early nineteenth century. The 1792 Synod confirmed the use of the Dutch Psalms of Dathenus but also recommended the use of the 1773 Dutch psalms. But the circulation of these new Psalms had not begun until 1775, a time when the colony was becoming an independent country, and with everything else that was going on, it was not an opportune time to introduce the new Dutch Psalms, especially as the Dutch Reformed church was moving inexorably in the direction of using only English. Therefore, those who sang in Dutch continued to sing the Psalms of Dathenus. But they would soon become a minority. Following the founding of the new nation of the United States the Dutch Reformed Church adopted an English title: The Reformed Protestant Dutch Church in North America. In 1793 its Synod adopted English liturgical forms for the whole church, a revision of the liturgies drawn up for use in New York city in 1767, and a few years earlier produced an English psalter/hymnal for general use: *The Psalms and Hymns of the Reformed Protestant Dutch Church in North America*, edited by John Henry Livingstone (New York, 1789). Thus, while the singing of Dutch Psalms continued in some churches it was declining and was ultimately and universally replaced by singing in English.

Conclusion
The Dutch Reformed were, however, different from the Swedish Lutherans in and around Delaware. They were persuaded to give up their language in favor of English at an early stage and, once they had done so, were effectively forced to use the *Book of Common Prayer* for their worship. They therefore became Anglicans and their national and cultural identity was absorbed into that of the English colonists, mostly before the end of the seventeenth century. The Dutch were different. They retained their language and customs so that they remained a clearly defined identity at the time the new American nation was born. And perhaps the singing of the Dathenus Psalms had quite a lot to do with the Dutch identity that was maintained throughout the eighteenth century.

Notes

1 On the background of the role of the *voorzanger* and congregational psalm singing in seventeenth- and eighteenth-century Netherlands, see Jan Luth, *'Daer wert om 't seerste uytgekreten...' : Bijdragen tot een geschiedenis van de gemeentezang in het Nederlandse gereformeerde protestantisme ±1550-±1852* (Kampen: Van den Berg, 1986), 182-209.
2 Gabriel P. Disosway, *The Earliest Churches of New York and Its Vicinity* (New York: Gregory, 1865), 2; see also Jonas Michaelius, *Manhattan in 1628*, ed. Dingman Versteeg (New York: Dodd, Mead, 1904).
3 For the background, see the introduction in Daniel Meeter, *'Bless the Lord, O My Soul': The*

New-York Liturgy of the Dutch Reformed Church, 1767 (Lanham: Scarecrow, 1998), 1-91.

4 See Dingman Versteeg, *Sketch of the Early History of the Reformed Dutch Church of Bergen in Jersey City* (New York: Versteeg, 1889), 23.

5 For the background, see Luth, *'Daer wert om't seerste uytgekreten... ,'* 177-182.

6 *Minutes of the Orphanmasters of New Amsterdam 1655 to 1663*, trans. Berthold Fernow (New York: Harper, 1902-1907), 2: 115-116; see also William Heard Kilpatrick, *The Dutch Schools of New Netherland and Colonial New York* (Washington: Government Printing Office, 1912).

7 Versteeg, *Early History of the Reformed Dutch Church of Bergen*, 24.

8 Bartlett Burleigh James and J. Franklin Jameson, eds., *Journal of Jasper Danckaerts 1679-1690* (New York: Scribner, 1913), 63.

9 Meeter, *'Bless the Lord, O My Soul,'* xiv.

10 Ibid., xv-xx. The Dominees of the Dutch Reformed churches of New Netherland supplemented the Heidelberg Catechism with their own books of catechetical questions and answers, among the first Dutch publications in the colony. Edelman records five such 'Nieuw York' imprints issued between 1700 and 1738; see Hendrik Edelman, *Dutch-American Bibliography 1693-1794: A Descriptive Catalog of Dutch-language Books, Pamphlets and Almanacs Printed in America* (Nieuwkoop: De Graaf, 1974), Nos. 2-3, 5, 15 and 26.

11 *New York Journal* (New York), No. 1420 (22 March 1770), 31.

12 *New York Journal* (New York), No. 1421 (29 March 1770), 32.

13 See C. A. Höweler and F. H. Matter, *Fontes hymnodiae Neerlandicae impressi 1539-1700: De Melodieën van het Nederlandstalig Geestelijk Lied 1539-1700* (Nieuwkoop: De Graaf, 1985).

14 According to Edelman, Jacob Goelet (1689-1769) was 'the most important bookseller and in New York for Dutch language books'; Hendrik Edelman, *The Dutch Language Press in America: Two Centuries of Printing, Publishing and Bookselling* (Nieuwkoop: De Graaf, 1986), 20.

15 *New York Gazette & Weekly Post Boy*, No. 992 (7 January 1762), 42. Such advertisements appeared in three or four successive issues of the newspaper as well as in other New York newspapers. Curtenius's advertisements which include direct and indirect references to psalm books can be found in various newspapers issued between 1760 and 1773.

16 *New York Gazette*, No. 197 (20 September 1762), 22.

17 *New York Gazette*, No. 268 (30 January 1764), 43.

18 *New York Gazette & Weekly Post Boy*, No. 1186 (26 September 1765), 32.

19 *New York Gazette & Weekly Post Boy*, No. 1346 (17 October 1768), 32.

20 *Political Intelligencer and New-Jersey Advertiser* (New Brunswick, New Jersey), No. 10 (16 December 1783), 33.

21 *The Diary of Samuel Sewall 1674-1729*, ed. M. Halsey Thomas (New York: Farrar, Straus & Giroux, 1973), 1: 257.

22 New York State Museum, Albany, New York, No. 76.255.1.

23 See the anthology of citations assembled by Andreas Andriessen, *Aanmerkingen op de Psalmberymingen van Petrus Dathenus: in welke uit het algemeen gebrek van taal- en dightkunde, onheblyke wartaal van Psalm tot Psalm voorkomende, en ongelykvormigheidt aan den text, derzelver onbestaanbaar gebruik, en Noodtzaaklykheidt der veranderinge vertoont en aangedrongen wordt* (Middelburg: Taillefert, 1756), sig. ***3ʳ-*****2ᵛ.

24 Cited Andriessen, *Aanmerkingen op de Psalmberymingen van Petrus Dathenus*, sig. ****2ʳ:
The poem, in dialogue form, can be translated thus:
'But that one of Datheen, that is what the world longs for.
Why so! It is the oldest child, and therefore good and sweet.
The pious are pleased with it in their heart.
That may be true, but I fear, they are all too content, and God is not.'

25 'In 1874 kocht ik op een stalletje te Middelburg een uiterst net geschreven *Vertaling der*

psalmen met zangnoten'; Frederik Nagtglas, *Levensberichten van Zeeuwen: zijnde een vervolg op P. de la Rue, Geletterd, staatkundig en heldhaftig Zeeland* (Middelburg: Altorffer, 1890-1893), 1: 147; trans., *Journal of Jasper Danckaerts 1679-1690*, ed. James and Jameson, xxiii.

26 *De CL | PSALMEN DAVIDS | op Nieus | Volgens de Nederduitshen Text | in Nederduits Sangh-Rym gebracht | door | J. D. | Liefhebber der Poësie | tot | Wiwert in Vrieslant.* Zeeuwsch Genootschap der Wetenschappen, Zeeuwse Bibliotheek, Middelburg. Accession No. 6293. The manuscript comprises three unnumbered leaves of prefatory material, and 202 leaves, numbered 1-404, containing the 150 Psalms, and metrical versions of the Commandments, Magnificat, Lord's Prayer, Creed, Benedictus and Nunc dimittis. Dathenus included metrical version of the same items but in a different sequence. Unlike the Dathenus, Danckaets did not include the 'Gebed voor de Predicatie,' by Jan Utenhove, nor his own version of such a prayer. Unlike editions of Dathenus, Danckaerts's manuscript does note repeat the musical notation with every stanza: each tune appears with the first stanza interlined with subsequent stanzas appearing underneath in poetic strophes. Danckaerts does not include a summary of the Psalm at its beginning as is commonly found in the Dathenus psalters.

27 On Jasper Danckaerts (1639- ca. 1702/04), see Pieter de La Ruë, *Geletterd Zeeland, verdeeld in drie afdeelingen, bevattende... de schryvers, geleerden en kunstenaaars*, 2nd ed. (Middelburg: Callenfels, 1741), 203-206. The biography is signed 'C. Vitringa,' and dated 'Franeker 1699. Mai 13,' that is, a few years before Daenckerts's death in Middelburg.

28 *De CL Psalmen Davids*, [ii] recto. Danckaerts's interest in translating the Psalms is seen in his visit to John Eliot in Roxbury, Massachusetts, in July 1680. Eliot, who had not only translated the Bible into an Indian dialect but also the Psalms in metre, presented Danckaerts a copy of his Indian Old Testament and metrical Psalms; see *Journal of Jasper Danckaerts 1679-1690*, ed. James and Jameson, 263-266. The Bible given by Eliot remains in the Zeeuwsch Genootschaap der Wetenschappen, Zeeuwse Bibliotheek, Middelburg, No. 1110 E23. The tipped-in manuscript note in Danckaerts's hand (*Onderichtingh*, dated June 1680) is now separate from the volume, No. 6651c; a translation of this document is given in *Journal of Jasper Danckaerts 1679-1690*, ed. James and Jameson, 265, note.

29 *De CL Psalmen Davids*, [ii] verso – [iii] recto; trans., *Journal of Jasper Danckaerts 1679-1690*, ed. James and Jameson, xxiv.

30 Nagtglas, *Levensberichten van Zeeuwen*, 147; repeated by J. Franklin Jameson in *Journal of Jasper Danckaerts 1679-1690*, ed. James and Jameson, xxiv.

31 *De CL Psalmen Davids* [iii] recto.

32 See H. Hasper, *Calvijns Beginsel voor de Zang in de Eredienst verklaard uit de Heilige Schrift en uit de Geschiedenis der Kerk...* 2 vols. ('s-Gravenhage: Stichting Geestelijkr Liederen, 1976), 2:665.

33 Cited in Orentin Douen, *Clément Marot et le Psautier huguenot, étude historique, littéraire, musicale et bibliographique...* (Paris, Imprimerie nationale, 1878-1879; repr. Nieuwkoop, De Graaf, 1967), 2: 392: 'Chaque vers, lisons-nous dans l'avertissment placé en tête du recueil, commence par une *note entière* et finit de même, tandis que toutes les notes intermédiaires sont *demies*. C'est ainsi que, depuis quelques années, nos pseaumes se chantent, dans diverses de nos Eglises. Que n'est-ce dans toutes!' On Chatelain's *Pseautier evangéliques*, see Hasper, *Calvijns Beginsel voor de Zang in de Eredienst...*, 2:147-151.

34 See *Protocol of the Lutheran Church in New York City 1702-1750*, trans. [from Dutch] by Simon Hart and Harry J. Kreider (New York: The United Synod of New York and New England, 1958), 8.

35 See, for example, Edelman, *Dutch-American Bibliography 1693-1794*, No. 4.

36 *Wy geloben in eenen Godt alley*, = Martin Luther's *Wir glauben all an einen Gott* (1524). *O Godt, die uw gedachtnis* = Wilhelm II of Saxe-Weimar's *Herr Jesu Christ, dich zu uns wend* (1648). *Herr Godt dyn tron w met g'naed heelers* = Johann Zwick's *Herr Gott, dein Treu mit*

Gnaden (1537), originally headed: 'Ein gesang vor anfang der Kinder predigt.'

37 *Protocol of the Lutheran Church in New York City 1702-1750*, 128 and 183. The *Protocol* (p. 60) also records that a copy of Johannes Hermanus Manné, *Nieuwe overgesette Lutherse gezangen* (Amsterdam, 1718) was offered for sale.

38 *Political Intelligencer and New-Jersey Advertiser* (New Brunswick, NJ) No. 10 (16 December 1783), 33.

39 *New York Gazette & Weekly Post Boy*, No. 1096 (5 January 1764), 32.

40 *New York Gazette & Weekly Post Boy*, No. 1180 (15 August 1765), 23.

41 *New York Weekly Journal*, No. 366 (8 December 1740), 41; see Edelman, *Dutch-American Bibliography 1690-1794*, No. 27. A number of manuscripts of hymns written by Dutch authors in New York State are extant; see Erich J. Roth, 'Vanderlyn's Song: A Story of Personal Conviction in Early New York,' *De Halve Maen* 76 (Winter 2003): 73-78.

42 See note 39.

43 See note 40.

44 *American Weekly Mercury*, No. 1131 (27 August-3 September 1741), 32.

45 *New York Gazette & Weekly Post Boy*, No. 726 (13 December 1756), 33.

46 *New York Gazette*, No. 10 (23 April 1759), 23.

47 *New York Mercury*, No. 419 (25 August 1760), 42.

48 *New York Gazette & Weekly Post Boy*, No. 966 (9 July 1761), 42.

49 *New York Mercury*, No. 484 (9 November 1761), 32.

50 *New York Mercury*, No. 803 (23 March 1767), 42.

51 New York Public Library, Performing Arts Center, shelf mark, Drexel 1936. The Houghton Library, Harvard University, Boston, has another copy that was once owned by the artist Vincent van Gogh, attested by his bookplate.

52 See Adriaen Valerius, *Neder-landtsche gedenck-clanck: Herdrukt naar de Oorsprunkelijke Uitgaaf van 1626*, ed. P. J. Meertens, N. B. Tenhaeff and A. Komter-Kuipers (Amsterdam: Stichting 'Onze Oude Letteren,' 1942), 4.

53 The literature on Wilhelmus is extensive; see for example, Jacobus Bernardus Drewes, *Wilhelmus van Nassouwe: Een proeve van synchronische interpretatie* (Amsterdam: Elsevier, 1946), 262-277, which is an annotated bibliography of literature published between 1891 and 1946; many more studies have been published subsequently.

54 *Pennsylvania Packet* [no number] (1 January 1780), 41, 42.

55 See Ruth van Baak Griffioen, *Jacob van Eyck's Der Fluyten Lust Hof (1644-c 1655)* (Utrecht: Vereniging voor Nederlandse Muziekgeschiedenis, 1991), 47; and Kees Otten in the facsimile of *Der Fluyten Lust Hof* (Amsterdam: Groen, [ca. 1970]), no pagination.

56 See van Baak Griffioen, *Jacob van Eyck's Der Fluyten Lust Hof*, 70-76, and 413-416 (Appendix D).

57 See van Baak Griffioen, *Jacob van Eyck's Der Fluyten Lust Hof*, 210-212, 239-242, 275-295.

58 See Rudolf Alexander Rasch, *De cantiones natalitiae en het kerkelijke muziekleven in de Zuidelijke Nederlanden gedurende de zeventiende eeuw* (s.l.: s.n. [Proefschrift Rijksuniversiteit Utrecht], 1985), 419-410; cited van Baak Griffioen, *Jacob van Eyck's Der Fluyten Lust Hof*, 168.

59 See Joyce D. Goodfriend, 'The Dutch in 17th-century New York City: Minority or Majority?' in Randolph Vigne and Charles Littleton, eds., *From Strangers to Citizens: The Integration of Immigrant Communities in Britain, Ireland and Colonial America, 1550-1750* (Brighton: Sussex Academic Press, 2001), 306-312.

60 Hugh Hastings, et al, ed., *Ecclesiastical Records, State of New York* (Albany: Lyon, 1901-1916), 3038.

61 Laidlie was contracted in the following terms: 'Your service in English is limited to the New Church'; *Ecclesiastical Records, State of New York*, 3872.

62 One who heard the sermon was an elderly lady who told Laidlie after the service: 'Oh Domi-

nee! We have prayed for you in Dutch, and the Lord sent you to us in English!' Jonathan Greenleaf, *A History of the Churches, of all Denominations, in the City of New York, from the First Settlement to the year 1846* (New York: Portland, French, *et al*, 1846), 16.

63 See Virginia L. Redway, 'James Parker and the 'Dutch Church,'' *Musical Quarterly* 24: 491.

64 Cited in Daniel Meeter, 'Genevan Jigsaw: the Tunes of the New-York Psalmbook of 1767,' in Frans Brouwer and Robin A. Leaver, eds., *Ars et musica in liturgia: Essays Preented to Casper Honders on His Seventieth Birthday* (Metuchen: Scarecrow, 1994), 151.

65 For the background, see Meeter, 'Genevan Jigsaw,' 151-153.

66 *New York Journal*, No. 1269 Supplement (30 April 1767), 22.

67 The music type was purchased from Daniel Crommelin of Amsterdam for 557 guilders, 12 stivers; see *Ecclesiastical Records, State of New York*, 4031.The Psalms were authorized for use from 1 January 1768. In March that year newspapers carried advertisements announcing where copies of the new psalter could be purchased; see *New York Journal*, No. 1315 (17 March 1768), 32; *New York Gazette & Weekly Post Boy*, No. 1316 (21 March 1768), 32.

68 This is acknowledged in the Preface: 'The Consistory of the Reformed Protestant Dutch Church in the City of New-York, having, by Reason of the Declension of the Dutch Language, found it necessary to have Divine Service performed in their Church in English; Have adopted the following version of the Psalms of David, which is greatly indebted to that of Dr. Brady and Mr. Tate; Some of the Psalms being transcribed verbatim from their version, and others altered...'; cited Meeter, 'Genevan Jigsaw,'158.

69 See Meeter, 'Genevan Jigsaw,' 157-163. The statement of the Consistory, that the Tate and Brady Psalms were 'transcribed... or altered, so as to fit them to the Music used in the Dutch Churches' (Meeter, *op. cit.*, 158), was only partially correct.

70 See Carleton Sprague Smith, 'The 1774 Psalm Book of the Reformed Protestant Dutch Church in New York City,' *Musical Quarterly* 34 (1948): 84-96.

71 See facsimile in Smith, 'The 1774 Psalm Book,' opp. p. 90.

72 This last point, that the four voices re all notated in the C clef, rather than in four different clefs, meant that it was easy to use.

73 Cited in Smith, 'The 1774 Psalm Book,' 86.

74 Speer Library, Princeton Theological Seminary, Princeton, NJ, call number SCB # 4403.

75 Gardner A. Sage Library, New Brunswick Theological Seminary, New Brunswick, NJ, call number BE6 Dut N55k.

76 See Charles H. Kaufman, *Music in New Jersey 1655-1860: A Study of Musical Activity and Musicians in New Jersey from Its First Settlement to the Civil War* (Rutherford: Fairliegh Dickenson University Press, 1981), 56. Kaufman also gives other examples, ibid., 56-57.

AN

ORATION

ON THE

UTILITY

OF

LITERARY ESTABLISHMENTS,

DELIVERED

(At the request of the Proprietors)

AT THE OPENING OF THE LITERARY ROOMS
IN NEW-YORK,

On the eleventh of February, 1814

BY JOHN BRISTED, ESQ

NEW-YORK:

PUBLISHED BY EASTBURN, KIRK & CO.
AT THE LITERARY ROOMS, CORNER OF WALL AND
NASSAU-STREETS.

1814

Coll. New York Public Library.

Marika Keblusek

NEW YORK, AMSTERDAM, LEIDEN: TRADING BOOKS IN THE OLD AND NEW WORLDS

Recently, the history of the book in America has received a good deal of scholarly attention. In 2000, the impressive first volume of the series *A History of the Book in America* was published, focusing entirely on the colonial period.[1] This early period of the printed book should, as one critic puts it, not be considered as 'simply the history of American books,' but rather as a history of printed matter imported from the Old World.[2]

In the colonial period, the majority of 'American' books originated from England, in particular London. Between 1701 and 1780, at least 23 percent of the English exports to America was intended for New England, followed by Virginia and Maryland (19 percent), New York (12 percent), Pennsylvania (9 percent) and the Carolinas (8.5 percent).[3] While other European cities exported books as well, this happened on a far less grand scale.[4] The British Navigation Acts of 1651, 1660 and 1696 limited the carrying and importation of foreign products (including books) to English and colonial ships, closing off the market for other European traders, or at least attempting to do so. This did not mean, of course, that books published outside England, for example in Holland, did not reach America at all. Indeed, in the period 1701-1780, especially in the first half of the century, over 60 percent of all unbound books (*i.e.* recent publications) imported into England came from Holland, and it is quite likely that at least some of these were subsequently exported to America.

Although the Dutch language press in America has been well documented by Hendrik Edelman, the nature and extent of book importation from the Netherlands has not been studied systematically.[5] For a large part, this is due to the lack of archival material. Booksellers' accounts and ledger books from the early modern period have not been preserved, frustrating an overview of the national, European and transatlantic trade until well into the nineteenth century. Whereas British custom records survive, enabling statistical analysis of the amount of books imported and exported, similar Dutch documents do not exist. Thus, it is only from incidental evidence that the early modern import of Dutch books into the New York area can be glimpsed.

Dutch Books in New York
This evidence seems to suggest books were distributed along private rather than commercial channels. Administrators and lawyers arrived in New Amsterdam, carrying their tools of trade: a copy of Damhouder's classic text on criminal law, Grotius's introduction

to Dutch law, or large folio editions of local and national Dutch ordinances and proclama-tions.[6] Relatives and friends enclosed newspapers and small pamphlets in their frequent letters to acquaintances in the colonies. In 1659, both his brother and a friend supplied Jere-mias van Rensselaer with Dutch newspapers; similarly, English colonists received written and printed newsletters from friends at home.[7] Early inventories of Dutch settlers listed religious texts, such as catechisms, psalm books and, above all, Bibles, while histories, dictionaries and romances were also found.[8] It must be assumed that these books had been among the possessions the immigrants had originally brought over, or were ordered and shipped privately. A survey of some 35 Dutch books in the Senate House Museum in King-ston, New York, clearly demonstrates the significance of religious reading in the settlers' community. Apart from two historical titles, an agricultural treatise and a Greek grammar, these are all theological texts, dating from the seventeenth and mostly eighteenth centu-ries, ranging from catechisms and Bibles, to sermons and devotional treatises.[9]

Devotional reading was an important means to confirm the immigrants' religious identity and to keep isolated communities together. In 1632, Kiliaen van Rensselaer provided the lay minister of Rensselaerswyck with a sermon book so services could be read, and in 1638 he sent eight copies of a practical catechism to be distributed amongst Dutch colonists.[10] In 1698, a Germantown minister wrote to Hermanus Schyn, his Mennonite colleague in Amsterdam, for 'catechisms and small Testaments for the young people,' and some Bibles for the elders. The Dutch Reformed Church in New York asked the Amsterdam classis to send over shipments of German Bibles for churches in Pennsylvania, while in 1745, a German clergyman ordered several hundred Amsterdam Bibles.[11] Practical texts – such as catechisms, almanacs, newspapers and school books – were imported at first, often with the intent of distributing them within the colony. In 1665, over three hundred school books and devotional texts were found in the library of Gijsbert van Imborch, who, in 1652, had ordered them from Holland to sell amongst his fellow-settlers. However, his business gener-ated so little interest that, in 1655, Van Imborch applied for permission to sell the books in a lottery; judging from the 1665 estate inventory, this plan did not work either.[12]

Rather than a systematic, commercial enterprise, then, book traffic between Amsterdam and the American colonies was marked by its incidental, private nature.[13] Even the ship-ments of Dutch books (mostly theological works) in the eighteenth century, which were advertised in New York newspapers, were imported by *general* traders, not by booksel-lers.[14] The merchant-bookseller Jacob Goelet – son of a Dutch settler in New York – con-tracted an (anonymous) Amsterdam printer for the 1725 issue of Gualterus Du Bois' *Kort Begryp der Waare Christelycke Leere*, a catechism which had originally been published (in 1706, and again in 1712) by William Bradford in New York. Although Goelet's motivation for commissioning a printer in Amsterdam, rather than in New York, remains unclear, the 1725-edition shows that there were some business contacts between New York and Amsterdam publishers.[15] Similarly, Joseph Bruyning Jr. may well have stocked his Boston shop with books from Amsterdam, where he had been trained as a bookseller, and where his mother was still active as a publisher.[16] Also, private customers may have ordered specific titles directly from Dutch booksellers, but even then, English intermediaries were often involved. The Puritan minister Increase Mather, for example, wrote to Utrecht for fifty Hebrew Bibles in 1689; the books were shipped to Harvard via the London bookseller Samuel Smith.[17]

Sometimes Dutch imprints were included in German imports. The 1702 estate inventory of bookseller Abraham dela Noy listed several imported German books in Dutch translation, and Dutch and German Bibles.[18] And in 1772, John Henry (Heinrich) Miller offered his Philadelphian customers three German translations of works by the mystic writer Jane Leade, which had been published in Amsterdam almost a century earlier.[19] Whereas booksellers and publishers catered to a growing German reading public with sale catalogues of imported books from Frankfurt or Hamburg, no such lists of Dutch books exist.[20] Admittedly, in 1747, a New York bookseller advertised 'a choice parcel of French and Dutch books,' and, half a century later, a Wall Street auctioneer promised a 'curious collection of Dutch and Latin books;' yet these are rare incidents, and the books may well have been part of private collections.[21]

Even after the Declaration of Independence, when, in 1784, British custom officials noted that Philadelphia and New York 'carried on an almost open foreign trade with Holland, Hamburgh, France, etc.,' the Dutch share in book imports remained marginal.[22] Although transatlantic export must at least have been easier than in the period of England's commercial dominance, it is unlikely that contemporary Dutch publications raised much interest in America, apart, perhaps, from theological works in Dutch which found their way to immigrants in Michigan and other Midwestern states. However, with American libraries and private collectors becoming increasingly interested in rare and valuable editions, it was in the developing antiquarian trade of the early nineteenth century that a number of Dutch booksellers found transatlantic business opportunities.

The Luchtmans-Eastburn Connection

In November 1816, the New York bookseller James Eastburn sent the Leiden booksellers Samuel and Johannes Luchtmans a commission, *i.e.* an order for books.[23] Luchtmans, an internationally renowned, scholarly publishing and bookselling firm, had survived the dramatic downfall of Dutch international book commerce after the 1750s. Indeed, around 1800, Samuel and Johannes Luchtmans were about the only booksellers still trading with colleagues in France, Switzerland and England. Their prominent role as antiquarian booksellers is evident from the specialized catalogues they put out, devoted to rare books.

Eager for business contacts in Holland, James Eastburn wrote to Luchtmans at the suggestion of a fellow New Yorker, John Brodhead Romeyn, an author whose collection of sermons Eastburn had published in 1816, and whose son would be among the first to publish documents relative to the Dutch colonial history of the state of New York.[24] An astute businessman, he had also sent similar letters to other Dutch booksellers, waiting to see who would offer the best and least expensive services. In his first letter, he laid out his conditions for business, urging Luchtmans to send the *exact* editions he had specified. All books should be in perfect condition and be bound, and would have to be well wrapped up for the journey. Eastburn's agent in Amsterdam, the trader Johannes Peter Wendorp, would take care of all financial transactions and would supervise the shipping. Indeed, the logistics of this transatlantic book commerce can be glimpsed from Wendorp's letters to Luchtmans, detailing the costs of packing, handling, shipping and insurance; the choice of ships and time of journey; the complicated exchange system and the inevitable financial complications; the books that were lost, or damaged or sent back.

In his first commission, Eastburn listed 161 different titles of which 113 titles – in multiple copies and multiple volumes – were eventually shipped. In February 1817, three boxes, containing a total of nearly 300 volumes, left Amsterdam, and the impressive sum of 1777 guilders and two stivers was entered in the Luchtmans account books under the name of 'James Eastburn & Co, Booksellers in New York'.[25] Five months later, Eastburn acknowledged the receipt of the boxes. Overall, he was quite content with the quality of the books, although some, he felt, had been too expensive. As for the fifty or so titles Luchtmans had been unable to find, Eastburn suggested that in future a 'catalogue' of missing books would be send to Wendorp, who could then search Amsterdam bookshops. Again, Eastburn stipulated that all books should be bound, preferably in vellum, 'since that pleases the eye best'.[26] Between 1817 and 1822, a total of 28 trunks, filled with 1236 different titles in almost 2000 multi-volume copies, left Amsterdam *en route* to New York. In five years time, Eastburn spent the capital sum of 12,000 guilders.[27]

According to contemporary witnesses, James Eastburn was 'a man of superior intelligence and high character,' 'one of the best known booksellers of the city,' and a 'learned bibliophile.'[28] Born in Leeds in 1756, he had emigrated to New York with his wife Charlotte and his children in 1802. At first, he had worked as a wool merchant, but in June 1812 he established himself in the book trade after taking over the shop and commercial library of Ezra Sergeant on 86 Broadway. In February 1813, he formed a bookselling and publishing company with Thomas Kirk from Brooklyn, which was liquidated in October 1816. He continued under the firm's new name 'James Eastburn & Co,' enjoying two very successful years, until he filed for bankruptcy in September 1819. However, he remained in the book business from 1820 to 1823 – still ordering from Holland, and occasionally putting out new publications – , returning, in 1824, to his former mercantile life, and working, until his death in October 1829, as a broker between England and New York.[29]

Eastburn's first commission at Luchtmans in November 1816 must have been directly related to the liquidation of his partnership with Kirk, for in October the complete inventory of their so-called 'Literary Rooms' had been sold off at auction.[30] Exactly three years before, in October 1813, Eastburn and Kirk had founded the Literary Rooms at the corner of Wall and Nassau Streets, a successor to Ezra Sergeant's library of the same name, which Eastburn had first helped to establish and had then taken over. The first of its kind in America, Sergeant's subscription library had been 'in great spirit, until the increasing difficulty of [importing] ... publications from Europe,' which were caused by the Napoleonic Wars.[31] Detailed plans for reviving the library were published in a small pamphlet, aimed at potential benefactors. Eastburn and Kirk intended their Literary Rooms 'to form a body of *reference*, for the Statesman, the Scholar, and the man of Science; to be as an *Encyclopedia* and *Index* to general knowledge, and to exhibit, in an abridged form, the history of the progress of the *mind*, at the various periods of its depression and elevation, among different nations.' The rooms would be stocked with a selection of the latest magazines, reviews and newspapers from Britain and France, while maps and atlases would enable 'constant reference.' A collection of historical and current pamphlets on any subject would be indispensable 'in a great city where conflicting opinions are for ever raising our curiosity.' Subscribers could consult grammars, dictionaries and bibliographical reference works, the proceedings of learned societies in England, France and Germany; as well public documents relating to national policy and finance. Apparently, response to the plans was favorable, for on 11 February, 1814, the clergyman John Bristed delivered a triumphant opening speech: 'This day, this hour, these *Literary Rooms*, all conspire to testify, that the wealth and mind of New-York, of the first city in the first state of our mighty union, have laid the foundations of this institution, for the improvement of public talent, for the embellishment of social existence.'[32] With the liquidation of Eastburn, Kirk & Co., and the auction of the library's inventory in October 1816, James Eastburn needed new material to restock the Literary Rooms, which he reopened, in 1817, in his new premises on the corner of Broadway and Pine Street.[33] Quite possibly, his purchases at Luchtmans were bought in order to refurnish the library's bookshelves. Also, Eastburn may have intended to reprint some of the titles, for, in the same year, he issued a prospectus for printing, by subscription, 'limited editions of scarce books, in the various branches of literature, from the sixteenth century down to the present time.'[34]

Right from the beginning of his career as a publisher, in 1812, James Eastburn had consistently focused on *modern* English texts: reprints from London imprints, mainly literary and historical works; collections of sermons and theological treatises by contemporary American clergymen; travel accounts; devotional poetry by contemporary authors; and topical publications, such as funeral speeches – in all, some 200 titles in ten years time. The books he commissioned from Luchtmans between 1816 and 1822 were of a different species altogether. In Holland, Eastburn mostly shopped for *antiquarian* texts, listing theological, historical and classical texts in Latin, Greek or Hebrew, published on the Continent in the sixteenth, seventeenth and early eighteenth centuries, for which he was willing to pay a substantial price. In 1817, for example, he paid 110 guilders for a 1498 edition of Aristophanes, and 238 guilders for a five-volume set of Aristotle, published in 1495-1498.[35] Eastburn's focus on antiquarian books explains why he ordered only a single copy of most titles; occasionally two or three copies.

One book that, according to Eastburn's commissions, seems to have been in great demand in New York, was, however, a recent publication – Johann Friedrich Schleusner's *Novum Lexicon Graeco-Latinum in Novum Testamentum* (Leipzig 1792). Ordering fifty copies in June 1817, and again, in December 1817, pressing Luchtmans for more, Eastburn explained he needed them urgently, 'as we have to supply a theological College with them.' He referred to the General Theological Seminary in New York, which had recently been founded and would open its doors to students in the Spring of 1818. One of Eastburn's sons, Edward, would become a student at the Seminary in the 1820s.[36] In fact, Eastburn's shop – and indirectly the Dutch firm of Luchtmans – must have been instrumental in supplying the college, and later its library, with books. In 1820, John Pintard, a highly prominent figure in the mercantile, cultural and intellectual circles of New York, founded the Seminary's library, and, to mark the occasion, presented it with a 55 volume set, in folio, of the Church Fathers, 'the only set .... now for sale in America,' which had been bought for $330 by several New York gentlemen 'by subscription of $25 each ... the whole sum was subscribed and paid by me into the hands of Mr. Eastburn bookseller, who himself gave $50.'[37] Eastburn also added the first edition of Luther's writings, which he had bought from Luchtmans in 1817.[38]

From Pintard's correspondence, meanwhile, it is clear that Eastburn not only played a crucial role in his personal life – Pintard called him 'my esteemed friend', 'my endowed intellectual friend' and was distraught when Eastburn died – but that the publisher was also actively involved in New York's many 'useful and benevolent societies'; in the Sunday

School movement, the Erie Canal enterprise, the First Savings Bank, the American Bible Society and possibly the New-York Historical Society, which had been founded by Pintard, in 1804. In October 1829, after Eastburn had died of consumption, Pintard contemplated his friend's many qualities, praising him, among many other things, as 'a Bookseller on a more extensive scale than had ever been attempted in this city ... His importation of the most valuable & rare works ... from the continent of Europe ... has enriched the public libraries of our country.'[39] A good number of these 'rare works' can now be traced back to the Netherlands. More importantly, Eastburn's business with the Luchtmans firm can be seen as an early example of the increasing commerce between Dutch antiquarian booksellers and American librarians and collectors; an example of the intellectual, bibliographical and commercial traffic that began in the nineteenth century, and continues to this day.

Notes

1 Hugh Amory and David D. Hall, eds., *The Colonial Book in the Atlantic World*. A History of the Book in America, vol. 1([Worcester, MA]: American Antiquarian Society/Cambridge: Cambridge University Press, 2000).
2 James Raven, 'The Export of Books to Colonial North America,' *Publishing History* 42 (1997): 30.
3 Giles Barber, 'Books from the Old World and for the New: The British International Trade in Books in the Eighteenth Century,' *Studies on Voltaire and the Eighteenth Century* 151 (1976): 219-224. Idem, 'Book Imports and Exports in the Eighteenth Century,' in Robin Myers and Michael Harris, *Sale and Distribution of Books from 1700* (Oxford: Oxford Polytechnic Press, 1982), 94. Raven, 'Export,' 30-38. See also Idem, *London Booksellers and American Customers: Transatlantic Literary Community and the Charleston Library Society, 1748-1811* (Columbia: University of South Carolina Press, 2002).
4 Raven, 'Export,' 21. On German export: Robert E. Cazden, 'The Provision of German Books in America during the Eighteenth Century,' *Libri* 23 (1973): 81-108. On books imported from Scotland: Warren McDougall, 'Scottish Books for America in the Mid 18th Century,' in Robin Meyers and Michael Harris, eds., *Spreading the Word: The Distribution Networks of Print 1550-1850* (Winchester: St Paul's Bibliographies, 1990), 21-46.
5 Hendrik Edelman, *The Dutch Language Press in America: Two Centuries of Printing, Publishing and Bookselling* (Nieuwkoop: De Graaf, 1986). Idem, *Dutch-American Bibliography, 1693-1794: A Descriptive Catalog of Dutch-Language Books, Pamphlets and Almanacs printed in America* (Nieuwkoop: De Graaf, 1974).
6 Jaap Jacobs, *Een zegenrijk gewest. Nieuw-Nederland in de zeventiende eeuw* (Amsterdam: Prometheus/Bert Bakker, 1999), 353.
7 Ibid., 532. A.J.F. van Laer, ed., *Correspondence of Jeremias van Rensselaer 1651-1674* (Albany: University of the State of New York, 1932), 149, 274, 347; David Cressy, *Coming Over: Migration and Communication between England and New England in the Seventeenth Century* (Cambridge: Cambridge University Press, 1987), 235-262.
8 Jacobs, *Zegenrijk gewest*, 350-352. A. Gregg Roeber, 'German and Dutch Books and Printing,' in Amory and Hall, *Colonial Book*, 301. Willem Frijhoff, *Wegen van Evert Willemsz. Een Hollands weeskind op zoek naar zichzelf, 1607-1647* (Nijmegen: SUN, 1995), 596-597.
9 I thank Jaap Jacobs for showing me this list.
10 Jacobs, *Zegenrijk gewest*, 353. A.J.F. van Laer, ed., *Van Rensselaer Bowier Manuscripts, being the Letters of Kiliaen van Rensselaer, 1630-1643, and Other Documents Relating to the Colony of Rensselaerswyck* (Albany: University of the State of New York, 1908), 418.

11 Cazden, 'Provision,' 82-83. The estate inventory of the Dutch immigrant Reynier Jansen, Philadelphia's second printer, contained a parcel of Dutch books, a large folio Bible and a small one with silver clasps: J.G. Riewald, *Reynier Jansen of Philadelphia, Early American Printer: A Chapter in Seventeenth-Century Nonconformity* (Groningen: Wolters Noordhoff, 1970), 198-200. See also Edwin Wolf II, *The Book Culture of a Colonial American City: Philadelphia Books, Bookmen, and Booksellers* (Oxford: Clarendon Press, 1988), 22.

12 A. Eekhof, *De Hervormde Kerk in Noord-Amerika (1624-1664)*. 2 vols. (The Hague: Nijhoff, 1913) 2: 163-164;.Frijhoff, *Wegen*, 596.

13 A 1654 invoice for goods to be shipped to America by Amsterdam merchants, 'to be sold to our best advantage,' lists six titles: Van Laer, *Correspondence*, 13. Jacobs, *Zegenrijk gewest*, 352.

14 See the essay in this volume by Robin A. Leaver. Edelman, *Dutch-Language Press*, 20.

15 Kenneth Scott, 'Jacob Goelet: Translator of Dutch for the Province of New York,' *De Halve Maen* 55-4 (Winter 1981): 1-6, 20-21. Scott wrongly attributes the 1706-edition to the press of Bradford and Goelet's father (5). Copies of the 1725 Amsterdam edition are kept in the New York Public Library.

16 P.G. Hoftijzer, *Engelse Boekverkopers bij de Beurs. De geschiedenis van de Amsterdamse boekhandels Bruyning en Swart, 1637-1724* (Amsterdam / Maarssen, APA-Holland University Press, 1987), 27.

17 P.G. Hoftijzer, 'The Utrecht Hebraist Johannes van Leusden and his Relations with the English Booktrade,' in *Miscellanea Anglo-Belgica. Papers of the Annual Symposium, held on 21 November 1986* (Leiden: Sir Thomas Browne Institute, 1987), 23. See also Hugh Amory, 'Reinventing the Colonial Book,' in Idem and Hall, *Colonial Book*, 31: 'we may assume that [Bruyning] dealt in Continental books, but the market cannot have been large. Latin literature was surely its most important sector, and by the eighteenth century European sales were mediated through London.'

18 Gregg Roeber, 'German and Dutch Books,' 301.

19 Cazden, 'Provision,' 96.

20 In 1773, for example, the Philadelphia bookseller Andreas Geyer advertised sixty titles that had been 'brought over by the latest ships from Germany,' while Francis Hasencleve boasted 225 newly imported German books. Robert B. Winans, *A Descriptive Checklist of Book Catalogues Separately Printed in America, 1693-1800* (Worcester: American Antiquarian Society, 1981), nos. 89 and 86. See also Cazden, 'Provision,' 88-89.

21 George L. McKay, comp., and Clarence S. Brigham, intr., *American Book Auction Catalogues 1713-1934. A Union List* (New York: New York Public Library, reprint Detroit: Gale Research Company, 1967), nos 46A and 132E. Compare two Philadelphia catalogues listing Dutch books in Winans, *Checklist*, no. 103 (1784; French books: 1600; Latin 475; English 175; German 42 and Dutch 68 titles) and no. 205 (1795: thirty pages of 'Hollandsche bockken' – *i.e.* German and Dutch books).

22 Quoted in Raven, 'Export,' 25. Compare James Raven, 'The Importation of Books in the Eighteenth Century,' in Amory and Hall, *Colonial Book*, 185: 'Imports from non-British sources are measurable with even less precision, but their overall contribution by about 1770 must have been extremely small.'

23 His letters and accounts are kept in the Luchtmans business archives, Bibliotheek van de Koninklijke Vereniging van het Boekenvak (KVB), deposited in the Amsterdam University Library.

24 Eastburn to Luchtmans, 29 November 1816, BLu 10-43, Luchtmans Archives, KVB. John Brodhead Romeyn, *Sermons* (New York: Eastburn, Kirk & Co., 1816), see Ralph R. Shaw and Richard H. Shoemaker, comp., *American Bibliography. A Preliminary Checklist for 1801-1819* (New York: The Scarecrow Press, 1958-1983), no. 38832.

25 Eastburn book order, 29 November 1816, BLu 12-21, Luchtmans Archives, KVB; Eastburn

Account, Grootboek Boekverkopers 1814-1818, ff. 300v-301v, Luchtmans Archives, KVB. Mysteriously, this first commission was sent in three boxes labelled nos 3-5.

26 Eastburn to Luchtmans, 20 June 1817, BLu 10-44, Luchtmans Archives, KVB. On the necessity of importing bound books for financial reasons, see McDougall, 'Scottish Books,' 37-38.

27 Eastburn Account, Grootboek Boekverkopers 1814-1818 and Idem 1818-1822, Luchtmans Archives, KVB.

28 Frederick de Peyster, Biographical Sketch of James Wallis Eastburn and Manton Eastburn, Members of the 'Literary Confederacy' of Columbia College, c. 1870, New-York Historical Society (NYHS). I thank Joseph Ditta, Reference Librarian of the NYHS, for providing me with this, and other, information. Biographical dates for James Eastburn and his family on the Internet: familysearch.org (January 2003). Nelson Frederick Adkins, Fitz-Green Halleck: An Early Knickerbocker Wit and Poet (New Haven: Yale University Press, 1932), 132, quoting John Francis, Old New York (1865).

29 George L. McKay, comp., A Register of Artists, Engravers, Booksellers, Bookbinders, Printers & Publishers in New York City, 1633-1820 (New York: New York Public Library, 1942), 26; Sidney F. & Elizabeth Stege Huttner, comp., A Register of Artists, Engravers, Booksellers, Bookbinders, Printers & Publishers in New York City, 1821-42 (New York: The Bibliographical Society of America, 1993), 80. I thank Jennifer L. Moore, Library Assistant of the American Antiquarian Society, for providing me with the Society's biographical information on Eastburn.

30 Catalogue of a Rare Collection of Periodical Works, Pamphlets, Portraits, Engravings, Maps, And Other Valuable and Curious Books: Belonging to the Literary Rooms of Eastburn, Kirk & Co.: To be Sold at Auction, by Franklin & Minturn, On Tuesday, the 8th Day of October (New York: [Eastburn, Kirk & Co.], 1816).

31 Plan of the Literary Rooms, Instituted by Eastburn, Kirk & Co. (New York: Eastburn, Kirk & Co., 1813), 3. I thank Elizabeth Wyckoff of the New York Public Library (NYPL) for providing me with a copy of this pamphlet, and of the following items.

32 John Bristed, An Oration on the Utility of Literary Estabishment, Delivered (At the request of the Proprietors) at the Opening of the Literary Rooms in New-York, On the eleventh of February, 1814 (New York: Eastburn, Kirk & Co., 1814). Printed announcement in the NYHS: New-York, February 7, 1814: Sir, We have the pleasure to inform you that the new literary rooms at the corner of Wall and Nassau-streets are at length completed (New York: [Eastburn, Kirk & Co., 1814]).

33 Plan of the Literary Rooms, instituted by James Eastburn & Co at the Corner of Broadway and Pine-Street, New-York (2nd corr. enl. ed., New-York: Abraham Paul, 1817). Copy in NYHS. Shaw and Shoemaker, Bibliography, no. 40715.

34 Shaw and Shoemaker, Bibliography, no. 40716.

35 Luchtmans Archives, KVB; Eastburn Account, Grootboek Boekverkopers 1814-1818, fol. 325v.

36 Powel Mills Dawley, The Story of the General Theological Seminary: A Sesquicentennial History, 1817-1967 (New York: Oxford University Press, 1969), 39-48. The online catalogue of the Seminary library does not list a copy of this title.

37 D.C. Barck, ed., Letters from John Pintard to his Daughter Eliza Noel Pintard Davidson 1816-1833 (New York: New York Historical Society, 1940), I, 326-327 (letter of 17 September 1820). See also Dawley, Story, 65 (letter of Samuel Turner to Jackson Kemper, 18 September 1820).

38 Luchtmans Archives, KVB; Eastburn Account, Grootboek Boekverkopers 1814-1818, fol. 301v. Eastburn paid 18 guilders for this 1564 edition (4 vols, fol).

39 Barck, Letters Pintard, 3:103-104 (27 October 1829).

Henry W. Lawrence

URBAN GREEN SPACES IN NEW YORK AND AMSTERDAM

The direct influence of the Netherlands on the New Netherlands in North America was brief, less than a generation in human lifetimes. Yet one of its lasting impacts may be seen in the shape of cities all across North America in the way trees are planted in the public landscape. The Dutch practice of planting trees along canals and streets, itself relatively recent in the seventeenth century, was brought to the New World. The planting of trees on the streets of Nieuw Amsterdam/New York City was later adopted by people in other American cities beginning in the second half of the eighteenth century and has become one of the most characteristic features of American urban landscapes. In the second half of the nineteenth century the urban green spaces of Amsterdam and New York City became more similar again, though as a result of stimulation from common foreign sources, British and French. This convergence is seen in the shape and location of large city parks in the second half of the nineteenth century, most notably New York's Central Park and Amsterdam's Vondelpark. These and other large public parks became very different landscape features in the rapidly growing commercial-industrial cities that Amsterdam and New York were becoming at the time.

Until the nineteenth century the nations of the western cultural realm had different ways of incorporating trees in the urban landscape.[1] In France linear allées were common in recreational spaces and promenades as well as in private gardens. The Tuileries gardens, the Cours la Reine, the Avenue des Champs Elysées and the Grands Boulevards on the periphery of Paris are prominent examples. By the late eighteenth century a few French cities also had trees in public squares, as at Nancy and Rochefort.[2] In Britain, linear promenades, called walks, were generally much smaller and more isolated. More important were private green residential squares such as Grosvenor Square, and large parks on the urban periphery, such as St. James's Park and Hyde Park at London.[3]

Urban Green Spaces in the Netherlands
In the Netherlands the most distinctive forms of urban green spaces were trees planted atop a city's walls or along its outer canals, and trees planted inside the city along its canals, and in some cases along a street. Amsterdam is the outstanding example, although the Hague provided an alternate model of green town with its many parks and promenades. In Amsterdam, trees were planted on some internal canals beginning at the end of

the sixteenth century and then more extensively with the expansions of the 'three canals' in the seventeenth century. The first such expansion, between 1610 and 1614 resulted in a new residential quarter for the well-to-do along the new Herengracht, Keizersgracht and Prinsengracht. Trees were planted one per building width, along the canal side, and protected by civic ordinances.

1. View of the Latin School in Amsterdam, from Casparus Commelin's *Beschryvinge van Amsterdam*, 1693-94, showing trees along the side of the canal. (Collection of the author)

In some towns, like Haarlem, Leiden, Amersfoort and Beverwijk, a canal or two were filled in and trees were planted along the new street that resulted. Open spaces were extremely limited in most Dutch towns at this time, around churches and in market places. Some of these were planted with trees, but not all. Often the tree-lined streets were used as marketplaces, but some seem simply to have been intended as shady promenades in the city.[4]

Evidence for planting trees along the canals comes primarily from graphic materials, in particular the plans of Amsterdam by Pieter Bast (1597, 1617) and Balthazar Florisz. Van Berckenrode (1625) and a variety of drawings, etchings and paintings throughout the seventeenth century.[5] Textual material is scarce. Much more was written about the plan of the city expansions and the buildings than about the trees. Contemporary travel accounts by foreigners in the Netherlands in the seventeenth century show the novelty and uniqueness of this way of planting trees within a city. A common comment was that one did not know if one was seeing a city in a forest or a forest in a city. John Evelyn, visiting Amsterdam in 1641, noted in his diary:[6]

The streetes so exactly straite, even, & uniforme that nothing can be more pleasing, especialy, being so frequently planted and shaded with the beautifull lime trees, which are set in rowes before every mans house, affording a very ravishing prospect.... Nothing more surpriz'd me than that stately, and indeede incomparable quarter of the Towne, calld the Keisers-Graft, or Emperors Streete, which appears to be a Citty in a Wood, through the goodly ranges of the stately and umbrageous Lime-trees, exactly planted before each-mans doore.

Large gardens accessible to the public, as found at Paris or London, were rare. With the exception of the Hague, Utrecht and Breda there were few towns with aristocratic gardens open to the upper classes for promenades. In Amsterdam, the Plantage was laid out in 1682 during a further expansion that continued the three canals of the 1610s around the eastern side of the city. The Plantage was an area where many small private gardens were leased out to citizens, organized around a series of long tree-lined allées that were used as public promenades.[7]

More commonly, people took their recreation along the city's walls or on paths leading out of town into the surrounding countryside. Some cities, like Rotterdam and Arnhem planted trees on the wall for promenades. In other cities, like Amsterdam, the walls were unplanted, but still popular places for walking, to take in the views of the countryside and breathe the clean air.[8]

In colonial towns Dutch East India Company around the world trees were commonly planted, either along canals as at Batavia or along streets as at Colombo and Cape Town. The early VOC towns were not replicas of Dutch towns, but they incorporated many features of the urban landscape of the Netherlands and planting trees along canals and streets was one of them.[9]

Urban Green Spaces in North America
In British colonial towns in North America the green spaces were much fewer than in towns in Britain. In Boston and Philadelphia, for example, there were no residential squares or royal gardens that could serve as parks, though Boston had its green municipal Common and Philadelphia was planned with five squares that would become important public spaces in the nineteenth century. No British colonial towns had trees along the street until very late.[10]

It is probable that trees were planted in Nieuw Amsterdam also, but has not yet not been documented. There are no records of trees along the two short canals in New Amsterdam, the Herengracht and the Bevergracht. There are no records of tree-lined streets or even of ordinances relating to trees.[11] The best visual document of the city is in the anonymous 'Castello' redraft of about 1670 of the plan of the town by Jacques Cortelyou, originally prepared in 1660. It shows individual buildings and private gardens behind most houses, but it shows no trees along streets or canals. The only trees in the public landscape are a group of four or five trees along the East River in front of the *stadhuis*. The 'Labadist' view of the city from the water in 1679 shows only one tree in the waterfront location.[12] The plan of 1660 seems excessively neat and clean, however, and it may be that trees along streets or canals were left out by the cartographers. Even some maps and views of Dutch towns in the seventeenth century omitted existing trees in order to show the buildings and streets more clearly.[13]

The best evidence for the Dutch type of tree planting in the city comes only after the British took control in the 1660s. Common Council minutes beginning in 1691 refer to a group of trees at the old Slip market, along the Burgers' Path, one block east of the old *stadhuis*, in the area of present day Hanover Square. These may have been native trees spared by the first settlers, however. By 1697 British visitors to New York City were remarking on the trees planted in front of many of the houses. 'N.Y. hath severall wide Large and orderly streetes, & athwart them sundry narrower, in which notwithstanding

2. William Burgis's view of the New Dutch Church in 1731, with trees planted along the street on three sides of the church. (Collection of the New-York Historical Society)

are many Very good buildings, & tradesmen of note, it being not regarded where a man lives in N.Y. as to his trade, for all are known, sundry trees are frequently sett at the doores.'[14] In 1708 the city council began to regulate street tree planting by residents on Broadway: 'Order'd that the Inhabitants of the Broadway of this City have Liberty to Plant Trees before their Respective houses & Lotts of Ground. According to such directions as they Shall Receive from the Alderman and Assistant of the Said Ward or Either of Them.'[15] In 1730 the New Dutch Church on Nassau Street was opened, and the view by William Burgis the next year shows it surrounded by street trees.

Swedish botanist Peter Kalm, a student of the great Karl Linné, visiting in 1748, left the most complete description:[16]

The streets do not run so straight as those of Philadelphia, and sometimes are quite crooked; however, they are very spacious and well built, and most of them are paved, except in high places, where it has been found useless. In the chief streets there are trees planted, which in summer give them a fine appearance, and during the excessive heat at that time afford a cooling shade. I found it extremely pleasant to walk in the town, for it seemed like a garden. The trees which are planted for this purpose are chiefly of two kinds: the water beech, or Linné's *Platanus occidentalis,* which is very plentiful and gives an agreeable shade in summer by its great and numerous leaves; and the locust tree, or Linné's *Robinia Pseud-Acacia,* which is also frequent. The Latter's fine leaves and fragrant scent which exhales from its flowers, make it very suitable for planting in the streets near the houses and in gardens. There are likewise lime trees and elms along these walks, but they are not by far so frequent as the others. One seldom met with trees of the same sort next to each other, they being in general planted alternately.

The city by this time had begun to lose its predominately Dutch culture, and some of the planting of trees could have been done by British or other nationalities. Distinctly British influences were becoming prominent, in the laying out of a Bowling Green at the foot of Broadway and private pleasure gardens (Vauxhalls) in several places. Yet the association of street trees with Dutch culture was noted by contemporaries. In Albany there were also street trees planted by individual residents, and British visitors often referred to the Dutch quality of the landscapes of both New York City and Albany, the former Beverwick, citing the trees planted along the streets as one of the main Dutch characteristics, in contrast to English-founded cities in the British colonies, which remained without street trees until just before independence. Former British colonial administrator Thomas Pownall, who lived in New York in the 1750s, wrote, 'The City however still retains the general appearance of a Dutch-town with its row of Gabel-ends & the rows of Trees on the sides of the Streets.'[17] Englishman Richard Smith, visiting Albany in the 1760s wrote, 'Some Lime or Linden Trees as well as other Trees are planted before the Doors as at N York and indeed

Albany has in other Respects much the Aspect of that City.'[18]

By the 1770s the practice of planting street trees had begun to spread to some other towns in British America, notably to Philadelphia, which by 1800 had many tree-lined streets. By the early nineteenth century street trees planted by individual residents were a common element in the American urban landscape. The Lombardy poplar was used widely, in a great fad that ended only when its undesirable qualities became apparent. Fads for the weeping willow and black locust followed, but by the middle of the century there were many species and varieties being planted.[19]

3. Wall Street, looking west past the City Hall (former Federal Hall) towards Trinity Church on Broadway, in a drawing by Archibald Robertson in the 1790s. The large tree on the right is in front of the house of Samuel Verplanck, one of the city's most prominent Dutch-American citizens. (Collection of the New-York Historical Society)

New York City was in the forefront of almost all these developments and it seems clear that the planting of street trees in American cities owes its origin to the example of New York. The practice was adopted by Americans of all backgrounds by the end of the eighteenth century. One interesting piece of evidence lies in the efforts of the Common Council of New York City to control tree planting on the city's streets at the end of the turn of the nineteenth century. In 1789 an ordinance was passed banning trees 'to the southward of Freshwater and Catherine-street, except before churches or other public buildings, under the penalty of five pounds for every offence.'[20] But between 1793 and 1802 exceptions were requested, and usually granted, by individuals named Watts, LeRoy, Varick, Murray, Ellis, Clarkson, Nielson and Scott, (many of them influential businessmen or politicians) to plant trees in front of their houses in the proscribed area.[21] Clearly the practice of planting street trees had become a general trait of the city's population not restricted to those of Dutch ancestry.

One important difference between the trees in Dutch and American cities, however, is that in America trees were planted by individual initiative, while in the Netherlands they were done as part of municipal policy. As noted above by Kalm and others, in American cities trees were planted in front of some houses and not others. Sometimes building developers paid to have trees planted along an entire block to make their properties more attractive, but the more usual pattern was an almost random distribution of trees along the street. This contrasts strongly with the uniform planting along almost all Dutch city streets. Municipal control of the process of street tree planting came rather late. Only in the 1890s did most cities begin to pass ordinances giving the city government responsibility for planting and maintaining street trees. From that point, on, though, planting of trees became more uniform in most American cities.[22]

Public open spaces in America were mostly in the form of small public parks which show neither clear British nor Dutch influences and were rather limited in most American towns before the middle of the nineteenth century. In New York City the major open spaces were the Battery (at the tip of Manhattan), the Bowling Green at the foot of Broadway, City Hall Park and a series of public and private squares laid out between 1800 and 1840, such as Washington Square, Union Square and Gramercy Park.[23]

4. New York City Hall and the Park, in the 1830s, depicted by William Bartlett. (Collection of the author)

Late Nineteenth Century New York City and Amsterdam

By the middle of the nineteenth century some American cities were very large and growing rapidly. Between 1850 and 1860 New York City (and Brooklyn) grew from 600,000 to over 1 million. Seven other cities were over 100,000. The needs for open space were increasing, but the creation of parks had not kept pace with urban growth. Street trees provided greenery but not open space for recreation.

Growth was also rapid in many cities in Europe. Amsterdam had reached 200,000 by 1850 and 300,000 by 1880. Public open space in most large European cities consisted mostly of (former) royal gardens, small squares and linear promenades. A few cities had begun to turn their old fortifications into parks, Bremen and Frankfurt early in the nineteenth century, Haarlem and Utrecht in the 1820s. In Britain the lack of publicly accessible open space sparked a movement in the 1830s and '40s to build public parks, and by 1850 many large public parks were created. They generally followed the example of London's royal parks, particularly Hyde Park. Another influential model was the Peoples Park at Birkenhead, near Liverpool, designed by Joseph Paxton, later of Crystal Palace fame.[24]

The influence of British city parks was felt soon in France where the renovations in the 1850s under Napoleon III and his agent, Baron Haussmann, included remaking the Bois de Boulogne and the Bois de Vincennes, transforming formal French hunting-parks into landscape-style parks. Haussmann is most famous for the many tree-lined boulevards he opened through the center of Paris and the many small green squares. But equally influential in other cities was the example of the new French city parks.[25]

In the 1850s and '60s many cities in Europe and North America began to create green spaces, building large city parks and small green squares as well as tree-lined streets. In the United States the most prominent example was the creation of Central Park in New York City. The design by Frederick Law Olmsted

5. Central Park on a portion of the United States Geological Survey topographical map Haarlem, New York, 1897. (United States Geological Survey, courtesy of the University of New Hampshire).

and Calvert Vaux was influenced by Paxton's design of Birkenhead Park in England, but began a new American urban design tradition. Its grassy meadows, winding paths and large lakes in the midst of a large city inspired dozens of similar parks in North America over the next fifty years.[26]

The Vondel Park was begun in 1864 as the result of a private subscription raised by a commission of prominent citizens, led by C.P. van Eeghen. To design the park the commission hired the Haarlem garden architect J.D. Zocher and his son L.P. Zocher, designers of many urban parks in the Netherlands. The Nieuwe Park, as it was first called, was soon renamed the Vondelpark, in honor of Joost van den Vondel, the seventeenth century poet. Much smaller than Central Park, the Vondel Park followed the international 'landscape style' with its flowing lines and interspersed trees and meadows. Given its site on low ground created from drained farmland it paid more attention to water features and there are few large open grass areas. The skillful design, however, allows the visitor to walk a long distance on the various intersecting winding paths and feel an illusion of a country ramble, except for the large number of fellow park-goers. The Vondel Park was built in stages over about fifteen years and as it was taking shape the city was growing around it.[27]

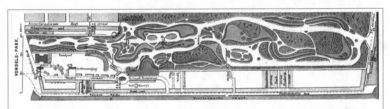

6. A plan of the Vondel Park from Braakensiek's 1883 plan of Amsterdam shows the intricate interweaving of paths, lawns, trees and waterways. (Gemeentearchief Amsterdam)

Central Park in New York City and the Vondelpark in Amsterdam share some striking similarities, even though their designers appear to have known little of each other's work. Both parks were just beyond the edge of the city but were soon surrounded by the urban expansion. Both were long rectangles cleverly divided by water features into separate areas of lawn and trees. They were also similar in that they were designed by members of great families of designers. The three generations of the Zocher family were responsible for dozens of major city parks in the Netherlands as were the three generations of the Olmsted family in the United States. The biggest difference between the two parks is their size. Central Park is 7 times as large as the Vondelpark (340 ha vs. 48 ha). Both were part of larger systems of parks in their cities. Other large parks were created in New York before the end of the nineteenth century, including Prospect Park in Brooklyn and Van Cortlandt Park in the Bronx. In Amsterdam other new parks were the Sarphatipark, the Westerpark and the Oosterpark. They also were designed in the landscape style.

These city parks served an important function by providing spaces for public recreation out

8. View of the Sheep Meadow
in Central Park in November,
2001.
(Photo by the author)

7. The entrance to the Vondel Park
from P. C. Hooftstraat in February, 2003.
(Photo by the author)

of doors. Olmsted had a clear vision for his parks, of an experience of nature which he felt would be therapeutic for city dwellers cut off from the world beyond the city. He felt that the pastoral scenery of a city's park would 'provide a poetic and tranquilizing influence on its people as comes through a pleasant contemplation of natural scenery, especially sequestered and limitless natural scenery.'[28] By the contradictory terms 'sequestered' and 'limitless' he was referring to the design of Central Park and Prospect Park, where large grassy meadows in the interior of the park were surrounded by groves of trees that cut off the sight of the city's buildings yet gave the impression of extensive views across a natural landscape.

However, even though they were public parks, they were created with a social bias. Provision was made mostly for the activities favored by the upper classes – walking, rowing, carriage and horseback riding, tennis – plus refreshment stands and band kiosks for music concerts. Expressly forbidden were team sports and alcoholic beverages. The working classes were welcome, of course, but only as long as they behaved in a proper manner. The parks were even seen as a vehicle for the improvement of the working classes. By imitation of their social superiors they were expected to acquire better manners, in dress and behavior. This was part of a larger group of social values attributed to public parks in the second half of the nineteenth in both Europe and America, and in turn part of a large movement to improve the urban environment, which was threatened by the tensions of rapid physical expansion, industrialization, pollution and social unrest based on class conflict. Parks were thought to help with many of these problems, by improving the aesthetic environment, by removing pollution and giving people a place to breath cleaner air, by providing places for healthful recreation, and by providing a place for improving public behavior.[29]

The large parks were also amenities for their surrounding neighborhoods. This had the effect of increasing the property values, and the increased revenue from property sales and/or taxes helped defray the cost of creating a park in the first place. Wealthy residential districts were built adjacent to new parks. In New York this was seen most clearly along Fifth Avenue, where millionaires like Vanderbilt, Morgan, Carnegie and Frick built palatial homes, most of which are museums today. In Amsterdam, a similar process took place around the Vondelpark especially prominently in the Willemspark project which built luxurious villas along the southwest side of the park beginning in the 1880s.

With the addition of the large new parks, late nineteenth century Amsterdam and New York City became more similar in their urban landscapes once again. After beginning with a similar pattern of urban green space created by trees along the streets and canals in the seventeenth century they had diverged substantially during the eighteenth and early nineteenth centuries. By the late nineteenth century, however, the combination of tree-lined streets and large public parks was making them more similar again. This was a landscape shared by other cities in Europe and North America as the design and ornamentation of cities had become cosmopolitan practices throughout Europe and the Americas by then. It is clear, though, that Amsterdam and New York City were extraordinary since the seventeenth century in their green urban landscapes and that they continue to share some common characteristics today.

Notes

1　Henry Lawrence, 'National Differences in Urban Green Spaces: France, the Netherlands, Britain and America, 1600-1800,' *Planning History* 20.2 (1998): 20-28.
2　Jean-Louis Harouel, *L'Embellissement des Villes: L'urbanisme Français au XVIIIe Siècle*, (Paris: Picard, 1993); Pierre Lavedan, Jeanne Hugueney, and Philippe Henrat, *L'Urbanisme à l'Epoque Moderne: XVIe - XVIIIe Siècles*, (Geneva: Droz, 1982); Daniel Rabreau, 'Urban Walks in France in the Seventeenth and Eighteenth Centuries,' in Monique Mosser and Georges Teyssot, eds., *The History of Garden Design: The Western Tradition from the Renaissance to the Present Day* (London: Thames & Hudson, 1991), 305-316.
3　Todd Longstaffe-Gowan, *The London Town Garden, 1700-1840* (New Haven, CT: Yale University Press, 2001); Susan Lasdun, *The English Park: Royal, Private and Public* (London: Andre Deutsch, 1991).
4　Ed Taverne, *In 't Land van Belofte: in de Nieuwe Stadt; Ideaal en Werkelijkheid van de Stadsuitleg in de Republiek 1580-1680* (Maarssen: Gary Schwartz, 1978); Leo Noordegraaf, *Atlas van de Nederlandse Marktsteden* (Amsterdam: Sijthoff, 1985).
5　W. Hofman, ed., *Historische Plattegronden van Nederlandse Steden, deel 1: Amsterdam* (Alphen aan den Rijn: Canaletto, 1978); Amsterdams Historisch Museum, and Art Gallery of Ontario, *The Dutch Cityscape in the 17th Century and its Sources* (Amsterdam: Amsterdams Historisch Museum, 1977).
6　John Evelyn, *The Diary of John Evelyn*, edited by E. S. de Beer (London: Oxford University Press, 1959) 27-28; For the reactions of French visitors, see, R. Murris, *La Hollande et les Hollandais au XVIIe et au XVIIIe Siècles Vus par les Français* (Paris: Librairie Ancienne Honoré Champion, 1925).
7　Erik de Jong, *Natuur en Kunst: Nederlandse Tuin- en Landschapsarchitectuur 1650-1740* (Bussum: Thoth, 1993), 190-202; Maurits van Rooijen, *De Groene Stad: Een historische studie over de groenvoorziening in de Nederlandse stad* (The Hague: Cultuurfonds van de Bank voor Nederlandse Gemeenten, 1984), 39-40.
8　See the delightful descriptions in Boudewijn Bakker et al., *Landscapes of Rembrandt: His Favourite Walks* (Bussum: Thoth, 1998).
9　James L. Cobban, 'Geographic Notes on the First Two Centuries of Djakarta,' in Y. M. Yeung and C. P. Lo, eds., *Changing South-East Asian Cities: Readings in Urbanization* (Singapore: Oxford University Press, 1976), 45-57; Ron van Oers, *Dutch Town Planning Overseas During VOC and WIC Rule (1600-1800)* (Zutphen, Netherlands: Walburg Pers, 2000); Nigel Worden, Elizabeth van Heyningen, and Vivian Bickford-Smith, *Cape Town, the Making of a City: An Illustrated Social History* (Claremont: David Philip Publishers, 1998).

10 See, for instance, Rudy J. Favretti, 'The Ornamentation of New England Towns: 1750-1850,' *Journal of Garden History* 2.4 (1982): 325-342.

11 E.B. O'Callaghan, ed., *Laws and Ordinances of New Netherland, 1638-1674* (Albany, NY: Weed, Parsons & Co., 1868); Berthold Fernow, ed., *Minutes of the Executive Board of the Burgomasters of New Amsterdam* (New York: Francis P. Harper, 1907).

12 I.N. Phelps Stokes, *The Iconography of Manhattan Island, 1498-1909*, 6 volumes (New York: Robert H. Dodd, 1915); John A. Kouwenhoven, *The Columbia Historical Portrait of New York* (Garden City, NY: Doubleday & Co., 1953).

13 See, for example, the varying depictions of trees in the maps in Joannes Blaeu's *Stedenatlas van de Vereenigde Nederlanden* (Amsterdam: J. Blaeu, 1649).

14 Wayne Andrews, 'A Glance at New York in 1697: The Travel Diary of Dr. Benjamin Bullivant,' *New York Historical Society Quarterly* 40.1 (1956): 55-73.

15 Stokes, *Iconography*, 4:461. The reference is to the meeting of the Common Council of the City of New York on 13 April 1708.

16 Peter Kalm, *Peter Kalm's Travels in North America, the English version of 1770*, repr. 1937, ed. Adolph B. Benson (New York: Dover Publications, 1964), 131.

17 Thomas Pownall, *A Topographical Description of the Dominions of the United States of America*, ed. Lois Mulkearn (1776; repr., Pittsburgh: University of Pittsburgh Press, 1949), 43.

18 Richard Smith, *A Tour of Four Great Rivers, the Hudson, Mohawk, Susquehanna and Delaware in 1769*, ed. Francis W. Halsey (Port Washington, NY: Ira J. Friedman, Inc., 1964), 17.

19 Daryl Gene Watson, *Shade and Ornamental Trees in the Nineteenth Century Northeastern United States* (Ph.D. dissertation, University of Illinois at Urbana-Champaign, 1978).

20 [New York] *Daily Advertiser*, 15 April 1789, 2.

21 Stokes, *Iconography*, 5:1294, 1306, 1307, 1364, 1365, 1393.

22 William Solotaroff, *Shade-Trees in Towns and Cities* (New York: John Wiley & Sons, 1912).

23 Elizabeth Blackmar, *Manhattan for Rent, 1785-1850*, (Ithaca, NY: Cornell University Press, 1989).

24 Lasdun, *English Park*; Hazel Conway, *People's Parks: The Design and Development of Victorian Parks in Britain* (Cambridge: Cambridge University Press, 1991); On the early landscape-style parks on the former fortifications, see, van Rooijen, *De Groene Stad*, 30-35.

25 Adolphe Alphand, *Les Promenades de Paris* (Paris: J. Rothschild, 1868-1873); David P. Jordan, *Transforming Paris: The life and labors of Baron Haussmann* (Chicago: University of Chicago Press, 1995); Pierre Lavedan, 'L'influence de Haussmann: 'L'Haussmannisation',' in Louis Réau, ed., *L'Oeuvre de Baron Haussmann, Préfet de la Seine (1853-1870)* (Paris: Presses Universitaires de France, 1954), 142-157.

26 David Schuyler, *The New Urban Landscape: The Redefinition of City Form in Nineteenth-Century America* (Baltimore: The Johns Hopkins University Press, 1986); Frederick Law Olmsted Jr., and Theodora Kimball, eds., *Frederick Law Olmsted, Landscape Architect, 1822-1903* (New York: Benjamin Blom, 1970).

27 Carla S. Oldenburger-Ebbers, Anne Mieke Backer, and Eric Blok, *Gids voor de Nederlandse Tuin- en Landschapsarchitectuur, Deel West: Noord- en Zuid-Holland* (Rotterdam: De Hef, 1998); Van Rooijen, *Groene Stad*, 46-50; Martha Bakker, Renée Kistemaker, Henk van Nierop, Wim Vroom and Piet Witteman, editors, *Amsterdam in de Tweede Gouden Eeuw* (Bussum: Thoth, 2000).

28 Schuyler, *New Urban Landscape*, 93.

29 George Chadwick, *The Park and the Town: Public Landscapes in the Nineteenth and Twentieth Centuries* (New York: Praeger, 1966). For a case study of the social roles of a large nineteenth century American city park, see, Terence Young, 'San Francisco's Golden Gate Park and the Search for a Good Society, 1865-80,' *Forest & Conservation History* 37.1 (1993): 4-13.

Elisabeth Paling Funk

KNICKERBOCKER'S NEW NETHERLAND: WASHINGTON IRVING'S REPRESENTATION OF DUTCH LIFE ON THE HUDSON

Washington Irving (1783-1859) was America's first internationally known author. A first-generation American of Scottish-English descent, he was born in New York City, as were his seven surviving older siblings. With about 23,000 inhabitants at that time, the town retained a recognizably Dutch character in structures, speech, and customs. Surrounded from birth by Dutch-American friends and in-laws, Irving's remarkable skill at bilingual punning and his ability to coin Dutch phrases prove that he had successfully absorbed Dutch as he had heard it spoken daily until he was twenty. Much of his reading was eighteenth-century neoclassical English literature, marked by realism and satire. Yet Gothic romances, notably Ann Radcliffe's, and later Sir Walter Scott's poetry, appealed to his antiquarian bent and romantic spirit, which had been nourished by his youthful explorations of rural Manhattan Island and the Hudson region, and by travel in Europe (1804-1806). These interests are reflected in the prominence of history and popular culture in his major works. Such material suited his abilities: Irving's talent was not for invention.[1] Rather, his imagination drew upon a superior ability to absorb what he read, heard, and observed, and to re-create his subject in a graceful, gently satirical manner.

Knickerbocker

Irving's portrayal of the seventeenth- and eighteenth-century Dutch on the eastern seaboard of America is located mainly in his comic *A History of New York, by Diedrich Knickerbocker* (1809), and in the Knickerbocker folk tales – 'Rip Van Winkle,' 'The Legend of Sleepy Hollow,' 'Dolph Heyliger,' and 'Wolfert Webber.'[2] For the *History*, he created Diedrich Knickerbocker, an old, crotchety, and comically inconsistent historian with a genuine New Netherland name, causing the appellation 'Knickerbocker' to become a household word. Unsuitable as history even in Irving's day because of its dominant use of the burlesque, the *History* is nevertheless more informative regarding New Netherland than are the straightforward accounts from his few immediate predecessors.[3] Irving availed himself of these, in addition to much if not all that could be located of seventeenth-century histories, journals, maps, and collections, and provided cryptic but genuine footnote documentation.[4] For his Dutch sources, he probably depended on the bibliophiles among his many friends of Dutch descent, notably Henry Brevoort. A New York City resident and Irving's friend from early youth, Brevoort owned a collec-

1. Washington Irving in 1820.
Portrait attributed to Charles Robert Leslie.

tion of some repute by 1807 and is known to have assisted him at that time by locating old and rare sources.[5]

Irving's access to hitherto untranslated, unexplored, or insufficiently examined sources include Dutch literature, notably *Spiegel van den Ouden en Nieuwen Tyt* (1632), an emblem book in three parts by Jacob Cats (1577-1660). Intended by its author as a guide for conduct in public as well as domestic life, it remained for centuries a counterpart of the Bible in Netherlandish families. It accompanied the seventeenth-century Dutch to New Netherland, continued to be imported, and remained a favorite into Irving's time among descendants of New Netherland's Dutch settlers.[6] Irving's acquisition for extensive use of this volume exemplifies his interest in and familiarity with the Dutch heritage of his native city. As a sketcher of some merit who had once contemplated a career in the visual arts, he must have been fascinated by the *Spiegel*'s portraits of seventeenth-century daily life, which contributed to his understanding of Cats's text and enriched the *History*'s content. His borrowings, in quotation and context, begin with the *History*'s title page couplet: '*De waarheid die in duister lag, | Die komt met klaarheid aan den dag,*' or, 'The truth that lay in darkness, (That) comes [clearly] (with clearness) into the [light of] day.'⁷ It sets the stage for his mock-heroic treatment of history and, in the figure of Knickerbocker himself, of historiography and the task of the historian. The impression of the *History* as fiction is mainly created by Knickerbocker's digressions and narrative manner. In the narrative itself, Irving is as accurate as personal observation, oral tradition, the limited historical records available in his day, and the demands of his work permitted. The couplet is not only part of the burlesque; it is also Irving's rightful motto.

Dutch Heritage

Irving's use of the Dutch heritage needs at least a book to do it justice.⁸ Here, representative selections from the *History* will serve to illustrate his method, which varies with the matter at hand. His preference is for gentle satire and wordplay. Matters that are too painful to permit such treatment are noted in passing or, more rarely, are related in a harshly satiric manner, such as the treatment of the native population by their European discoverers and New England's witch hunts and religious intolerance. Beginning with Hudson's exploration, the narrative covers New Netherland's existence up to and including the English takeover in 1664. New Netherland's underpopulation in comparison with that of the New England colonies is obliquely addressed in his emphasis on Yankee squatters. The relatively bloodless nature of armed conflicts with these neighbors and with the Swedes on the Delaware permits comic treatment. Serious incidents of Indian warfare, such as the destruction of Swanendael on the Delaware(1632) and the 'Peach War' invasion of Manhattan (1655), are characteristically downplayed. Irving also created a homogeneous New Netherland through the extensive use of Dutch first names and surnames that is at variance with its cosmopolitan character. Nevertheless, nearly all had their origins in the seventeenth-century Dutch colony, frequently in the area where Knickerbocker places them. These approximately one hundred residents probably did not result from research, except for major figures. Rather, the names in the Knickerbocker canon and their locations demonstrate the existence of clusters of Dutch-Americans into Irving's day and attest to the validity of his repeated assertion that the New Netherlanders and their descendants tended to put down roots. They also confirm the author's profound familiarity with these Dutch New Yorkers and their antecedents.

The *History* treats in detail only three of New Netherland's directors, or governors: Wouter Van Twiller (1633-1638), Willem Kieft (1638-1647), and Petrus Stuyvesant (1647-1664). Of these, Van Twiller's portrayal is the most at variance with historical truth. Kieft's is a satire of president Jefferson's democratic and scientific experiments, yet it closely resembles the historic figure. That period is correctly credited for the beginnings of popular participation in public affairs, which continued, in the *History* broadly outlined, through the Stuyvesant era. However, following the scant information at hand, Irving mistakenly locates the creation of New Amsterdam's municipal government, with *schout*, *burgermeesters*, and *schepenen* in Van Twiller's day. Like Knickerbocker's Kieft, his Stuyvesant shares traits with the historical counterpart: dictatorial, volatile, but also 'the best, of our ancient dutch governors.'⁹

In 1828, James Fenimore Cooper remarked that 'a few old Dutch dwellings yet remain' in the city.¹⁰ The *History* reveals that Irving likewise drew upon observations of New York architecture, but his often remarkably detailed descriptions depend as well on written

2. Partial copy of the *History*'s 'View of New Amsterdam,' a modified version of the inset of Justus Danckerts' map of New Netherland.

and oral sources. Early construction on Manhattan began, says Knickerbocker, when the Dutch 'settled upon the south-west point of the island, and fortified themselves strongly, by throwing up a mud battery, which they named FORT AMSTERDAM' (449). Regarding the construction of the wall, Stuyvesant's 'care... was to strengthen and fortify New Amsterdam. For this purpose he reared a substantial barrier that reached across the island from river to river.' Knickerbocker elaborates by giving the *Land-poort,* the *Water-poort,* and *Smits Vleye* in their locations (589, 589n). His text reflects uncertainty about the materials for the wall's construction, but goes on to place it within the correct time frame: 'Some traditions... have ascribed the building of this wall to a later period, but they are wholly incorrect; for a memorandum in the Stuyvesant manuscript, dated towards the middle of the governor's reign, mentions this wall particularly.... And it mentions moreover the alarming circumstance of a drove of stray cows, breaking through the grand wall....' (589). Ordinances to keep livestock from roaming freely notwithstanding, unfenced cattle indeed caused damage in New Amsterdam; in fact, pigs still roamed the city's streets in Irving's day.[11]

Folded into the *History*'s first edition is a 'View of New Amsterdam' credited to 'an ancient Etching of the same size, Published by Justus Danckers, at Amsterdam,' and to 'Justus Danker' in a textual note (527n). Justus Danckerts was a seventeenth-century art dealer, publisher, and engraver who copied and may have slightly retouched a map of New Netherland and its surrounding areas, published in the early 1650s by Nicolaes J. Visscher. In all pertinent details, however, including the legends, Danckerts copied the view of New Amsterdam that occurs on the Visscher, or Prototype, map as a rectangular inset in its lower right.[12] The *History*'s print, entitled, 'NEW AMSTERDAN (NOW NEW-YORK) [a]s it appeared about the year 1640, while under the Dutch Government,' is somewhat predated, perhaps deliberately, to fit within the Kieft narrative. As in the original, the *History*'s identifications move roughly from left to right, omitting those for the windmill and the flagpole; but in the text, Kieft is credited with raising 'a stupendous flag-staff' and 'a great windmill,' 'a novelty in the art of fortification' (527). The remaining eight occur in Irving's translations: 'A. The Fort; B. Church of St. Nicholas, [Nicholas' addition serving to justify his presence in the *History*]; C. The Jail; D. Governor's House; E. The Gallows; F. The Pillory; G. West India Companie's Stores; H. City Tavern.' Similarly, the Gallows' identifying letter is placed behind the lower of two prominent structures at the southeast corner of Manhattan. This structure is likewise occupied by a single figure; but Irving's view includes another, dangling by the waistband from the higher of the two. Facing left, its arms and legs are free and widespread.

Added to conform to the author's amplifications in the Kieft narrative, this figure is not Irving's invention. A seventeenth-century, square view of New Amsterdam, located in Arnoldus Montanus' *De Nieuwe en Onbekende Weereld* ('The New and Unknown World'), demonstrates the tall gibbet's purpose and use by adding an occupant who is facing to the right, with legs and arms tied together. Montanus' description reads: 'Aan de waterkant staet [sic] galg en wip,'[13] or, 'At the water's edge stand(s) [the] gallows and strappado.' Using Montanus' work, Irving's acknowledged source John Ogilby adopted this print for his book *America*, where Irving encountered it.[14] Preferring Danckerts' view with its wide panorama and more differentiated structures, Irving borrowed the suspended figure to add a small but significant detail to his view of Manhattan. He translates Danckerts' *'t Gerecht* with the imprecise 'The Gallows,' but in his text correctly distinguishes between the two objects. The lower, says Knickerbocker, is 'a goodly gallows':

> Hard by also was erected another gibbet... on which the ingenious William Kieft valued himself not a little, being a punishment entirely of his own invention.... [T]he culprit instead of being suspended by the neck... was hoisted by the waistband, and was kept... dangling and sprawling between heaven and earth... [Kieft] called them... his *gallows birds*, which ingenious appellation... had since grown to be a cant name given to all candidates for legal elevation. This punishment, moreover..., gave the first hint for a kind of harnessing... by which our forefathers braced up their multifarious breeches...[15] It still bears the name of the object to which it owes its origin; being generally termed a pair of *gallows-es*... sometimes vulgarly denominated *suspenders*. (540-41)

Irving correctly interpreted the function of these two instruments of justice, but went on to exploit the one less known in his place and time to invent two humorous, explanatory tall tales: the origin of the expression 'gallows bird' and the invention of modern suspenders. Unquestionably, the sight of the dangling figure on the Montanus map in Ogilby prompted his composition of Kieft's breeches-gallows episode and the concomitant addition to the *History*'s copy of Danckerts' view. The substitution of the constrained figure in the Montanus print with the droll, spread-eagled manikin conforms to the *History*'s comic spirit.

In contrast, thus being hoisted aloft was torture, for centuries the most common in Europe and inflicted for purposes of interrogation and punishment. It involved lifting the subject by the hands, usually tied behind the back, by means of a rope or chain and a pulley, and quickly dropping him again. The practice was applied in varying degrees of severity, ranging from merely positioning the subject at the strappado to adding weights and flogging.[16] By the 1630s, corporal punishment, including the death penalty, and interrogation under duress could be administered in New Amsterdam as it was in Amsterdam, where, as throughout Europe, public chastisement was still practiced. But by the seventeenth century, wooden structures such as the gallows and strappado were not permanently in place. Instead, they were erected from ready material at a customary site as their need arose and then knocked down again.[17] Therefore, the representation of these temporary structures in the several views of New Amsterdam probably must be seen as symbolic. Aimed at a European public, these views were intended to present the Dutch colony in a favorable light. Their inclusion of *'t Gerecht* conveyed that this city in the New World was an orderly *locus* of European civilization; these instruments of justice proclaimed New Amsterdam's status as the equal of the familiar, well-established cities of the Netherlands and thus helped to promote New Netherland's settlement. Irving must have been aware that the occupied, tall gibbet he so fortuitously discovered in Ogilby had some harsh purpose. But, unlike the more common gallows next to it, it was probably no longer within living memory in the North America of his day. Hence, the gallows is barely acknowledged; the strappado's relative antiquity set him free to create another humorous passage in his Kieft narrative.

Source of Dutch Folk Life
Not primarily thought of as a treasure trove of early Dutch-American folk life, the *History* is precisely that. Structures and interiors; dress; food and drink; customs of social and family life; legendry, tall tales, and folk belief provide a rich texture that consists unmistakably of transplanted Old-World Dutch traditions. Dutch-American popular culture is the mainstay of the Knickerbocker tales. Ostensibly tales of the supernatural, these were intended as realistic portrayals of country manners, related with a comic touch.[18] Many particulars were gathered through personal observation and chosen from those that had withstood the changes of time. People and their customs are set in a material culture that is sufficiently detailed to indicate the historic seventeenth-century Dutch province; however, without violating literal accuracy, Irving created a New Netherland that in its early years seems less rude, because emphasis on hardship would not have suited Knickerbocker's comedy. An implicit contrast is drawn between the scrupulously maintained Dutch structures and New England's rickety ones to underscore the differences between the two groups. These are accentuated in specific Dutch details such as the rarely used front door (478) and the contrast between best room and daily living quarters:

> The grand parlour was the sanctum sanctorum, where the passion for cleaning was indulged without controul. In this sacred apartment no one was permitted to enter, excepting the mistress and her confidential maid,.... leaving their shoes at the door, and entering devoutly, on their stocking feet. After scrubbing the floor, sprinkling it with fine sand, which was curiously stroked into angles, and curves, and rhomboids, with a broom... the window shutters were again closed... and the room carefully locked up until the revolution of time, brought round the weekly cleaning day. As to the family, they always entered at the gate, and most generally lived in the kitchen.... The fire-places were of a truly patriarchal magnitude, where the whole family, old

and young, master and servant, black and white, nay even the very cat and dog... had each a prescriptive right to a corner.' (478-79)

Passages in Irving's journals kept while traveling in the Netherlands in 1805 do not reflect this gentle ridicule of obsessive cleanliness; instead, they indicate appreciation for his Hudson Valley heritage: 'The Inn was simple... but very clean. The tea service..., the well sanded floor, the decent clean old fashioned look of the landlady and her dutch language reminded me forceably of some of our dutch country inns in the state of New York.'[19]

The *History*'s ostensibly seventeenth-century dietary customs are probably based on Irving's own experience, and the tenacity of eating habits in general accounts for their verisimilitude. All serve his satire, directed at both the colonial and his contemporary worlds; nevertheless, they present realistic portrayals of Dutch-American family and social life:

> The tea table was crowned with a huge earthen dish, well stored with slices of fat pork, fried brown, cut up in mouthfuls, and swimming in doup or gravy. The company being seated around the genial board, and each furnished with a fork, evinced their dexterity in launching at the fattest pieces in this mighty dish.... [T]he table was always sure to boast an enormous dish of balls of sweetened dough, fried in hog's fat, and called dough nuts, or oly koeks – a delicious kind of cake, at present scarce known in this city, excepting in genuine dutch families; but which retains its preeminent station at the tea tables in Albany. (480)

In the Netherlands, *doop* (here 'doup') for sauce or gravy had disappeared from general usage by the late eighteenth century, but evidently survived among the Hudson Valley Dutch into Irving's day. The modern doughnut, in taste and appearance far removed from the Dutch *oliekoek* or *oliebol*, is its descendant. The description continues with a slightly predated 'majestic delft tea-pot' and 'a huge copper tea kettle.' 'To sweeten the beverage, a lump of sugar was laid beside each cup – and the company alternately nibbled and sipped with great decorum, until an improvement was introduced by a shrewd and economic old lady, which was to suspend a large lump directly over the tea table' (480-81).[20]

To accentuate the separation between population groups and the struggle between them, Irving assigned a common courtship tradition to one, the English. '[B]undling,' says Knickerbocker, is responsible for 'the marvellous fecundity' of New England's population and the 'amazing number of sturdy brats' that were born 'without the license of the law, or the benefit of clergy' (496-97), an alteration that underscores the unsettled and unregulated Yankee ways as they are satirized in the *History*. Practiced throughout Europe and known in the Netherlands as *kweesten* (to talk) or *nachtvrijen* (to go night courting), bundling continued in some areas well into the twentieth century. A young man known to the family would enter the girl's bedroom by the window, leaving quietly an hour before sunrise. Bundling was one of two major ways for parents to guide their children's social contacts so that a 'wrong' choice of marriage partner could be prevented. The other consisted of a close-knit organization of contemporaries that resulted in regular gatherings of the marriageable young,[21] indicated in the *History*'s festivities that here precede bundling. These gatherings still existed in the Hudson Valley of the mid-eighteenth century. Formed early, the exclusive 'companies' continued into adulthood; as a result, 'it was reckoned a sort of apostacy to marry out of one's company,' which rarely happened. As in the Netherlands, 'companies' went on unchaperoned outings or met at the home of a member whose parents would be absent, leaving 'some old domestic' in charge. These liberal ways for the young to become acquainted were possible because they occurred in small communities among mutually dependent people in similar economic and social circumstances. However, a stranger to the community was never allowed to take part; and, in the Hudson Valley, 'no person that does not belong to the company is ever admitted to these meetings.'[22] Similarly, when the *History*'s Yankee squatters try to introduce bundling in New Netherland, the Dutch girls are favorably disposed, but 'their mothers... strenuously discountenanced all such outlandish innovations' (501). In contrast, the fictive trumpeter Antony Van Corlaer, Irving's benign, comic version of the promiscuous Cornelis van Tienhoven,[23] gleefully adopts Yankee courtship traditions. He readily follows Stuyvesant on his eastern voyage, for he remembers 'the frolicking and dancing and bundling,' from which, as a stranger, he should have been barred. His previous forays into New England have already had consequences: 'strapping wenches' are joyful at the sight of Antony, who is pleased to have 'a crew of little trumpeters crowding around him for his blessing' (685, 688). Irving's fiction illustrates that to the extent that ethnic groups adopted each other's customs, they lost their own distinctive cultural identity and became colonial Americans.

Dutch Tales

All major elements of Dutch folk belief occur in the *History*, representing whatever Irving gathered of the Dutch oral tradition of the Hudson River Valley. They were adapted by the literary artist and augmented by his fiction that, while it too does not possess the simple narration of the oral tale, remains within the Dutch tradition. In a brief digression, Knickerbocker refers to the legend of the 'Flying Dutchman,' which contains several elements of that legend's earliest forms, without the literary embellishments it subsequently received at other hands. The ship itself is personified as the Dutchman. It is a 'phantom' and a 'spectrum' or specter, reflecting the unsubstantial nature of the legendary Flying Dutchman and its kinship with the ghost ships of the world's maritime tradition. It is 'shadowy,' conforming with the legendary ship's most frequent description as black or dark in color; and it is 'of the night,' which agrees with the phantom's most usual appearance at night or at sundown. The apparition is 'portentous,' an omen, in view of the 'terror' it engenders, of bad luck (428). An encounter would forecast disaster: a heavy storm, a shipwreck, or damage to the vessel.[24] Irving's literary use of the legend, to be expanded in *Bracebridge Hall*'s tale-within-a-tale 'The Storm-Ship,' is one of the earliest in world literature and the first by an American author.

Many of the Hudson Valley Dutch traditions that are part of the *History*'s fabric survived to become part of the regional or even the national popular culture. None of them is more remarkable than Irving's adoption and transformation of the Dutch St. Nicholas in that work. In 1809 and 1810, the recently founded New-York Historical Society evinced an awareness of Nicholas' importance for the region. Further, a broadside commissioned by one of its founders portrays Nicholas in bishop's garb, without miter but with the punishing birch twig, with text consisting of old Dutch St. Nicholas songs. Their survival lends further credence to the continuity of domestic St. Nicholas celebrations in former New Netherland, as does that of the traditional bakery products mentioned in a letter of

1819: "In old times... St. Class [sic] used to cross the Atlantic and brought immense supplies of cookies etc. from Amsterdam."[25]

Legendary saint and popular hero, the latter growing out of his portrayal in medieval miracle plays, St. Nicholas had survived the Reformation because the secular celebration of his feast day, December 6, had become too firmly entrenched in Dutch domestic life to be eradicated along with the veneration of other saints.[26] It is, therefore, the saint as secular folk hero who accompanied the Dutch settlers to New Netherland, where his celebration survived into Irving's day. In the *History*, all attributes of the legendary saint are revived. For example, the church in
the fort, says Knickerbocker, 'they dedicated to the great and good ST. NICHOLAS, who immediately took the infant town of New Amsterdam under his peculiar patronage, and has ever since been... the tutelar saint of this excellent city' (454). The history of the St. Nicholas legend in the Netherlands upon the Reformation indicates that such a dedication is impossible: the official church of New Netherland was the Dutch Reformed; other rites were permitted only in seclusion. Nicholas as folk hero is present, but with altered appearance and a change in character. Instead of bishop's garb, his attire is that of a seventeenth-century Dutch settler.[27] He still rides through the skies, but it is a farmer's wagon rather than a white horse that serves as transport. He has lost his tall, lean figure along with his dignified demeanor and his austere and occasionally punitive traits; in Irving's hands, he has become an entirely benevolent, folksy, pipe-smoking elf. Much of this portrait was complete with the *History*'s first edition; the second provided more detail in Oloffe Van Kortlandt's dream of the metropolis that would be New Amsterdam:

[T]he good St. Nicholas came riding over the tops of the trees in that selfsame wagon wherein he brings his yearly presents to children.... And the shrewd Van Kortlandt knew him by his broad hat, his long pipe, and the resemblance he bore to the figure on the bow of the Goede Vrouw [which brought the *History*'s first settlers]. And he lit his pipe by the fire and he sat himself down and he smoked.... And when St. Nicholas had smoked his pipe, he twisted it in his hatband, and laying his finger beside his nose gave the astonished Van Kortlandt a very significant look; then mounting his wagon he returned over the treetops and disappeared.[28]

Others completed the transformation, including the removal of gift-giving to Christmas Day, but it is Irving's adoption and treatment of the Dutch *Sinterklaas* that became the origin of the most widespread character in native folklore: the American Santa Claus. In all, Irving's imaginative re-creation of the essentially Dutch life on the Hudson of his day ensured its survival and made him into America's first folklorist. His successful attempt to make his own fiction a part of this Dutch tradition has placed him early and prominently in a long procession of American storytellers.

Reception
Washington Irving's *Knickerbocker History* was privately published on St. Nicholas Day, 1809. Its success brought the author instant fame. Most appreciated the book, the first entirely devoted to New Netherland after the colony ceased to exist, for what it was: a tolerably accurate portrayal for its day of New York's beginnings, related in a humorous

vein. Nevertheless, several Dutch New Yorkers were offended by the irreverent treatment of their ancestors, and the *History*'s earthy humor also drew some adverse commentary. Gulian Verplanck, in his address of December 7, 1818, to the New-York Historical Society, deplored the *History*'s 'coarse caricature.'[29] Irving was sensitive to both: some of its low comedy disappeared by the second edition; and, in a letter written in 1837, he mentioned with regret specific families whom he had unintentionally caused distress.[30] It is not known whether he was aware of criticism in the Netherlands, but there too offense was taken. In a sharply critical 1841 poem 'Aan New-York,' E.J. Potgieter mentions Irving as one who unjustly ridicules and denigrates the seventeenth-century Dutch colonists.[31] Unlike several of Irving's other works, the *History* was never translated in Dutch, perhaps not so much because its satire was unacceptable than that the work was too topical and, therefore, deemed insufficiently accessible to Dutch readers.

Irving's private commentary on expressions of dismay was as good-natured in tone as was that which prevailed in his satire. This was not solely directed at the Dutch New Netherlanders. The Swedes on the Delaware and, most severely, the New Englanders were satirized as well for their respective foibles. The universality of such foibles is further extended when we recognize that the *History*, in part, served as satire of Irving's own times and, indeed, remains applicable today. His work, along with the straightforward histories that appeared at least before the mid-nineteenth century, cannot be regarded as a reliable historical resource, but neither should it be totally disregarded. Errors, burlesque, and literary embroidery notwithstanding, it deserves attentive reading, for its rendering of New Netherland may suggest areas of inquiry or challenge received wisdom.

By his own admission, Washington Irving 'look[ed]... at things poetically.'[32] He also clearly foresaw that, in time, the disappearance of tangible evidence of Dutch life and history on the Hudson and, perhaps, his own narrative manner, might cause the substance of his Knickerbocker works to be dismissed. Speaking specifically about Sleepy Hollow in 1839, he wrote: 'the antiquarian visitor,... in the petulance of his disappointment, may pronounce all that I have recorded of that once favored region, a fable.'[33] Such dismissal would be unfortunate. The tenacity of the Dutch popular culture as that had been transmitted from seventeenth-century New Netherland ensured its survival well into nineteenth-century New York. Knickerbocker's *History* and tales provide a unique window on this essentially Dutch life on the Hudson.

Notes

1. Irving's inability to invent, Henry A. Pochmann, Introduction, *Washington Irving: Representative Selections* (New York: American Book, 1934), xl. The latter half of Irving's career was mainly spent as a straightforward biographer and historian. His final work was a five-volume *Life of George Washington* (1855-1859), which remained definitive until well into the twentieth century.
2. The *History* saw several more editions, the most important being the third (1819) for its illustrations by Washington Allston and C. R. Leslie, and the second (1812) and final (1848) editions for significant changes in the text. For the tales, ostensibly found among the effects of the late Knickerbocker, see *The Sketch Book* (1819-1820), *Bracebridge Hall* (1822), and *Tales of a Traveller* (1824).

3. William Smith's *History of the Province of New York* (1757), with some 30 pages on New Netherland, much of them quotation of a few documents, and Benjamin Trumbull's inaccurate, biased *History of Connecticut, 1630-1764* (1797).

4. For Irving's sources, see Stanley T. Williams and Tremaine McDowell's Introduction to *Diedrich Knickerbocker's A History of New York by Washington Irving* (New York: Harcourt Brace, 1927), xxvi-xxvii, xliv-li. The authors conclude that 'Irving, apart from his obvious nonsense, is a kindly and a surprisingly dependable historian' (lii). Their discussion of his Dutch sources is incomplete and erroneous. These include his acknowledged source David Pietersz. de Vries's *Korte Historiael* (1655) and seventeenth-century maps and views. Internal evidence demonstrates his unattributed use of Adriaen van der Donck's *Vertoogh van Nieu-Nederland* (1650). Irving credits some unidentifiable old manuscripts for historically correct material.

5. See Vol. 1 of *The Life and Letters of Washington Irving* by Irving's nephew and first biographer, Pierre M. Irving (New York: Putnam, 1869), 222.

6. Alice P. Kenney, 'Dutch Traditions in American Literature,' *De Halve Maen* 48.4 (1973): 7. Irving's unattributed use of Cats's work was first recognized in Elisabeth Paling Funk, 'Washington Irving and His Dutch-American Heritage as Seen in *A History of New York*, *The Sketch-Book*, *Bracebridge Hall*, and *Tales of a Traveller*,' (Ph.D. dissertation, Fordham University, New York, 1986).

7. Except for differences in spelling, Irving's text is identical. Jacob Cats, 'Spiegel van den Ouden en Nieuwen Tyt,' *Alle de Wercken van den Heere Jacob Cats*, vol. 1 (1712; Utrecht: De Banier, 1962), 622. All translations are the author's. Parentheses indicate omissions; brackets, added text.

8. Elisabeth Paling Funk, 'Washington Irving and the Dutch Heritage,' manuscript in progress.

9. Washington Irving, 'A History of New York... by Diedrich Knickerbocker' (1809 edition), James W. Tuttleton, ed., *History, Tales, and Sketches* (New York: Library of America, 1983), 468, 564. Irving's anomalies of spelling, capitalization, and punctuation are copied without comment. Further references to this volume will appear in the text.

10. James Fenimore Cooper, *Notions of the Americans*, vol. 1 (New York: Ungar, 1963), 129.

11. For 'an accurate representation of this wall,' Irving refers to 'an antique view of Nieuw Amsterdam, taken some few years after the above period [of its construction]' (589). This is probably the Restitutio view dated 1673, which shows the wall but is actually quite inaccurate. For this view and commentary, see John A. Kouwenhoven, *The Columbia Historical Portrait of New York* (New York: Doubleday, 1953), 45. The 'Stuyvesant manuscript' is unidentifiable and may have been invented for items Irving collected pertaining to that director's period, yet facts attributed to it hold up (see note 4). *Council Minutes, 1652-1654*, trans. and ed. Charles T. Gehring. *New York Historical Manuscripts*, vol. 5 (Baltimore: Genealogical Publ., 1983), 14, 69; J. Paulding, *Affairs and Men of New Amsterdam in the Time of Governor Peter Stuyvesant* (New York: Childs, 1843), 34-35. For Irving's time, Mary W. Bowden, *Washington Irving* (Boston: Twayne, 1981), 42.

12. Abraham van der Aa, *Biografisch Woordenboek der Nederlanden* (Amsterdam: Israel, 1969), 2: D 18; G.M. Asher, *A Bibliographical and Historical Essay on the Dutch Books and Pamphlets Relating to New Netherland* (Amsterdam: Israel, 1960), 11; I. N. Phelps Stokes, *The Iconography of Manhattan Island, 1498-1909* (New York: Dodd, 1915) 1: plate 7a.

13. Arnoldus Montanus, *De Nieuwe en Onbekende Weereld* (Amsterdam: Jacob Meurs, 1670), 123. A secondary meaning of '*wip*' is '*wipgalg*,' or, 'strappado.'

14. John Ogilby, *America: Being an Accurate Description of the New World* (London: Johnson, 1671), 171.

15. One of the *History*'s references to layered clothing. Common among the seventeenth-century Dutch, the habit persisted among Hudson Valley Dutch-Americans into Irving's day.

Paul Zumthor, *Daily Life in Rembrandt's Holland*, trans. George Weidenfeld et al. (London: Weidenfeld and Nicholson, 1962), 56. Into the nineteenth century, the Dutch outside of New York City adhered to their accustomed attire (Cooper, *Notions*, 189).

16. Henry C. Lea, *Superstition and Force* (Philadelphia: Lea, 1892), 466-67, 516, 543; Leo Lensen and Willy Heitling, *Tussen Schandpaal en Schavot* (Zutphen: Terra, 1986), 32, ill., 37; *Oxford English Dictionary*, 'strappado,' *n*. Strappado occurred indoors in New Netherland, during Stuyvesant's tenure, involving the Quaker Robert Hodstone for continuing to preach in public. Edmund B. O'Callaghan, *History of New Netherland*, vol. 2 (New York: Appleton, 1846), 347-49, 457.

17. Philip Mackey, 'Capital Punishment in New Netherland,' *De Halve Maen* 47.2 (1972), 7; Joyce Goodfriend, 'Crime and Law Enforcement: Dutch,' in Jacob Ernest Cooke, et al, eds., *Encyclopedia of the North American Colonies*, vol. 1 (New York: Scribner, 1993), 403-04; Pieter Spierenburg, *The Spectacle of Suffering* (Cambridge: Cambridge University Press, 1984), 111, 186.

18. Irving's letter to his brother Ebenezer in December 1819, *Letters*, vol. 23, Ralph M. Aderman et al, ed., *The Complete Works of Washington Irving* (Boston: Twayne, 1978), 573.

19. *Journals and Notebooks, 1803-1806*, vol. 1 of *The Complete Works of Washington Irving*, ed. Nathalia Wright (Madison: Wisconsin University Press, 1969), 445. On this visit, Irving did not travel further north than Rotterdam. His second stay in Europe (1815-1832) occurred after the first two editions of the *History* had appeared and did not affect its content in later versions of this work.

20. G.D.J. Schotel, *Het Oud-Hollandsch Huisgezin der Zeventiende Eeuw*, ed. H.C. Rogge, 2nd rev. ed. (Arnhem: Strengholt-Guisbers & Van Loon, 1903), 377, 381, 384; J.J. Voskuil, 'De Verspreiding van Koffie en Thee in Nederland,' *Volkskundig Bulletin* 14 (1988): 71, 74; Charlotte Wilcoxen, *Seventeenth Century Albany: A Dutch Profile* (Albany: Albany Institute of History and Art, 1984), 105. Those of small means in Europe and the Hudson Valley would dip a suspended piece of sugar for a few seconds to conserve this commodity. Rufus A. Grider, Ms. 'Travels in Mohawk, Cherry and Schoharie Valleys, 1886-1900,' Grider Collection, New York State Library, Albany, New York, box 8, file 73.

21. Donald Haks, *Huwelijk en Gezin in Holland in de 17de en 18de Eeuw* (Assen: Van Gorcum, 1982), 109-11.

22. For the Hudson Valley, Anne Grant, *Memoirs of an American Lady*, 2 vols. in 1, vol. 1 (Boston: Wells, 1809), 38-39, 55-58. J. L. de Jager, *Volksgebruiken in Nederland* (Utrecht: Spectrum, 1981), 48-49; Haks, *Huwelijk*, 112-13; Schotel, *Huisgezin*, 217.

23. Van Tienhoven arrived in New Netherland in 1633 and served in various functions until his dismissal in 1656. His personal and public behavior is part of Van der Donck's *Vertoogh* (see note 4).

24. Helge Gerndt, *Fliegender Holländer und Klabautermann* (Gottingen: Otto Schwartz, 1971), 115.

25. Charles W. Jones, *St. Nicholas of Myra, Bari, and Manhattan* (Chicago: Chicago University Press, 1988), 338, 341-42; Katharine Schuyler Baxter, *A Godchild of Washington: A Picture of the Past* (New York: F. Tennyson Neely, 1897), 651.

26. Martin Ebon, *St. Nicholas* (New York: Harper & Row, 1975), 57-58; J.L. de Jager, *Volksgebruiken in Nederland* (Utrecht: Spectrum, 1981), 148-49.

27. Irving was not the first to change Nicholas' attire. Rare wooden cookie molds from areas in the Netherlands that became Protestant upon the Reformation show him as a horseman, for example, with filled baskets and a miter, a beard, or a staff hinting at his identity. J.J. Schilstra, *Prenten in Hout* (Lochem: De Tijdstroom, 1985), 46-47, 133-34.

28. Washington Irving, *A History of New York*, ed. Edwin T. Bowden of the 1812 ed. (New Haven: New Coll. and University Press, 1964), 109.

29. Gulian C. Verplanck, 'Historical Discourse,' *Discourses and Addresses on Subjects of Ameri-*

can History, Arts, and Literature (New York: J. & J. Harper, 1833), 63.

30. The Van Cortlandt, Stuyvesant, Schuyler, and Bleecker families. Washington Irving, _Letters_, vol. 2, vol 24 of _The Complete Works of Washington Irving_, ed. Ralph M. Aderman et al (Boston: Twayne, 1979), 886.

31. E. J. Potgieter, 'Aan New-York,' _Poezy 1832-1868_, vol. 9 of _De Werken van E. J. Potgieter_, Comp. Joh. C. Zimmerman (Haarlem: H.D. Tjeenk Willlink, 1890), 22-28.

32. Washington Irving, _Bracebridge Hall_, in Herbert F. Smith, ed., _The Complete Works of Washington Irving_, vol. 9 (Boston: Twayne, 1977), 6.

33. Washington Irving, _Miscellaneous Writings, 1803-1859_, vol. 2 in Wayne R. Kime, ed., _The Complete Works of Washington Irving_, vol. 29 (Boston: Twayne, 1981), 113.

THE CUNARD LINE R.M.S. "CAMPANIA" & "LUCANIA" 12,950 TONS.

In August 1898 Abraham Kuyper crossed the ocean on the 'Lucania'. Coll. Historical Documentation Center for Dutch Protestantism, Vrije Universiteit Amsterdam.

George Harinck

HOMEWARD BOUND: NEW YORKER'S QUEST FOR AMSTERDAM AT THE END OF THE NINETEENTH CENTURY

Introduction

For a long time in our Western culture, traveling had a well-defined aim. People traveled, because it brought inner and outer fulfillment. They wrote in essence about traveling as an allegory of the path to salvation. Voyage had to do with destination. From the *Odyssey* to John Bunyan's *Pilgrim's Progress* a transcendental vision on traveling was dominant. The passage from Europe to America can be understood within this framework. For a long time crossing the Atlantic Ocean to the west has been a journey to a better world. America was the New World, the city upon a hill, the land of freedom. But if this vision of pilgrimage is the one pole in the history of travel, modern travel is the other pole. Since the nineteenth century traveling is an open-ended process. This does not mean that modern travelers do not carry the desire for a sacred vision. There are more destinations and more visions than ever. But the point is they never reach for it. The modern traveler does not look forward to a goal, but is motivated by a loss. He senses an absence of something richer, and fuller than the present. Consequently, modern travel writing is a literature of disappointment. Behind this lies in essence the ambivalence of our culture of modernity: it is constituted in opposition to a past, for which there is also a desire.[1]

This ambivalence is presented in modern travel writing. There is a conflict between progress and futility, between fulfillment and desire. As Henry Adams, one of the great travelers between Europe and America in modern times put it: 1900 showed itself as the key year, the year when 'the continuity snapped'.[2] The world had ceased to be a unity, and become a multiple, the present was no longer a continuation of the past but its own novel self. There is always traveling, but there is never a homecoming. This caused deep disappointment, and that is why we keep on reading and keep on traveling.

This unending quest for fulfillment is illustrated in the history of New York travelers to and travel writing on the Netherlands and Amsterdam at about 1900. The Netherlands were popular in the United States at the turn of the century. From the 1880s on, for about three decades the Netherlands were a regular topic in American newspapers and magazines, in the art scene, and in historic research. One author coined this interest for our country in the period between 1880 and 1914 with the term 'Holland Mania'. The popularity is clear, but as we will see, the reasons for it are complex.

To throw a light on the popularity of the Netherlands we have to ask why the people of the greatest nation on earth were interested in this small and unimportant country? For when it came to names and places, most Americans knew nothing about the geography of Europe. Holland could as well be Denmark.

There is a general explanation for the interest in Holland, and there is a special one. The general goes like this: Since Columbus' discovery we speak of the New World of America and consequently of the Old World of Europe. These were two worlds that did not seem to belong to each other, the one representing the future, the other the past, the one vibrant, the other tired, the one hopeful the other desperate. But history has shown time and again that both worlds were intimately entangled.

Towards the end of the nineteenth century America was in its Gilded Age. The United States had enjoyed material progress in the past decades, and the World's Columbian Exhibition of 1893, held in Chicago, was meant to prove that American power and progress were now outrunning the European.[3] American industry was not just competing with the two other great industrial powers, England and Germany, but outstripping their industrial production combined. Machines now made machines, the nation was committed to energy, capitalism and exponential growth. Europe was beaten, the West was won and the Frontier was closing. America seemed to have reached the gates of Eden. But right at that moment of ultimate fulfillment the Americans ran into uneasiness. As America presented itself as a country of power and fact, more exposed to sociological, economic and material forces, in short more than real, it was also less shaded by the mitigating influence of tradition, culture, and romance. At their new, unprecedented level of civilization the Americans needed a new stimulus, a new tradition. This was exactly what Europe had to offer, and not in the least the Netherlands. Our country had a name for its painters already, and for its history. John Lothrop Motley's books on Dutch history, published in the 1850s and 60s, placed our country on the American map of Europe. He explored the era of the founding of the Dutch Republic and pointed at parallels between the Dutch Republic in the 16th and 17th century and the American Republic in the 18th and 19th century. With his history books he provided the Americans with 'a landmark in the development of the future United States of America'.[4] In his trail, quite a few American historians stressed the similarity and consequently the inspiration of the history of the Dutch Republic to Americans, sometimes described as Europe's United States.[5] 'For about three quarters of a century,' one American travel writer noted in the early 20th century, 'when British or American readers thought about the Netherlands, it was the prose of Motley's *Dutch Republic* they had in mind.'[6] And ultimately it was themselves and their future they had in mind.

Consequently, although Motley's work was criticized by the best representatives of the sophisticated Dutch historical scholarship and in the United States as well,[7] this had no impact on the popularity of his books. Motley was, in fact, an anachronism from the start,[8] but in 1908, about half a century after its first publication, the Holland maniac William Elliot Griffis still thought it appropriate to edit and introduce a condensed edition of the work of the discoverer of Holland: *Motley's Dutch Nation, Being the Rise of the Dutch Republic*. Another image-builder was Mary Mapes Dodge's book *Hans Brinker, or, The Silver Skates*, published in 1865. Rowen stated that the American picture of the Netherlands was shaped 'most strongly not by formal guidebooks but by [this] book for boys and girls written by a woman who had never been to the country.'[9] The smallness of the Netherlands, its cleanliness, its wooden shoes, windmills and tulips, all contributed to the American's association of the Netherlands as an idyllic place, the absolute and contrast to the modern, harsh American city. Holland was the perfect nation to fulfill American dreams at that time: distant and yet so near, alien and akin at the same time.

It was in this context that the Holland Societies arose. The Holland Society of New York was established in 1885, the Holland Society of Chicago in 1895. Their aim was to collect and preserve information relating early Dutch history in North America, and to perpetuate, foster and promote the principles and virtues of their Dutch ancestors.

The American interest for the Netherlands was ignited by a sense of loss, but fuelled by the growing fear that the established American culture would be overwhelmed by the cultures of new immigrants from Southern and Eastern Europe.[10] As Theodore Roosevelt stated in his 1890 address to the Holland Society of New York, of which he was a prominent member: 'The thoroughness with which the Hollander has become Americanized... makes him invaluable as an object-lesson to some of the races who have followed him to America at an interval of about two centuries.'[11] The assumption was that American and Dutch culture and character were closely allied, and that the word Holland stood for liberty and Puritan heritage.

The New Amsterdam Frame

This brings us to New York as the special explanation for the American interest in Holland. Between 1860 and 1890 ten million Europeans immigrated into the United States. The American urban population quadrupled in the four last decades of the 19th century. By 1900, the foreign-born made up three-quarters of the population of New York. Americans were rapidly becoming urban people with urban values. Of course, the same urbanizing process was taking place all over Europe too; Paris, Vienna and Berlin went through great civic reconstructions at the same time, and Amsterdam grew fast since the 1870s. But American cities were distinctive. The frontier West was officially closed in 1890, but the frontier was now extended to the city. Cities like New York were a cultural and social novelty, a laboratory for urban planning and landscape. Cities were places of confusion and contrast, and they were very modern and commercial places too. New York became a modern metropolis, and the index of American character. Skyscrapers started to dominate the skyline of New York, aided by new features like steel construction, the elevator, and the revolving door. The metropolitan underground entered the scene, as did Edison's electric light. The key figures in William Dean Howells' novel *A Hazard of New Fortunes* (1890), returning to Manhattan after many years, 'looked down [Broadway], and found it no longer impressive... all that certain, processional, barbaric gaiety of the place is gone.' On the other had, the city had become the place of radicals, bohemians, beggars, and strikers, and they 'engage this world with urbane fascination, preferring its shocks and pleasures to the virtues of the civilizing periphery.'[12] But there were dark and gloomy places too, as police reporter Jacob A. Riis showed in his famous *How the Other Half Lives: Studies among the Tenements of New York*, published in the same year. He qualified the New York tenements as 'a storm-centre forever of our civilization.'[13] There were riots and massive strikes in the early 1890s; there was financial panic in 1893. In this dynamic, contrasting and confusing New World the original population of New York had a hard time getting to grips with modern life.

These New Yorkers tried to get a hold on the situation by stressing their roots. Confronted by rapid urban development that blurred the class boundaries and social credentials, they constituted a community of feeling that was locally based and delimited by class and heritage. The Victorian ideal of sharp cultural distinctions yielded to the modernist project of integrating human nature and social experience. These New Yorkers successfully constructed their own past and wrote 'patrician histories' of New York in which they idealized the colonial past of the city. These histories of 'Old New York' stressed the continuity and viewed the city history as a steady forward march and the New Yorkers as a seamless whole, and Dutch in its culture. What mattered was not so much a specific time period or geography but rather that this idealized colonial New York – devoid of immigrants, skyscrapers and rapid transit – offered upper- and middle-class New Yorkers an emotional alternative to the modern city. To improve the level of knowledge of Old New York several devices were employed. Historic tours were organized, historic tablets erected at places like the sites of Fort Amsterdam, dozens of educational courses were given – Theodore Roosevelt and the Princeton Professor Woodrow Wilson often appeared as guest lecturers in classes of the City History Club of New York, founded in 1896 - , and historic houses were saved from demolition and opened its doors to the general public, like the Van Cortlandt House (1896) and the Dyckman House Museum (1915). The three hundredth anniversary of Henry Hudson's discovery of the Hudson River and the two hundredth anniversary of Robert Fulton's invention of the steamboat were celebrated in 1909 by a parade - according to one journalist 'a "city history lesson three miles long"' – watched by more than two million spectators. The organizing committee gave a touch of Dutchness to the celebration: except for the Iroquois and the Dutch no ethnic elements were allotted in the parade. In the Netherlands a Hudson-Fulton Commission had been founded, and its members, among them the prominent Dutch politician and theologian Abraham Kuyper, were honorary foreign councilors of the Hudson-Fulton Celebration Commission of the State of New York.[14] The Dutch Commission built and sent a replica of Hudson's Dutch ship 'De Halve Maen' to New York to enhance the celebration.[15]

It is no surprise that in this sentimental mood a direct link was forged between the modern New Yorkers and the colonial Dutch, between New Amsterdam and the capital of the Netherlands. The heyday of the Old New York myth lasted from 1880 till 1920 and was part of the Holland mania. But the link between New Amsterdam and Amsterdam was not much elaborated upon: 'The imagined city was distinguished less by its physical space than by its promise of community and personal meaning.'[16] Amsterdam was not necessarily a place to visit. It functioned in the background in imagined histories and picture books of old New York and no one needed to leave the city or even his house to go on a historic pilgrimage. The New Amsterdam frame offered a solution to concerns about identity – indeed the very problem of modernity.

How Dutch Can You Get?
Other American regions took up the Netherlands as a novelty, but residents of New York and other old Dutch communities in the East had a deeper stake in the national focus on Holland. In 1896 the City History Club was founded out of the conviction that New York

was being overrun by 'hundreds of thousands of illiterate Hungarians, Italians, Slavs, Jews, Turks, Armenians, Greeks and Bohemians – the rag-tag and bobtail of the earth, most of whom never heard of history, do not know what it is, and herd in the tenements like rabbits in a warren.'[17] Clashes like in Scorcese's *Gangs of New York* were history, but the uneasiness about the new type of immigrants still existed. Feeling ambivalent in the new metropolis, the Club clung to the Dutch heritage of New York as an anchor in a modern city life full of uncertainties, and at the same time as a means to participate in it. The heritage was turned into a herald of the future. This feeling spread among New Yorkers. Many histories of New York and colonial America were published, in which the Dutch influence was actualized.

The Club's publications included the *New Amsterdam Year Book*, but it was preceded by *The New Amsterdam Gazette*, first published in July 1883.[18] It was a ten-cent weekly, later on monthly, published by Morris Coster, and 'devoted to the history and customs of the founders of New York'. The magazine was meant to be a 'medium between the old and new, recalling to the New Yorkers of today the early foundation of their city, by acquainting them with the current history of Holland', as the editorial in the first issue stated. The subscription price was kept low to underline the will that the *Gazette* would come within the reach of all, 'so that the pride hitherto taken in the Dutch, instead of being almost wholly of a traditional character, may become a thing of to-day.' This pride was for New York use only. When on February 27, 1885, the *Gazette* acknowledged the receipt of the first issue of *De Moederland* (The Motherland), devoted to promote international connection between Dutchmen in foreign countries and those at home, the editor doubted its success in the United States, as 'we hardly believe our Dutch friends have time to spare for attending to new periodicals of the Fatherland, considering also the vast amount of English literature on hand.'

The only institute that still represented the old country in the New World was the Dutch Reformed Church, prominently present in New York as well. Though the *Gazette* promised to keep its columns clear of all religious controversies, preference was given to this church in noticing special events of a religious character. Especially here the Netherlands came close by. The editor did not have to wait long for religious news, for Abraham Kuyper was stirring the Reformed Church in the Netherlands. On occasion of the centennial of the Theological Seminary of the Dutch Reformed Church at New Brunswick (an hour south of New York), Ph.J. Hoedemaker, theology professor at Kuyper's Free University in Amsterdam, informed the readers of the *Gazette* that 'a revival of the old principles which are ever new, is changing the aspect of our Church, our State, and our theology.'[19] When two years later, Kuyper from his Amsterdam headquarters led a secession from the Reformed Church, the *Gazette* reported that suspended ministers preached to Amsterdam crowds in large halls procured for preaching places. Eager to be a medium between Old and New Amsterdam, the *Gazette* observed in this Amsterdam struggle 'precisely the same influences and issues which agitate churches' in the States as well.[20] However, in the issue of August 1, 1888, the Dutch Reformed minister Henry Dosker (born in the Netherlands) was reported to have said that 'the charm of the movement is greater at a distance than at close quarters.'[21] While the magazine showed some interest in the actual Dutch church struggle, without a living ecclesiastical link even this Dutch connection was not strong enough to get the New Yorkers interested in present day Holland. For the same reason a plan to found a church in Brooklyn of the Reformed denomination with services in the Dutch language did not get support in the 1880s. It was Dutch New York that was at stake, not the Dutch.

Ancestry seemed to forge a tighter link. In August 1888 a group of members of the New York Holland Society organized a trip to the Netherlands for the first time, 'to become personally convinced of the beauties of that country of which they had heard and read so much, and also to offer a tribute to the principles of freedom of the Dutch people',[22] as the secretary of the Holland Society George W. Van Siclen put it eloquently. The company was composed entirely of men whose Dutch ancestors colonized North America. The trip turned into a media event. The editor of the European edition of *The Herald of New York* appointed a Dutch journalist, Lehman Israels (a brother of the painter Jozef Israels), to join the company and report extensively about the trip. The Dutch newspapers *Algemeen Handelsblad* and *Nieuwe Rotterdamsche Courant* did the same, and the *Gazette of New Amsterdam the Gazette* devoted two issues to this event. The group visited the Dutch towns and were officially welcomed everywhere. The *Gazette*'s account of their arrival in Amsterdam on Thursday, August 9, was impressive:

When the train containing the visitors arrived at the Central Station in Amsterdam, an immense crowd was assembled. The procession [of twenty-five landaus] itself was imposing; the people cheered, waved their hats, and the sentries and police saluted. The hotels where they alighted [Doelen Hotel and Hotel Rondeel] were surrounded by people. The American and Dutch flag were entwined with the banner of the Society, on which was inscribed: 'Eindelyk wordt een spruit een boom'. The Kalverstraat – the Broadway of Amsterdam – resounded with American airs. Since the anniversary of the 70th birthday of the King [February 19, 1887] no such enthusiasm was shown in the capital of Holland.[23]

The love the members of the Holland Society bore for the Netherlands was expressed not only in their pride, bearing Dutch names like Voorhees or Van Wyck, 'but also by the throbbing of the blood in our veins'.[24] The Dutch connection after all was a living thing, the Netherlands still being there. It was no surprise then, that quite a few of the New York visitors used their stay in Holland to trace their ancestry or relationship to families still living in the Netherlands. Others associated with the Netherlands by becoming a member of the Leyden Third of October Society.

Burghers or Burglars
After the Civil War American mass tourism to Europe started to blossom. The steamship lines carried Americans out of the various ports of the country to Europe, at the rate of four or five thousand a week: 'Everybody was going to Europe – I, too, was going to Europe', as Mark Twain wrote at the start of his *The Innocents Abroad* (1869).[25] This was the era of Thomas Cook (1808-1891), and the organized tour. Having started with his travel business in 1841, in the early 1850s Thomas Cook introduced 'vacation packages' to the continent, including tickets, sleeping accommodations, guides, and so on. In 1860, something like a 1000 American tourists visited Rome; at about 1900 the numbers were 40,000. About 90,000 American tourists returned from Europe through the New York customs by

1891. Paris became such an important stop on the social trail that the *New York Herald* established an edition there, filled with society news. Mobility became a distinguished aspect of modern life, offering possibilities that were unthinkable in the times before the Civil War. The New York clergyman William E. Griffis traveled to the Netherlands more than ten times. And Mark Twain crossed the Atlantic 39 times.

Americans were all looking in Europe for education and cultural acquisition. The old continent had to redeem them with something they missed at home. Quite a few settled in Europe for some time. In about 1890 an American colony was founded in the Latin Quarter in Paris, and in 1900 about 50,000 Americans lived in London. Europeans observed a wandering, oddly-dressed white tribe who expected Europe to be more like America, cleaner and simpler and more respectful.

England, Germany, France, and Italy were popular, but the Netherlands had never been a regular stop on the grand tour of the Americans. Tourist travel to the Netherlands remained negligible until the 1880s. If this country was part of the trail, it was often because their ships lay in the harbors of Rotterdam and Antwerp. Not more than a few days were spent here. The first record of an American tourist in The Netherlands was the account of Elkanah Watson in 1784. The first Baedeker, Murray or Bradshaw guidebooks on the Netherlands were published in the 1830s.

Increased awareness of America's Dutch heritage meant that also inhabitants without personal Dutch ancestry were apt to tour Holland. The Nederlandsch-Amerikaansche Stoomvaart Maatschappij (NASM) started a regular passenger service between Rotterdam and New York in 1872. The Red Star Line was founded in 1873, and sailed between Philadelphia and Antwerp, its fares being somewhat lower than those of the NASM. In the 1880s the NASM had a fleet of passenger ships and the crossing time had been cut from 16 to 9 days. A roundtrip second class fare cost $ 90, well within the means of the more affluent members of the middle class.[26] To aid advertising itself in the United Sates the name of the company was changed in 1896 into Holland-America Line. At about 1900 the Netherlands was visited by approximately 30.000 American visitors a year, tourists and business, but only a dozen Americans actually lived in Amsterdam.

At first the Dutch hardly realized the popularity of their country, but this changed when by the 1890s American publishers began producing many more American accounts of travel in Holland. Till 1914 about 200 American travel accounts on the Netherlands were published, of which 15 were devoted to this country alone, while 100 accounts dealt with the Netherlands up to 10 percent.[27] A clear sign of the rising popularity of the Netherlands was the inexpensive popular edition of Edmondo De Amici's *Holland and its People* by the New York publisher G.P. Putnam's Sons, which went through five printings in its first two years, 1880-1882.[28] Rather than using analogies between Dutch and Italian cities, Putnam's edition compared Amsterdam to New York and The Hague to Washington, D.C. An illustrated edition followed suit.

American tourists generally made the same tour in the Netherlands, directed by the guidebooks. They did not visit the Netherlands for the roaring city life, but for a quick glance at some renowned paintings and to get a quick glance of a country modern life had passed by, as indicated in the guidebooks. Characteristic is how Mark Twain went like a whirlwind through Holland and Belgium in 1879 and made some short notes. On the country: 'No wonder Wm III pined for Holland, the country is so green & lovely,

& quiet & pastoral & homelike.' On Rotterdam: 'How very pretty & fresh & amiable & intelligent the middle class Dutch girls are. Wish they would come over to us instead of the Irish.' And on Amsterdam: 'bricked square filled with cheap trash (Jews)... Went to the Museum & saw Rembrandt's Night Watch & his portraits of some burghers, or burglars.'[29] Burghers or burglars: this ambivalence is present in many travel accounts of the Netherlands.

In many travel books Dutch sites were described as famous pictures from two centuries previous, ensuring that the reader would form a clear mental picture, and reinforcing the notion that Holland was old-fashioned and unchanging. This sense of history controlled the American view of Holland. According to the Americans the Dutch were liberty-loving people. They came to Holland expecting to see their democratic and republican values at work. For this reason the House of Orange was in high esteem as a safeguard of liberty. When King William III died on November 23, 1890, a memorial service was held on December 3 in the Holland Reformed Church, Houston Street, New York. The service was presided by Rev. Daniel Van Pelt, who had resided for six months in The Hague in 1889. Psalm 24 was sung in Dutch, followed by an address in Dutch by Maurice Ossewaarde of New Brunswick Theological Seminary. Special mention was made of the fact that the church owed its foundation directly to the policy of Maurice of Orange, as opposed to that of his adversary John of Barneveldt. King William III was hailed for securing perfect liberty of opinion and worship, making him worthy of honorable remembrance by the Dutch Reformed emigrants of 1847, and also for having contributed a considerable sum of money to purchase the present building of the New York congregation.[30]

Because of its cosmopolitan and industrial character Rotterdam failed to satisfy the American image of Holland. Rotterdam was too much like modern New York. Marken and Volendam were considered to be real Dutch. In the real world, even Amsterdam was disappointing to the Americans. Hare wrote in 1884: 'Now we entered Amsterdam, to which we had looked forward as the climax of our tour, having read of it and pondered upon it as the 'Venice of the North', but our expectations were raised much too high.'[31] In 1888 Smith Ely was struck by the changes that had taken place since she visited the Netherlands twenty years ago: 'Amsterdam was a disappointment to me, everything is so modernized... The windmills are diminished in number and many of the canals have been filled in.'[32]

Added to the prosaic reality of Amsterdam was the realistic character of the seventeenth century paintings. As the popular illustrator Felix Darley put it, after having seen Rembrandts and Potter's bull: 'subjects are often disgusting, but their art, splendid'.[33] Another American judged he could have chosen a better subject than a 'scrubby-eight-months-old bull calf that would not be permitted to invade the Panhandle of Texas.'[34] Artists also had a more idyllic view of the Netherlands, and were attracted by the closed communities that still existed in modernizing Holland: Katwijk, Volendam, Egmond. But the greatest of them all, the painter and etcher James Whistler, in 1883 went to Amsterdam and did picture the reality of a modern city. He challenged the Amsterdam myth. His series of etchings of city views of 1889 was much appreciated by the Dutch critics and he himself counted them among his best etchings: 'He considered Amsterdam as a sunny, gay Southern town,' as one of the critics wrote.[35]

The civil authorities of Amsterdam did not really understand what the Americans were looking for and presented their town as a modern city. They facilitated the New York visitors of the Holland Society in 1888 with a 'Guide to Amsterdam', containing information on fares for cabs and carriages, the different streetcar routes, on steamboats, restaurants, coffee houses, refreshment rooms, oyster houses and confectionary establishments. The directory of post and telegraph offices, exchange offices, and bathing establishments were also mentioned in the book, followed by the locality of the principal churches of all denominations, places of amusements, and institutions. A map was added to the guide, as well as a description of the city. In this description the history of the city was told, with stress on its importance for international trade and as the home of the famous Dutch school of painting and sculpture. The importance of the Amsterdam harbor was underlined, the amelioration of the North Sea Canal, opened in 1876, and the construction of a new canal to the Rhine, which was in the course of construction. This guide made clear that there was an interest vice versa in the New Yorkers as well, but this interest was more commercial than culturally or historically oriented.[36]

American tourists who published on their Dutch journey were usually well-to-do, educated, white, male Protestants. Their prototype was Charles R. Erdman (1866-1960). Before he was called to the newly created chair of practical theology in 1906 to become 'the best loved man in the Presbyterian Church,' he had already traveled a lot. His journeys already started in the days he was a well-to-do student at Princeton Theological Seminary (1888-1891). He traveled throughout Europe for the first time in 1888, with a friend. They made a bicycle tour and did the Netherlands in a week. He had no Dutch ancestry, and his father had left the Dutch Reformed Church before he was born. So he had no special acquaintance with the Netherlands. They came from Germany and went via Arnhem, Utrecht and along Dutch windmills and waterways to Gouda. He noted what he saw, not what he had expected or envisioned: 'All day we have followed the course of one of the main canals', he wrote in his diary on August 29, 'and have had the full opportunity of examining this method of transportation: countless boats were moving along the still waters but were moved, not by *mules* but by *men*.'[37] They went to The Hague and saw the statue of 'the grand man, William of Orange'. Here Motley resonates, but no more than that. Erdman was hardly interested in paintings, but he did see Rembrandt's 'The School of Anatomy' and one or two other works by him – 'of great interest and great value when we remember that the one named was sold for $150.000.' The tour ended in Rotterdam, where the young Americans, tired of the strong wind, took the night boat to Antwerp.

The second time he visited Holland was the following year, with some American friends or relatives, among whom his wife to be, Mary Estelle Pardee, daughter of the Pennsylvania coal magnate Calvin Pardee. He traveled Europe, and also did Amsterdam this time. To him Amsterdam was just another European town. Coming from Scandinavia he and his company arrived on July 26, 1889. They stayed in the Amstel Hotel – together with Hotel Oude Doelen a popular place to stay for Americans. What did these well to do people from New York and vicinities do to entertain themselves in Amsterdam? While the ladies slept Erdman strolled through the town with a guidebook in his hand, and learned why the town was called a 'vulgar Venice', as he wrote in his travel diary: 'vulgar because the green water which stagnates in the canals is by no means cologne – because those narrow streets are even less pure, and are thronged with dirty children and odour and cheese and Jews.'[38] The Jews crossed his way again at another 'must see' of the guidebook: the

Jewish quarter. There were so many of them, that the theology student believed to have discovered the dwelling place of the ten lost tribes of Israel, having 'lived in that ghetto for centuries without even having purchased new clothes, or making any advance towards civilization... Let me advise the judo-maniac to never carry his researches or investigations into the odour and darkness of Prague or Amsterdam.' He ended the notes on his Amsterdam stay with a complaint on the Dutch who 'argue with you as to the amount of the gratuity you are expected to offer him... – we are no longer in civil Sweden or honest Norway.'

Holland was presented in the guidebooks as a pastoral Eden, but the reality of Amsterdam was often grim indeed. Lilian Leland wrote in 1890 to her relatives in the United States: 'I departed from Holland very much depleted in pocket, for my ancient countrymen are the worst in Europe, I believe, when it comes to fleecing the unhappy traveler.'[39] Most of Erdman's impressions were also quite negative: Holland was a country of burglars. But in the afternoon he took a drive with the ladies and when they crossed bridge after bridge he was impressed by 'a long vista of water overarched by trees', by the docks with their abundant shipping and by the new Central Railway Station. They had the next day at their disposal to visit the museums – in his diary he mentioned just one painting, Rembrandt's 'Night Watch' - and to leave for 'beautiful' The Hague, which he appreciated much better. On July 30 they crossed the border into Belgium.

The Best-Informed American in New York
As the United States and New York were confronted with a huge mass of catholic and other non-protestant ('sectarian') immigrants, the fact that the Netherlands were a protestant country turned out to be an attractive feature. It was a special attraction that once the Pilgrims had lived in Holland. As the Netherlands became a more popular destination, the short period of their stay began to loom larger in American interpretations of Pilgrim history. There was a lively interest in places where the Pilgrims were said to have lived, like Brownists's Alley in Amsterdam or John Robinson's house in Leiden. Griffis noted that in 1914 that Americans had erected thirteen memorials in Holland to their own historical roots there.[40]

In the early 1880s no one knew exactly where in Delfshaven the Pilgrims had spent their last hours in Holland. But after Horace Scudder in 1882 published his children's book *The Bodley Grandchildren and Their Journey in Holland*, in which the literary heroes walked the whole length of Delfshaven waterfront to be sure they had not missed the point of embarkation,[41] lots of tourists did the same. So many came to walk the waterfront, that in the 1890s the Delfshaven civil authorities decided to give imagination a hand and renamed one of their quays Pelgrim Kade – Pilgrim Quay.

While not always accepted in its entirety, no historian in about 1900 could afford to ignore the Dutch contribution to America's democratic origins. One of main contributions to this view was made by William Elliot Griffis (1843-1928), the most experienced New York traveler of the Netherlands, who visited the country eleven times and published several well read books on the topic. They differ from other books on the Dutch-American connection by personalizing the transatlantic connection, thus making it 'relevant and believable to the average American'.[42] He constantly stressed the similarities between the United States of America and what he called the United States of the Netherlands. The Dutch were very important in shaping the American mind. They imported religious toleration, free press, free schools, local self-government, written ballots and a written constitution. Reading Griffis' pages, a Dutchman cannot but blush.

Though he had no Dutch ancestry, Griffis — better known as Japan specialist, who lived in Japan and wrote *The Mikado's Empire* (1876), the first general introduction to Japanese history and culture in English - had a special interest in the Netherlands and its culture.[43] He studied at the seminary of the Dutch Reformed Church in New Brunswick (1869-1870) and with his sister and a friend, he visited the Netherlands for the first time on a European tour in 1869, to return there many times, including 1891, 1892 and 1898. He learned to read Dutch, and in 1892 took daily Dutch lessons with father and son Lelieveld in Rotterdam. From the 1890s on, he published a lot on his trips to the Netherlands and on Dutch history. As minister of the First Reformed Church in Schenectady (1877-1886) he researched Dutch-American documents in the New York State Library and the City Hall of Albany. Known as a Dutch specialist he was named an honorary member of the Netherlands Society of Philadelphia, founded in 1892, and was appointed a member of the Dutch Society of Arts and Letters in 1896. In the 1890s Griffis was the best-informed American on the East coast on Netherlands and Dutch culture.

When in the Netherlands, Griffis did not act like an ordinary American tourist, but went off the beaten track. He toured all the provinces, attended services in the various churches, protestant and Roman Catholic, shared in Dutch festivities, like the *kermis* in Franeker ('at the kermis 10.30- 12.30 [P.M.] watching the people. Retired at 1 but no sleep till 4. Streets full of singing people and all night starlight.'[44]), attended a Princess Wilhelmina organ concert in the St. Laurens Church in Rotterdam in 1892, and collected Dutch fairy tales. He considered a visit to the Netherlands as a healthy resort from the stress of daily New York life: 'the country in general induces a spirit of quiet restfulness, so grateful to the overwrought American'.[45]

In the debates in the 1890s about the historical relevance of Holland to the United States, a special area of interest emerged in church history. Douglas Campbell and Griffis accepted the Dutch origin of American religious toleration as a basic part of their thesis. The predominant Protestant experience of many New Yorkers predisposed them to take a positive view of the Netherlands. The churches in Amsterdam were not appreciated very much, but the fact that the protestant religion was dominant certainly contributed to the positive view of the city.

Their books became popular in the United States, Campbell's history on the Dutch impact on American history having three editions in 1892. The new interest for Holland changed the image of the colonial Dutch as lazy dreamers and stupid humorists, set by Washington Irving's absurd wonderful legends of old Knickerbocker New York, published in 1809 and the best known discussion of the colonial Dutch published before 1880.[46] In its place for example Campbell offered this much more positive image: 'if an American of the present generation could go back to the Dutch Republic of two centuries and a half ago, he would find himself in a familiar land, because he would be among a people of the nineteenth century.'[47] Campbell considered the ideas of seventeenth-century Holland essentially modern, as they correlated so well with ideas he saw operating in the United States.

Griffis appreciated Motley's books, but his historical research in a time that the link between the self image of the American of the 1890s and the Dutch Republic became substantial, created room for a critical approach of the master: 'If here and there I have disagreed with Motley', Griffis wrote in 1894, 'it is because I have thought that illustrious writer more dramatic and subjective than scientific in some of his statements. Brave little Holland taught our fathers many things which the true historian of the American republic can no longer afford to ignore.'[48] He adapted Motley's views on some points. In his eagerness to tell a thrilling story, Motley for example had ignored 'those forces which are more powerful in their energy than picturesque in their expression (...) The story of Holland, and especially her great struggle with Spain, cannot properly be told without due and proportionate emphasis being laid on all the forces in play, and *the religious motive was the deepest and strongest.*'[49] Griffis was clearly influenced by the recent historical publications of Fruin and Groen and introduced their opinions in the United States. But he hardly used the word Calvinism to describe this religion – a clear sign he was no Kuyperian.[50] Instead he wrote that the Netherlands fought 'for Christendom and for humanity'.[51] Griffis judged that Motley as a Modernist and Unitarian was unable to do justice to the Calvinistic religion of the Dutch. But it is exactly for this religion that the American must feel indebted to the Dutch.

On another point, Griffis pushed the comparison between the Dutch and the American Republic further than Motley had done. The recent experience of the civil war had not alienated the course of American history from its Dutch predecessor. Quite the contrary, it had increased the appreciation of the Dutch republic, its trials and triumphs. According to Griffis, Motley's depiction of Maurice, Barneveldt and the Synod of Dordt 'reminds one of the typical denominational sermon... Motley shows himself too much the partisan':

We who knew at the time, and understand now, the real meaning of Chancellorsville, of Gettysburg, and of Appomattox, need not be told what the civil troubles of 1619 meant. Barneveldt, despite all his noble services to the State, and 'the deep damnation of his raking off,' stood for Calhounism and disunion. (...) Maurice stood for national unity, for the life of the commonwealth... the real question at issue was like ours in 1861 – the existence of the Republic.[52]

Apart from his historical knowledge based on study and his regular visits of all provinces, he knew many important Dutchmen in religious, cultural and academic life personally. In 1892 he met among others Abraham Kuyper, and the Leiden professors J.H.C. Kern and G. Schlegel. Especially his notes of the 1892 trip offer a vivid impression of his contacts: on July 18 he met in Amsterdam J.A. Sillem, publisher of *De Gids*, and the medical professor T. Place, on July 19 he went to Leiden and had a 'pleasant evening with professor Blok on historical matters'. The next day he went to Utrecht, 'called on professor Doedes, and spent nearly two hours in his study, talking on first translations and editions of the Scriptures in Dutch, his daughter translating.' Thursday July 21 he had a conversation with theology professor J.J.Ph. Valeton on Utrecht University. He then traveled to Den Bosch ('fine old Catholic Church'), Zeist ('beautiful avenues, trees, houses and gardens'), talked with the minister of the Moravian Church. July 22 he took the train to Kampen, called 'the New Brunswick of the Christian Reformed Church',[53] where the Theological Seminary of this denomination was ('called on prof. Noordtzij, piloted around by his son [Arie], and another young man from South Africa'), and went off for Groningen and the historic site of Heiligerlee, to end his tour in Groningen on July 24, where he went to a service of the Free Evangelical Church, where Rev. [A.M.] Mooij preached.[54]

His most interesting contact was Abraham Kuyper. In his diary he described how on Sunday June 14, 1891, he stayed in the Bible Hotel in Amsterdam, and went out with his Japanese friend Rev. T. Harada to experience Dutch church life:

Entered first the Nieuwe Kerk, nearly all seats full, heard slow, grand congregation singing, large bibles on desks, and heard prayer, salutation, text and exortium of Rev. [E.] Barger. On leaving, was directed by elderly gentleman and let out by section, with key. Going down to Begynhof, 5 minutes in a catholic church, and in English church built 1609 (200 members, mostly Dutch people who speak English), heard the prayer and looked in. Then, went to the Dolerende ('remonstrant') church on Keizerstraat [Keizersgracht], built in modern style borrowed largely from America, fine, large, handsome, crowded. Sermon by Dominie Rynier [C.A. Renier], well written, enunciation clear, effect good. Lay reader, elders and deacons in special pews. We visited study – fresh cigar smoke – saw Sunday and day schools in the rear... After dinner, with Harada, called on Dr. Kuyper, leader of the dolerende party, or remonstrants. In his lovely Dutch home [Prins Hendrikkade], we were most cordially welcomed by the great man, and so pleasantly did the hours pass that ten o'clock was soon come and gone. Prof. [D.P.D.] Fabius and [space left open for name; presumably F.L. Rutgers] also came in and joined in conversation. All spoke English well. In Dr. Kuyper's study he showed me his edition of John A Lasco's works, and some of his own other writings, large bronze bust of John Calvin in the hall. Rich talk and much suggestive conversation. Left at 10.30 glad to have spent an evening with the great leader.[55]

When he stayed in the Netherlands again in 1898, to report on the enthronement of Queen Wilhelmina from within the Nieuwe Kerk, he again visited Kuyper on August 4 who was about to leave for the United States: 'Dinner with Dr. A. Kuyper, wife, 2 daughters, miss [room left open for name] of Hilversum, son, and English lady, correspondent of The Gentlewoman, of England. Tea in the garden, 6 – 8.30.'[56]

Confusion

All this traveling and travel writing, combined with a feeling of snapping continuity, had a strange effect on the notion of place and time. The Americans traveled to see the original paintings of Rembrandt and Hals and Ruysdael they knew from their guidebooks, and expected more or less also to see the living models. Most American travel books did not pay enough attention to the Netherlands to correct this view, and if they did, they usually agreed with the consensus image of Holland as a land of windmills and wooden shoes. Staying in Holland for such brief periods, they naturally misunderstood some of what they saw and modernizations were easily overlooked. The Dutch cities facilitated this view of Holland, for quite a few of them contained an old quarter dating back to the Middle Ages, and Amsterdam had its Jews in rags. The Holland-America Line promoted this historic view by publishing *A Journey through Old Holland*, a travel book in which the narrator fell asleep and in his dreams toured the Holland of the old masters with a seventeenth century Dutch-American colonist, just like Twain's Connecticut Yankee who after his car accident woke up in King Arthur's times. The voyage to Holland was a form of time travel. As Annette Stott put it:

> The character of Holland Mania depended upon a profound confusion of time... It is not surprising that many Americans began to associate colonial America with nineteenth-century Holland, and nineteenth-century America with the seventeenth-century Dutch Republic, or that the importance of Holland for many tourists was its role in American history – which they now believed they could readily see in the land and people around them as they traveled through the Netherlands.[57]

Some truth is hidden in Robert Louis Stevenson's famous saying: 'There is no foreign land. It is only the traveler that is foreign.' There is always traveling, and the travelers are homeward bound always and everywhere, but there is never a coming home. After his visit to the Netherlands the American travel writer Ernest Talbert reversed the usual formula of declaring a Dutch town in Holland unchanged through the centuries. In his opinion it was not Amsterdam, but New York that preserved 'the serene, unchanging atmosphere Americans admire so greatly in Holland, though they decry it at home'.[58] The search for American identity was not geographically bound. Griffis recognized America in the newly built Keizersgracht Church, just as Holland could be identified in the Collegiate Church and School of New York, built in 1892 on West End Avenue. This church's design was based on the Haarlem Vleeshal, which was considered a model of Dutch Renaissance architecture and the crowning achievement of Lieven de Key. The architect undoubtedly considered an early-seventeenth-century building a particularly appropriate model for a Dutch reformed church and school in an American city founded by the Dutch. Griffis, who for several years lived in the New York area, saw reminders of the city in several Dutch towns he visited, like Bloemendaal (Bloomingdale), Haarlem (Harlem) and Breukelen (Brooklyn). Many other Dutch inspired buildings appeared in New York City in de mid 1880s, like the John Wolfe Building, erected in 1895, and several blocks in New York's West End.

This sense of Dutchness could not be pushed too far. At the 40th annual dinner of the St. Nicholas Society of Nassau Island, held in Brooklyn on December 6, 1888, the president John W. Hunter 'was arrayed in his finest cocked hat, with the silver insignia of office hanging from a chain suspended from his neck. He looked that evening like a genuine Dutch Burgomaster, a type that Rembrandt loved to paint'.[59]

When Abraham Kuyper visited the United States in 1898, the confusion was complete. Griffis', Campbell's, and above all Motley's images of Holland were known in the English speaking world, and applied to all Dutch phenomena. When Albert Venn Dicey, professor of English Law at Oxford University, in October 1898 heard and saw Abraham Kuyper speech in Princeton, he recognized a seventeenth century Dutchman. He wrote to his wife:

> ...the most remarkable speech I have heard for a long time. Kuyper... looked like a Dutchman of the seventeenth century. He spoke slowly and solemnly. His English was impressive, with here and there a Dutch idiom. He told us he was a Calvinist; that he had been persecuted by anti-Calvinists – this itself sounded like the language of

another age. All the good in America had its roots in Calvinism, which was as much a legal and an ethical as a religious creed. The Continental States had sympathized with Spain [in the Spanish American War of 1898]. Not so the Dutch Calvinists. 'We have not forgotten our contest with Spanish tyranny; we fought it for a hundred years. In six weeks you have given Spanish power its *coup de grace*, but neither England nor the United States would have been free but for Dutch heroism. Spain has in all countries and in all ages been a curse to the world...' This was the tone of the whole speech. There was not a word of flattery to America. One felt as if the seventeenth century had visibly risen upon us to give the last curse to Spain.'[60]

In historic Amsterdam the American identity was searched for in vain, but it was recognized in a modern Dutchman who criticized the Americans for forsaking the mission they had inherited from the Dutch. The circle was closed.

Notes

1 Jaś Elsner and Joan-Pau Rubiés, 'Introduction,' in Ibidem, ed., *Voyages & Visions: Towards a Cultural History of Travel* (London: Reaktion Books Ltd., 1999), 8-15.

2 Quoted in Malcolm Bradbury, *Dangerous Pilgrimages: Trans-Atlantic Mythologies and the Novel* (London: Penguin Books, 1996), 251.

3 Winfried Kretschmer, *Geschichte der Weltausstellungen* (Frankfurt/New York: Campus Verlag, 1999), 139: 'Amerika nahm die Schau als massive Demonstration seiner Stärke, als Aufschein seiner neuen Weltmachtrolle.'

4 O.D. Edwards, 'John Lothrop Motley and the Netherlands,' in J.W. Schulte Nordholt and Robert P. Swierenga, eds., *A Bilateral Bicentennial. A History of Dutch-American Relations, 1782-1982* (Amsterdam: Meulenhoff), 179.

5 So did Willam Elliot Griffis. See: Annette Stott, *Holland Mania: The Unknown Dutch Period in American Art Culture* (Woodstock: The Overlook Press, 1998), 86.

6 G.W. Edwards, *Thumb-nail Sketches* (New York: Century & Co., 1891[4]), 173. Cf. O.D. Edwards, 'John Lothrop Motley and the Netherlands', in Schulte Nordholt and Swierenga, *A Bilateral Bicentennial*, 173: 'He [Motley] and he alone had created a Dutch awareness on a wide scale'.

7 See: Henry E. Dosker, 'Barneveldt, Martyr or Traitor,' *The Presbyterian and Reformed Review* 9 (1898): 289-323, 438-471, 637-658. Being a Calvinist, Dosker questioned Motley's view on John of Barneveldt and the Arminians. Edwards, 'Motley and the Netherlands,' 581, stated that Motley's sympathy for the Arminians was motivated by the hostility to his Unitarian faith in Massachusetts, in his youth. Griffis called the Dutch historian G. Groen van Prinsterer 'Motley's severest critic,' William Eliot Griffis, *Motley's Dutch Nation being the Rise of the Dutch Republic (1555-1584) by John Lothrop Motley. Condensed, with Introduction, and a Brief History of the Dutch People to 1908.* New edition (New York/London: Harper Brothers Publishers, 1908) 933.

8 Edwards, 'Motley and the Netherlands,' 178: 'His work stood strangely between pre-scientific partisanship and archivally dominated modernity of approach.'

9 Herbert H. Rowen, 'American Travelers in Holland Through Two Centuries' in Schulte Nordholt and Swierenga, *A Bilateral Bicentennial*, 228.

10 Stott, *Holland Mania*, 95.

11 *New Amsterdam Gazette*, 25 January 1890.

12 David M. Scobey, *Empire City. The Making and Meaning of the New York City Landscape*

(Philadelphia: Temple University Press, 2002), 266.

13 Scobey, *Empire City*, 267.

14 Clifton Hood, 'Journeying to "Old New York". Elite New Yorkers and Their Invention of an Idealized City History in the Late Nineteenth and Early Twentieth Centuries,' *Journal of Urban History* 18 (September 2002): 699-719. See: Henry W. Sackett to A. Kuyper, 28 June 1909. Kuyper Collection. Historical Documentation Center for Dutch Protestantism. Vrije Universiteit Amsterdam. A recently built replica of 'De Halve Maen' is operated by the New Netherland Museum, Albany NY.

15 On the history of this 1909 replica of 'De Halve Maen' see: Lincoln Diamant, *Hoopla on the Hudson: An Intimate View of New York's Great 1909 Hudson-Fulton Celebration* (New York: Purple Mountain Press, 2003), 122-125.

16 Hood, 'Journeying to 'Old New York',' 703.

17 Stott, *Holland Mania*, 95, quoted from *Harper's Bazar* 43 (August 1909): 766.

18 I made use of the first six volumes of the *New Amsterdam Gazette* (21 July 1883-7 January 1891), held in the library of Rutgers University, New Brunswick, NJ. The last issue of this *Gazette* appeared in January 1895 (vol. 8, nr. 4).

19 *New Amsterdam Gazette*, II, nr. 10, 30 May 1885.

20 *New Amsterdam Gazette*, V, nr. 4, 17 April 1888. See also on this topic: John Cairns, 'The present struggles in the national church of Holland,' *The Presbyterian Review*, 9, (January 1888): 87-108.

21 See: George Harinck, 'Henry Dosker, between Albertus C. Van Raalte and Abraham Kuyper,' *Origins. Historical Magazine of the Archives. Calvin College and Calvin Theological Seminary*, 19, 2, (2001): 34-41.

22 *New Amsterdam Gazette*, V, nr. 7, August 1888.

23 Idem.

24 G.W. Van Siclen, 'Valediction of the members of the Holland Society of New York on their departure from the Netherlands,' *New Amsterdam Gazette*, V, nr. 8, 17 September 1888. This valediction was inserted in some of the leading newspapers in Holland as well.

25 Quoted in Bradbury, *Dangerous Pilgrimages*, 158.

26 When the World's Conference of the Young Men's Christian Association was held in Amsterdam in August 1891, the Netherlands-American Steamship Company ran steamers from New York direct to Amsterdam, charging reduced excursion rates of $92, or $107 first class. *The Christian Intelligencer*, 17 June 1891.

27 Erika van der Linden, 'American Tourists in the Netherlands, 1784-1914,' MA Thesis, Katholieke Universiteit Nijmegen, 1990, 3. I am indebted to Van der Linden for her overview of American travel literature in the Netherlands, on which I relied heavily.

28 De Amici's book was popular in the United States, but was – and is – hardly purchased in the Netherlands. The only library that has the cheap 1880 edition is the Rijksdienst Monumentenzorg in Zeist; the Royal Library, The Hague, has a de luxe 'Zuyderzee' edition of 1885 and the Zeeuwse Bibliotheek has a 'Van Dyke' edition.

29 Frederick Anderson, Lin Salamo and Bernard L. Stein ed., *Mark Twain's Notebooks and Journals, volume II (1877-1883)* (Berkeley: University of California Press, 1975), 331, 329, 330.

30 A report of the service in *The Christian Intelligencer*, 10 December 1890.

31 A.J.C. Hare, *Sketches in Holland and Scandinavia* (New York: Rouledge, 1884), 39.

32 Quoted in: Pieter R.D. Stokvis, 'Some American Views of the Netherlands During the Nineteenth Century,' *De Negentiende Eeuw* 6 (1982): 67.

33 Felix O.C. Darley, *Sketches Abroad with Pen and Pencil* (New York: Hurd and Houghton, 1869), 85; quoted in Annette Stott, *Holland Mania*, 43.

34 Ibid., 134, 135.

35 Hans Kraan, *Dromen van Holland. Buitenlandse kunstenaars schilderen Holland, 1800-1914*

(Zwolle: Waanders, 2002), 224-249; quotation 231.

36 A description of the guide in *New Amsterdam Gazette*, V, nr. 8. The editor had received a copy of the guide from the secretary of the Holland Society. He had also seen the guide the Rotterdam authorities offered to the visitors, 'twice as well made up as the Guide issued for the same purpose at Amsterdam'.

37 Travel diary, 1888. Charles R. Erdman Collection, Box 1. Archives and Special Collections. Princeton Theological Seminary, Princeton, NJ, United States.

38 Travel diary, 1889. Charles R. Erdman Collection, Box 1.

39 Van der Linden, 'American Tourists,' 14.

40 Stott, 100. For a complete list see W.E. Griffis, 'Thankful America,' *The Outlook*, 106 (10 January 1914): 88-90.

41 Horace E. Scudder, *The Bodley Grandchildren and Their Journey in Holland* (Boston: Houghton Mifflin, 1882).

42 Stott, *Holland Mania*, 87.

43 There is no literature on Griffis and the Netherlands, except a short essay by A. Lammers, *De jachtvelden van het geluk. Reizen door historisch Amerika* (Amsterdam: Balans, 1998) 132-138; for a general introduction to Griffis, see: Robert A. Rosenstone, *Mirror and the Shrine. American Encounters with Meiji Japan* (Cambridge: Harvard University Press 1989), 9-18, 87-119, 185-205, 249-296.

44 Notebook trip to Europe, July 1 – September 14, 1892. Archives William Elliot Griffis. Special Collections, Alexander Library, Rutgers University, New Brunswick NJ. That year he made a 16 day tour through the Netherlands.

45 Stott, *Holland Mania*, 128; quoted from Griffis, *The American in Holland*, 198-199.

46 Stott, *Holland Mania*, 94.

47 Douglas Campbell, *The Puritan, in Holland, England, and America: An Introduction to American History*, 2 vols. (New York: Harper & Brothers 1892), 2: 358.

48 William E. Griffis, 'Preface,' *Brave little Holland and what she taught us* (Boston/New York: Houghton Mifflin Company, 1894), IX.

49 W. Elliot Griffis, 'The American in Holland,' *The Christian Intelligencer*, 5 August 1891.

50 See on the rise of the word Calvinism as characterization of the Protestant religion in the Netherlands: J. Vree, ''Het Réveil'en 'het (neo-)calvinisme' in hun onderling samenhang,' *Documentatieblad voor de Nederlandse Kerkgeschiedenis na 1800* 38 (juni 1993): 24-54.

51 Griffis, 'American in Holland'.

52 Idem.

53 Daniel Van Pelt, 'Kampen; or, the Protest Against State-Churchism,' *The Christian Intelligencer*, December 12, 1888.

54 Notebook 1892. Griffis Collection.

55 Notebook Summertrip to Europa, May 28 – September 24, 1891. Griffis Collection. The following year Griffis used these notes for the article 'An evening with Dr. Kuyper,' written in London on August 6 and published in *The Christian Intelligencer*, 31 August 1892.

56 Notebook trip to Europe, July 23 – September 25, 1898. Griffis Collection. The English lady presumably was Ethel Ashton, who gave English conversation lessons to Kuyper's daughters and helped him to prepare his Stone lectures on Calvinism, to be delivered at Princeton Theological Seminary in October 1898.

57 Stott, *Holland Mania*, 101, 102.

58 Ernest Talbert, *Old Countries Discovered Anew: A Motor Book for Everybody* (Boston: Dana Estes 1913), 64-65.

59 *New Amsterdam Gazette*, 17 December 1888.

60 Quoted in Peter S. Heslam, *Creating a Christian Worldview. Abraham Kuyper's Lectures on Calvinism* (Grand Rapids: Eerdmans, 1998), 65.

J.R. Planten, Consul-general
(1883-1911)
in New York City.

Hans Krabbendam

CAPITAL DIPLOMACY: CONSULAR ACTIVITY IN AMSTERDAM AND NEW YORK, 1800-1940

Introduction

Consuls are usually no heroes in literature. They often appear as intoxicated, indecisive, melancholic, cut loose from their roots – a sorry lot. The 'Consul,' Malcolm Lowry's protagonist in *Under the Volcano*, is a perpetual drunk. Charley Fornum, the 'Honorary Consul' in Graham Greene's book of the same name, suffers from the same quality and is a victim, rather than a creator of history. And yet the activities of these 'literary losers' offer a window to assess the importance of the cities of Amsterdam and New York in the foreign policies of the United States and the Netherlands.[1] I am interested in the role played by the official diplomatic representatives in these two powerful cities to find out whether the cities were able to use diplomatic channels to promote their own interests. The position of consul general seemed to offer a local instrument to influence opinion and policy in another country.

The title of this essay 'Capital Diplomacy,' refers to the role played by two capitals: Amsterdam and the unofficial 'capital' New York, as well as to the importance of the financial sector in diplomatic relations. It searches for parallel developments in the consular history of these cities, set in a historical context. The effectiveness of consular representatives in the cities depended on a combination of international, national, and local factors. Internationally, the global trade network and geo-political clashes influenced the bilateral exchange of goods and services. Nationally, the economic policies of the respective nations, the organization of the diplomatic corps, and internal developments of nation building determined the role of the consuls. Locally, swings in economic fortune and city organization affected the position of foreign diplomats, making them more or less important according to the changing conditions.

Even less than fictitious consuls, real-life consuls found biographers. While ambassadors and ministers are frequent subjects of serious studies, consuls as individuals rarely see the limelight.[2] Whereas American historians have assessed the efficiency of their consuls abroad, a Dutch counterpart has not yet emerged beyond the footnotes in works on Dutch-American commercial and political relations.[3]

American Consuls in Nineteenth-Century Amsterdam

It would have been nice for this volume were I able to start with the statement that Amsterdam and New York were the locations of the first consulates in Holland and America, but they were not. The first American consul was not appointed to Amsterdam, but to Surinam, Curacao, and St. Eustatius, and did not come from New York. The first Dutch consul in the young United States was not from Amsterdam, neither did he settle in New York. He was not even a success, this Mr. J.H.Chr. Heineken, a flimsy son of a pastor at Elburg, who arrived in Philadelphia, the provisional capital of the United States in 1784.[4]

The first American consul appointed to Amsterdam, the Bostonian James Greenleaf (1765-1843) was not to be trusted with money or women. His noble wife proved his best asset, providing an entry into the Amsterdam moneyed circles through her relation to president Willem Scholten van Aschat van Oud-Haarlem of the Amsterdam court.[5] With this introduction he tried to raise money in Amsterdam for the purchase of 6,000 city lots in America's new capital Washington, D.C., in the early 1790s.[6] However, few banks joined in, judging it too risky after the revolution in France, leaving Greenleaf in a painful position amidst various contesting claims. This failure delayed the building of the capital city severely. This young speculator was more interested in strengthening his credit line and growing rich than in being a diplomat. Therefore, the task to shape the consular post in Amsterdam was left to his successor, Greenleaf's business associate and fellow Bostonian Sylvanus Bourne (1761-1817).[7]

In Bourne, the consulate received a man with contacts in high places – he had been one of the messengers of Congress to George Washington to inform him of his election as president in 1789 – and some experience – Bourne had served as consul in Hispaniola since June 4, 1790 (also called Cape François /Santo Domingo). He was appointed vice consul on 29 May 1794 and was promoted to consul general in 18 June 1815.[8]

Despite his previous position, Bourne had no exact ideas about what his duties involved. His specific instructions were to protect the interests of American citizens and assist American sailors, but the circumstances inevitably moved him into diplomacy. His tenure between 1794 and 1817 covered a period of great upheaval and political tension in the Atlantic world. The appointment of John Quincy Adams as American Minister suspended Bourne's political tasks, but only temporarily, since during the majority of his stay the Netherlands was under French rule, no American political officer was stationed in The Hague, leaving Bourne the main U.S. representative in Amsterdam.[9] Bourne found himself in an awkward position, especially towards the end of his term, when Holland and England fought France, but England fought the US as well in the War of 1812. Bourne was promoted to Consul-General in 1815, but suffered from poor health and died in the spring of 1817, leaving a widow and two teenagers. He had accomplished much for Dutch-American trade. He had founded and solidified the American consular presence in the Netherlands, made a connection between commerce and politics and had proven that the consulate was indispensable in establishing confidence in international trade with America. His early death was mourned by the English Reformed Church of Amsterdam, in which he had occupied a prominent place.[10]

In order to execute his tasks Bourne advised his superiors how to shape the consular service and urge his government to use the navy against aggressors, for instance the Emperor of Morocco, to protect American interests. He liked his job and lived up to the expectations. He realized his era was one of fundamental and positive change, 'Revolutionary principles become daily more fashionable and the state of society in the old world is threatened with a total change – may this change advance the cause of human happiness.'[11] At the same time he felt the consequences in his own pocket. He complained about the obstructions of commerce for American vessels in October 1794, while his other main concern, the discharge of crews of American vessels in foreign ports, made a serious dent into his income.[12] Despite his commitment to his consular status, Bourne could not live off the consular fees he collected for his services. They were infrequent and too small to cover his standard of living. Bourne had to be involved in business activities in partnership with Johann Wilhelm Lange, trading and selling ships for Baltimore merchants George Salmon and William Taylor.[13]

His two successors built on this foundation. They continued the tradition of a merchant banker who served for a lengthy period of time as consul – the next merchant-consul also served for two decades, but soon the spoils system thwarted this trend.[14] With the exception of David Eckstein, the U.S. consular officers had no consular efficiency in the nineteenth century.

The spoils system, introduced by President Andrew Jackson in 1828, meant that consular posts became rewards to political supporters of the party that won the presidential election. The only Dutch citizen who served as U.S. consul, Jan Willem van den Broek of Amsterdam, was the first to experience this change. He had succeeded John Parker in 1839 after he had secured U.S. minister Auguste Davezac's approval and served satisfactorily until October 1842.[15] In that month Van den Broek read in a New York newspaper that he had been unceremoniously replaced by Charles Nichols. In the future only American citizens would serve as consuls.[16]

As was to be expected, political appointments did not recruit the best and the brightest. Nichols failed to pay his debts, and his successor C. Goethe Baylor spent most of the time of his appointment in the United States, trying to establish direct trade relations between the Southern cotton planters and Dutch traders.[17] He was forced to resign in March 1853 because he was hardly ever at his post in Amsterdam. His successor Robert G. Barnwell was single, lived on his own means and was recalled at the breakout of the Civil War since he fostered Southern sympathies.[18]

Between 1860 and 1893 a string of consuls carrying names such as Klauser, Marx, Mueller, Eckstein, and Schleier, showed that Amsterdam had become a prize for political supporters from German immigrant stock in the Midwest who had become loyal Yankees. Most of them had accepted the Amsterdam consulate because they could not get appointed to their preferred posts in German-speaking countries.[19]

The consuls complained as usual about their low salaries. The $ 1000 offered for Amsterdam was half the amount of the consul's salary in Rotterdam. The Amsterdam post was ranked at the bottom of the consular posts, since the port was hardly called on by American ships in the 1860s.[20]

The only outstanding consul was David Eckstein. He began his appointment in the summer of 1878 with a poor showing because he missed the opportunity to meet the most prominent American tourist in Holland of his time, former president Ulysses S. Grant (20-22 June 1878), because he was struck down with hemorrhoids. However, he made this up in the remaining 12 years of his posting. When he retired because of failing health in August 1890 he received unprecedented public praise from the Dutch captains of industry for his active promotion of Dutch-American trade.[21] His success was the overture for the improved quality of American consuls in the early twentieth century. They needed this injection to successfully compete with Rotterdam as the center for Dutch-American commerce. The initiatives of the American consuls in the twentieth century greatly advanced the volume of trade.[22]

Dutch Consuls in Nineteenth-Century New York

The first Dutch consuls in America were similar to the early American consuls in Amsterdam: experienced merchant bankers who already had strong ties with the country. The first consul in New York was an American merchant Herman Le Roy in 1784, who had learned his trade in various Amsterdam firms.[23] During the Batavian Republic (1800-1806) the consul general resided in Charleston, South Carolina. After the reconstruction of the Dutch state into a Kingdom, the first consul in New York was an American merchant with Dutch connections, Frederick Gebhard. He served for only a year, giving up his commission caused by to the frequent calls for financial assistance made by destitute Dutch immigrants.

The nineteenth century consular history is really the history of three gentlemen, who filled the post from 1816-1911, an average of 32 years each: Johannes C. Zimmerman, Rudolph C. Burlage and Jan Rutger Planten. These three Amsterdammers were paragons of stability.[24]

The 27 year-old Zimmerman applied for the job in 1816 and served a record of forty years, dying in office in 1855. Nothing notorious happened during his long consular term. The main obstacle was the lack of a solid and reciprocal trade agreement since the validity of the 1782 commercial treaty was still in dispute.[25] The Americans requested equal treatment of their vessels in the East Indian colonies, but the Dutch feared that granting the Americans free access would thwart the profitability of the Nederlandsche Handel Maatschappij. The negotiations failed and no commercial treaty was concluded. Only in 1839 did a separate tractate grant equal rights to ships from both countries while reducing the tariff to 20 per cent, but trade disagreement continued during the entire nineteenth century.[26]

Despite the protectionist measures introduced in 1842, which especially hurt Dutch exports of coffee, tea, and gin to the United States, American exports at mid-century consisting mainly of staple crops such as tobacco, cotton, and grain continued to increased. After 1850 the export from America to the Netherlands increased eleven-fold over the next four decades.[27] The New York consulate therefore became an attractive post from the 1850s onwards. That showed in 1852 when this location was promoted to the level of consulate general. In 1855 the first consul general Zimmerman suddenly died and a real competition broke loose over his successor.[28] The first to be recommended was a fellow Amsterdammer Rudolph Christian Burlage, since he was well versed in commercial and shipping affairs and was of a respectable family.[29] Interestingly enough, Burlage's brother, also called Rudolph, with the middle name Wilhelm, had already expressed his desire for the same post earlier. Apparently R.C. was more decisive and likable than R.W. and he was endorsed by some Amsterdam commercial firms, while others recommended Wilhelm.[30] More applicants turned up so that nine names circulated for the job.[31] In April 1855 an Amsterdam group of businessmen recommended R.C., a Rotterdam faction petitioned the foreign minister on behalf of R.W. and the largest petition signed by over 100 Amsterdam business men supported J.E. Zimmerman Jr., the 23 year-old son of the deceased.[32] Apparently the family had built up some rights to this position. Unfortunately Zimmerman Jr. occupied a low business rank, had little knowledge of the Dutch and French languages, and a shallow understanding of business operations.[33] Dutch Foreign Minister Van Hall found a compromise by appointing Rudolph Christian as consul general and Zimmerman Jr. as vice-consul.[34] The Amsterdam lobby had won.

After the American Civil War the Dutch consular service began to modernize, publicizing occasional reports after 1867 and annual overviews after 1878 and stimulating new business ventures.[35] The most important issue of the tariffs was conducted in Washington by the legation.[36] Burlage reported the up and downs of the import of Dutch gin in the late 1870s circulating at the 1.3 million liters. The lines of transport were few and trade was not strong. In 1877 only five steamers made 26 trips to New York, in addition to seventeen sailing vessels. Most cargo from America to Holland was shipped under a foreign flag, which amounted to 116 ships. More than half of the ships coming from the Netherlands were in ballast, while the ships to the Netherlands were fully loaded. With business at a slow pace and low immigration, Burlage could not be overworked.[37]

In 1873 and 1874, the Dutch parliament attempted to formulate a new policy for the consuls. The main point of debate was how to pay for the diplomatic service. Business interests sought to reduce the consular fees, but this meant an extra demand on the treasury. Some representatives pointed towards the US as a model for the payment of the costs involved by making the consular fees pay for the consul's salary, while a strict check on passing ships prevented fraud.[38] The skippers' interests won the battle over the fees, but a coherent commercial policy had to wait for three more decades. As a concession to the desires of the chamber of commerce a position of apprentice consul was created to prepare future personnel with training on the spot. However, the dependency on honorary consuls prevented a real career track, and discouraged qualified personnel from applying.

In 1878, Burlage published his first annual report with statistics covering the entire economy in the United States, describing the effects of the depression of 1873 and reporting signs of recovery. Though new Dutch consulates opened in the western parts of the country, which were not supervised by the New York consul general, the national trends were left to the New York post to be described. In 1883 John R. Planten succeeded Burlage. He had been born in Amsterdam, had acted as consul for nine years and was financially independent. His bid for the consulship was endorsed by influential Dutch-Americans in New York City who had noticed his generosity to destitute Dutch immigrants.[39] During his posting the exchange transportation from the Netherlands increased to over 90 arrivals in 1892, carrying almost 36,000 passengers. He also witnessed the birth of Dutch interest in the life insurance business in the United States, which he investigated to ascertain its commercial solidity. In 1901 he stopped submitting annual statistics because the figures became available too late, and instead he started to give an overall assessment of the American economic situation. Economic statistics showed that from 1869, the first year of the overview including the trade with North-America, till 1922, the trade balance between the United States and the Netherlands was always in favor of the first nation. During this half century the import from the U.S. and Canada was three to four times larger than the value of Dutch exports to North America (see tables 1 and 2). In percentages, U.S. imports accounted for 9-11 percent of total imports, while Dutch exports to the U.S. was valued between 3-4 percent of total Dutch exports. In 1877 the u.s. ranked sixth in the list of import countries and eighth in export destinations.[40]

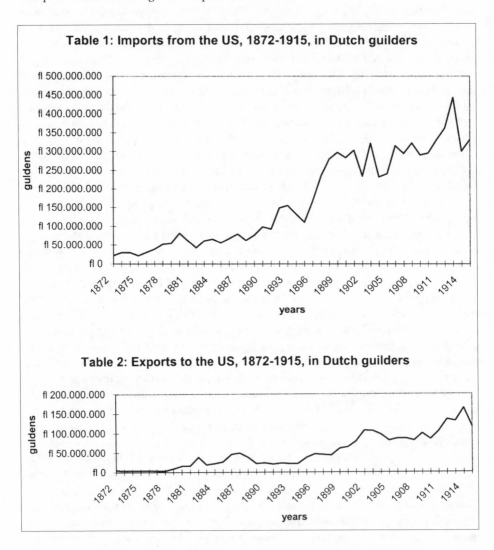

Table 1: Imports from the US, 1872-1915, in Dutch guilders

Table 2: Exports to the US, 1872-1915, in Dutch guilders

American Careers in Amsterdam in the Twentieth Century
In Amsterdam the series of German immigrant consuls changed into a succession of consuls from Anglo-Saxon stock, carrying names such as Downes, Corey, Hill, and Morgan. Their most publicized act was a constant warning against the hoax of rich estates left by deceased Dutch citizens two centuries ago, that could be claimed by their American descendants. For once the Americans sought their fortunes in the Old World. The rumors continued for two decades and were constantly refuted, even by official circulars.

In terms of personnel, the quality of the post improved after 1900, but the great impetus for consular reform came in 1906, when President Theodore Roosevelt, a longtime supporter of Civil Service reform, succeeded in changing the consular service into a career service.[41] The new system provided a biennial review of the consuls, introduced efficiency ratings based on consular reports, which were submitted for review to the newly created Department of Commerce and Labor. President and Secretary personally reviewed the files of the candidates up for promotion to better posts or consulates general. A diplomatic historian has drawn a parallel with the assembly line innovation in industrial production: 'Like the officers themselves, the consulates were also beginning to resemble interchangeable parts in a large mechanism.'[42] The inspection was a useful instrument to professionalize the service by rewarding efficient officers, recruiting junior staff, and – if necessary – closing a consular office when the consul was hopelessly ineffective. By 1924 consuls and diplomats were absorbed into one Foreign Service.

The inspection reports offer a detailed view of the operations at the posts. When Inspector Horace Lee Washington brought the first inspection visit to the American consulate at Amsterdam on 23 October 1906, he found a small two-room office at Keizersgracht 766. He met consul Frank D. Hill, stationed since 1899, assisted by a vice consul, two messengers, and a very loyal Dutch clerk who had served under five successive consuls since 1877. Washington rated Hill as excellent, thanks to the consul's command of the Dutch language, his first-hand knowledge of business transactions, and his close contacts in the community.[43]

Unlike many other American consuls who were occupied with registering American vessels and taking care of destitute sailors, the Amsterdam office had little to do in this field. Before World War I, hardly any American ship sailed from the port of Amsterdam. In 1906, trans-Atlantic shipping was conducted by 48 Dutch ships and a few foreign ones. After the Great War this pattern changed. In 1920, one percent (i.e. twelve) of all ships calling on Amsterdam were American-owned, and this rate rose to meet a level of 25 per cent of all ships in the mid-1920s. The situation in Rotterdam had been similar to Amsterdam in 1906, where the liners of the Holland America Line dominated the trade, with an occasional American flag ornamenting the port. But during the Great War American ships gained ground in the Rotterdam port. In 1916 they counted for 10 per cent of the America-bound ships (36 of a total of 379) and three years later for more than 50 per cent: 379 ships against 314 others.[44] In 1923 Amsterdam consul Carl Kuykendall admitted 'Amsterdam is decidedly inferior to Rotterdam as a port of general activity.'[45] The number of American citizens in the Dutch capital remained at a low level till the 1930s, when it increased from a handful to 50 in the city and 600 in the entire district.

The inspection reports actually improved the efforts of mediocre personnel, as Frank W. Mahin, who occupied the post between 1910 and 1924, experienced. He was temporarily suspended for abusing postal privileges for personal correspondence and seeking petty pecuniary profits at the government's expense, but was reinstalled because of his new-found efficiency.

In the 1920s the dominance of diamonds in the Amsterdam exports to the U.S. dwindled and the consulate became more involved in trade promotion. Trade opportunities with the Netherlands increased, but to effectively trigger new contracts much personal attention was needed.[46] In 1924 the Amsterdam post was recognized for its future potential. No other than the consul general residing in Rotterdam suggested a transfer of the consulate-general to Amsterdam, because Amsterdam offered much better contacts with the business community, cities close to Amsterdam became industrialized, the American Chamber of Commerce was located there, as well as all the other foreign consuls-general. The strong international banking activities in the city also requested close American attention. Adding a personal note, the consul general added that the social and cultural life in Rotterdam was depressing.[47] And so it happened that Amsterdam became the center for trade with America once more. Its position was strengthened even more with the promotion of two Batavia consul generals to the Amsterdam post in the 1930s, indicating an increase in American interest in trade with the Dutch colonies. At the end of the decade the Amsterdam post became very important for scrutinizing the flow of German capital and immigrants. So as in the beginning of the consular system, a temporary political role for the consul emerged. After World War II the Amsterdam consul general continued to have a political function, gauging the political climate through his contacts in local society.

Professionalization in New York, 1911-1940
Meanwhile the professionalization of the Dutch consular service diminished the Amsterdam influence in New York, because the foreign ministry demanded that its officers became more active and began routinely transferring its officers. The celebration of Planten's 25th anniversary as Consul in New York in 1909 was the occasion to seriously consider the installation of a professional consul, since Planten openly hinted at his own retirement.[48] Two years later his successor, lawyer A. van de Sande Bakhuyzen, became the first paid consul in the United States.[49] This late appointment was caused by the long-held opinion in the Dutch foreign office that government should not interfere with business in order not to disrupt free trade by introducing tariffs. Dutch businessmen operating internationally called on the consulates for information about business opportunities and tariffs to protect their manufacturing. Disappointed with the slow pace of the Dutch government in building a strong service, the business clubs founded an office for trade information in Amsterdam in 1903.[50]

At the turn of the century, Dutch Foreign minister Willem H. de Beaufort (1897-1901) was in the best position to assess the consular service. A patrician, he identified three problems with the service. It offered no opportunities for advancement to able young officers, while it demanded high expenses for social events. The consuls represented a small European country, which had little leverage and few new commercial relations could be established. Moreover, the consuls had to deal with fellow countrymen of a lower class. De Beaufort concluded that the generation that had enthusiastically joined the foreign service after the reorganization of 1875 had grown disappointed and the lack of appealing prospects had prevented the influx of able young officers.[51]

Consulships demanded more from the civil servants than a position in the Netherlands. The culture and expectations of foreign countries and reciprocal relations in the international community influenced the importance and efficacy of the Dutch consulates to a large degree. De Beaufort advocated the appointment of diplomats in the Near East because these attributed much prestige to a title. Consuls frequently compared their own position with their immediate colleagues representing other countries.

De Beaufort realized that managers of substantial firms which had sufficient funds to explore, invest, and wait for profits were in a better position to start new business than consuls. He feared that the consulates found only the second bests to fill their vacancies, since successful merchants stayed in business. Another problem was the lack of career advancement, since the consular hierarchy was restricted to four levels with no prospects to move to so-called better places. This lack of quality caused the Dutch Chambers of Commerce to advocate the transfer of the role of advancing commerce to businessmen, thereby weakening the function of the consulates even more.

Pressure from without and within the government resulted in the announcement of the reorganization of the consular service in 1906. However, the internal dispute about responsibilities between the foreign office and the newly created ministry of Agriculture, Industry and Trade prevented an efficient organization. The Foreign Office supervised the personnel, but was mainly interested in the standard bureaucratic and diplomatic functions. Trade and Industry had the expertise knowledge, but could not touch trade relations. The compromise that the Trade Department edit and distribute the consular reports worked too slow for launching new business ventures and was abandoned. Only in the 1920s did trade relations become an integrated part of the consular service, while the foundation of professional organizations for consuls reduced their isolation.[52] By that time the consular service had come of age. After World War II New York became part of the career pattern of the Dutch foreign service, while Amsterdam became an American post that was held for an average of three years.

Conclusion

The consulates in Amsterdam and New York had no special relationship with each other, nor strong ties with the municipal authorities. However, the posts were important anchorages for commercial activities and offered first-hand experience of national and international developments. In the course of two centuries the consular representation in both cities showed many parallels: the first generation of consuls were merchant bankers with strong local contacts and personal interests in maintaining the commercial relation. The control by Amsterdam interest groups in the nineteenth century was much stronger than the New York interest. In fact, the interest of the Boston/Baltimore commercial elite in Amsterdam was stronger than New York.

After 1840 the trends diverged. For sixty years (and ten consuls-general) the United States administrations used consular appointments as part of the patronage system. The Dutch opted for continuity and let their officers serve almost for life. At the end of this period the services in both countries began to converge again in their efforts to professionalize. The reorganization of the American consular corps was far-reaching and transformed the corps into an efficient operation. The Dutch reforms were piece-meal and far less rational. In both cases the influence of Amsterdam in New York and vice versa disappeared.

The history of the Dutch and American consular representations in New York and Amsterdam reveals the important role of consuls in the processes of integration of commerce and government, of the bureaucratization of diplomatic relations, and of the globalization of trade and traffic. Apart from this, they supplemented important additional political information in the absence of diplomats.

2-21 March 1793	James Greenleaf
1797-1817	Sylvanus Bourne
1818-1839	John W. Parker
	(vice consul, in 1820 consul) since 1802 in Holland,
1839-Oct 1842	Willem van den Broek
Oct. 1842-1849	Charles Nichols (Connecticut)
March 1851-8 March 1853	C. Goethe Baylor
	(Kentucky-born, from Texas)
Sept. 1853-4 Nov. 1861	Robert G. Barnwell (South Carolina)
4 Nov. 1861- 23 Aug. 1863	F. J. Klauser (German-born from Ohio)
28 Sept. 1863- 6 Sept. 1866	Joseph E. Marx
	(native of Baden, from Ohio)
27 Oct. 1866- June 1878	Charles Mueller
	(German by birth, from Ohio)
26 June 1878-Oct. 1890	David Eckstein
	(Bavaria, from Cincinnatti, Ohio)
Nov. 1890-6 July 1893	Theodore M. Schleier
	(born in Prussia, from Tennessee)
1 Aug. 1893-10 Dec. 1897	Edward Downes (Connecticut)
10 Dec. 1897-8 July 1899	George Corey
12 July 1899-June 1907	Frank D. Hill
1907-July 1910	Henry H. Morgan
5 July 1910-1 July 1924	Frank W. Mahin
	(with interruption between 1913-Dec. 1915)
1925-Oct. 1927	William H. Gale (consul general)
18 Oct. 1927-June 1934	Charles L. Hoover (Iowa)
20 June 1934-Oct. 1937	Kenneth Stuart Patton (Virginia)
5 Jan. 1938-1941	Frank C. Lee (Nebraksa)
2 July 1945	Albert M. Doyle
Nov. 1947	Jesse F. Van Wickel
Oct. 1949-1954	Frederik van den Arend
Aug. 1954-1956	Elvin Seibert
July 1956-1958	Robert P. Chalker
June 1959-1961	G. Edward Clarke
Jan. 1962-1964	Byron E. Blankenship
Aug. 1964-1967	Warde M. Cameron
Sept. 1967-1971	Harold E. Howland
Sept. 1971-1974	Eugene M. Braderman
July 1974-1976	Alexander J. Davit
Nov. 1976-1979	Henry A. Lagasse
June 1979-1983	S. Morey Bell
June 1983-1985	Hawthorne Q. Mills

Jan. 1986-1987	Thomas R. Reynders
Aug. 1987	Jake M. Dyels, Jr.
Oct. 1989	Kenneth Longmyer
Oct. 1990-1994	Roger D. Pierce
Aug. 1994-1997	John W. Shearburn
Febr. 1997-2000	Dianne M. Andruch
July 2000-2003	Arnold H. Campbell

Appendix 2: Dutch Consuls in New York, 1784-2003

1784-1815	Herman LeRoy
1815-1816	Frederick Gebhard
1816-1855	J.C. Zimmerman
1855-1883	R.C. Burlage
1883-1911	J.R. Planten
1911-1915	Mr. A. van de Sande Bakhuyzen
1916-1919	H. Spakler
1920-1921	Van Steyn Parvé
1922-1923	Mr. D.H. Andrae
1923-1939	W.P. Montijn
1939-1942	J.A. Schuurman
1942-1945	T. Elink Schuurman
1945-1947	Jhr. Mr. G.R.G. van Swinderen
1947-1951	Mr. W. Cnoop Koopmans
1951-1956	Mr. J.A.G. Baron de Vos van Steenwijk
1956-1960	Jhr. Mr. M.Th. A.M. van Rijckevorsel
1960-1964	Mr. B.J. Slingenberg
1964-1966	Mr. J.I.M. Welsing
1966-1972	Mr. D.A. van Hamel
1972-1977	W.S.J. Campagne
1977-1983	Jhr. L. Quarles van Ufford
1983-1986	Mr. C.J.M. Kramers
1986-1989	Mr. A.F. Tieleman
1989-1994	Mr. C.W.A. de Groot
1994-1997	Mr. Tj.T. van den Hout
1997-2003	Drs. B. Hiensch

Notes

1 The minutes of the Amsterdam city council show no direct dealings with foreign consuls. If connections were made this was done through the services of the Amsterdam Chamber of Commerce. Gemeentearchief entry 5287, inv. 69. Dutch author Arnon Grunberg's description of his meeting with a Dutch consul in New York also confirmed the poor reputation of

the consul as being shallow and self-centered. Arnon Grunberg, 'Ontmoetingen met consul Pierre P. van der Velden II,' *Hollands Maandblad* 38.5 (1997): 3-5.

2 C.A. van Minnen, *American Diplomats in the Netherlands 1815-1850* (New York: St. Martin's Press, 1993). Hans Krabbendam, 'Mooie woorden. Het geletterde leven van Henry van Dyke, 1852-1933,' in E.F. van de Bilt and H.W. van den Doel, eds., *Klassiek Amerikaans. Opstellen voor A. Lammers* (Leiden: Universiteit Leiden, 2002), 103-124. Willem Melching, ''I have the honor to report'. De Amerikaanse consulaire reportage uit Nederland, 1940-1941,' *Oorlogsdocumentatie '40-'45. Vierde Jaarboek van het Rijksinstituut voor Oorlogsdocumentatie* (Amsterdam 1993), 65-88; Hans Krabbendam, 'Valentine's Days: The Experiences of Marshall Mission Chief Alan C. Valentine in the Netherlands, 1948-1949,' in Tity de Vries, ed., *Dynamics of Modernization: European-American Comparisons and Perceptions* (Amsterdam: VU University Press, 1998), 121-134.

3 A brief general overview is H.J. de Muy-Fleurke and S. Plantinga, 'Hulp in het buitenland. De consulaire dienst,' in R.E. van Ditzhuyzen a.o., eds., *Tweehonderd jaar Ministerie van Buitenlandse Zaken* (Den Haag: Sdu, 1998), 124-142. Albert Kersten, *Buitenlandse Zaken in ballingschap. Groei en verandering van een ministerie 1940-1945* (Alphen aan den Rijn: A.W. Sijthoff, 1981), 74-129, 157-175, 198-248. A revealing memoir about the internal working of the Dutch foreign service offers H.N. Boon, *Bagatellen uit de diplomatieke dienst: herinneringen van 35 jaar Buitenlandse zaken* (Rotterdam 1972). The New York Consulate-General published a commemorative booklet in 1984: *200 Years of Consulates of the Netherlands in New York, Boston, Philadelphia, 17 September 1784-1984;* Charles S. Kennedy, *The American Consul: A History of the United States Consular Service, 1776-1914* (New York 1990). Henry E. Mattox, *The Twilight of Amateur Diplomacy: The American Foreign Service and Its Senior Officers in the 1890s* (Kent: Kent State University Press, 1989). Richard Hume Werking, *The Master Architects: Building the United States Foreign Service 1890-1913* (Lexington: University Press of Kentucky, 1977). The only biographical article is from M.C. Vernon, 'General Benjamin Butler and the Dutch Consul,' *Civil War History* 5 (1959): 263-275; G.J. Kloos, *De handelspolitieke betrekkingen tusschen Nederland en de Vereenigde Staten van Amerika 1814-1914* (Amsterdam: H.J. Paris, 1923); Walter Salzmann, *Bedrijfsleven, overheid en handelsbevordering. The Netherlands Chamber of Commerce in the United States, Inc. 1903-1987* (Leiden, 1994) 36-42; Rob van Vuurde, *Engeland, Nederland en de Monroeleer, 1895-1914* (Amsterdam 1998); George M. Welling, *The Prize of Neutrality: Trade Relations between Amsterdam and North America 1771-1817: A Study in Computational History* (Amsterdam 1998) 188-227; J.C. Westermann, *The Netherlands and the United States: Their Relations in the Beginning of the Nineteenth Century* ('s-Gravenhage: Martinus Nijhoff, 1935); P.J. van Winter, *Het aandeel van den Amsterdamschen handel aan den opbouw van het Amerikaansche Gemeenebest* 2 vols. ('s-Gravenhage: Martinus Nijhoff, 1927-1933). Frances Gouda with Thijs Brocades Zaalberg, *American Visions of the Netherlands East Indies/Indonesia: US Foreign Policy and Indonesian Nationalism, 1920-1949* (Amsterdam: Amsterdam University Press, 2002).

4 Van Winter, *Het aandeel*, vol 2:283. He quotes a letter from John Quincy Adams to the Secretary of State, 25 September 1796. NA, RG 59, Despatches form United States Ministers to the Netherlands, 1794-1906, Microfilm M 42 roll 2: frame 215. Van Winter, *Het aandeel*, vol. 1: 93. He left his post in 1797, vol. 2: 82.

5 He married baroness Antonia Cornelia Elbertin Scholten van Aschat van Oud-Haarlem. Greenleaf accepted his appointment in a letter dated 10 May 1793. Allen C. Clark, *Greenleaf and Law in the Federal City* (Washington, DC: Press of W.F. Roberts, 1901), 79-90.

6 J. Rogge, *Het handelshuis Van Eeghen. Proeve eener geschiedenis van een Amsterdamsch handelshuis* (Amsterdam: Van Ditmar, 1949), 125.

7 Bob Arnebeck, *Through a Fiery Trial: Building Washington 1790-1800* (Lanham, MD: Madison Books, 1991), 232-238.

8 For a list of appointments see Microfilm M587 List of U.S. Consular Officers, 1789-1939, reel

1 (Amsterdam).

9 John Quincy Adams presented his credentials on November 6, 1794 and presented his recall in June 20 1797, his successor William Vans Murray left on September 2, 1801. Bourne was the highest ranking diplomat till William Eustis arrival in 1815. A letter took two months to reach Washington or Philadelphia from Amsterdam. J.C. Westermann, *The Netherlands and the United States: Their Relations in the Beginning of the Nineteenth Century* (The Hague: Martinus Nijhoff, 1935), 97-108.

10 A. MacIntosh, D.D., *An Address, at the Internment of Sylvanus Bourne, Esqr, Consul-General of the United States in the Netherlands, Who died 25th April 1817. Aged 56 years* (Harlem: John Enschedé & Sons, 1817) 16 pp. Microfilm M42, *Despatches from United States Ministers to the Netherlands, 1794-1906*, Reel 6.

11 Bourne to Secretary of State, Amsterdam, 25 september 1794 and 21 April 1795, Reel 1 of M446.

12 Ibid., 6 August 1795.

13 Gemeentearchief Amsterdam, Notarieel Archief ingang 5075, inv. Nrs. 17333/345, 17338/140 (J.H. Zilver). Sale of his properties by Claude Crommelin, after his death: 17362/380 to benefit his under age sons: George Salmon Bourne, 18 years, and William Taylor Bourne, 16 years.

14 In 1820 the new consul John W. Parker, who had lived in Holland since 1802, had a partnership with exporters in Boston and Amsterdam in the trade firm Van Baggen, Parker & Dixon. This firm was the largest firm trading with America, which counted 27 ships from the U.S. calling at the port of Amsterdam in 1832. See Joost Jonker, *Merchants, Bankers, Middlemen: The Amsterdam Money Market During the First Half of the 19th Century* (Amsterdam: NEHA, 1996), 199; Rogge, *Handelshuis Van Eeghen*, 173-4; J. Rogge 'Inlichtingen omtrent een aantal handelshuizen in Amsterdam, in het najaar van 1816 verstrekt door de firma Van Eeghen & Co,' *Economisch historisch jaarboek* 22 (1940-1942): 193-195.

15 John Parker to Secretary of State, 21 February 1839, NA RG 59, Despatches from United States Consuls in Amsterdam, Netherlands, 1790-1906, M446 reel 2.

16 Correspondence Van den Broek to Christopher Hughes, who forwarded the letter with his comments to Daniel Webster, 17 October 1842, M446 reel 2.

17 *New York Times*, 4 November 1851, and Baylor to Secretary of State, 13 August 1852, M446 roll 3. In 1858 and 1859 he tried to establish a cotton staple market in Belgium in his capacity as American Consul in England in an effort to help Georgian merchants to circumvent the Northern middlemen. See H. Coppejons-Desmedt, 'De overzese expansie van de Belgische kantoonindustrie. Van het afsluiten van de Nederlandse koloniale markt tot het uitbreken van de Amerikaanse Secessieoorlog,' in *De Belgische expansie onder Leopold I (1831-1865). Verzameling Studies* (Koninklijke Academie voor Overzeese Wetenschappen) [1965]), 98-105.

18 Likely he was related to a member of the Confederate Senator Robert W. Barnwell. He later asked for his remainder of the balance and claimed to have been a loyal citizen.

19 Microfilm collection M873: Letters of Application and Recommendation, Presidents Polk and Fillmore, reel 6, Goethe Baylor, applied for a German consulate. Baylor later recommended Robert G. Barnwell, see Microfilm collection M967: Letters of Application and Recommendation, Presidents Pierce-Buchanan, reel 2. Microfilm collection M650: Letters of Application and Recommendation, Presidents Lincoln to Johnson, reel 27, Dr. F.J. Klauser, 13-26 March 1861, and reel 32, J.E. Marx, 1 September 1863. The latter wrote that 'ere long this cursed rebellion will be entirely crushed' but he had to deal with a lot of ignorance in the Netherlands about the stakes in the Civil War, (Marx to William Hunter, 4 May 1865, M 446 reel 3).

20 The diplomatic reform act passed by Congress in 1856, categorized the consulates in B and C (A being reserved for diplomatic posts), with B consuls entitled to a salary between $ 1000

to $ 7,500, and could not participate in trade, while they had to hand over the fees. The 40 consuls in category C, could be commercially active, but could not keep the fees, Kennedy, *American Consul*, 83.

21 Microfilm M446, *Despatches from United States Consuls in Amsterdam, the Netherlands, 1790-1906*, reel 6, 15 December 1890. Eckstein monitored all kinds of products and trade opportunities in the Netherlands.

22 Consul George J. Corey presented lectures on the history and current conditions of Holland to American audiences in June 1899 (M466, reel 7, frame 249.) Frank D. Hill received praise from the *Algemeen Handelsblad* on 7 March 1901 for his efforts to find American trade partners. See his article on American trade in the Netherlands in the *New York Times*, 1 January 1900. He also promoted the idea of a Dutch Chamber of Commerce in New York, see *New York Times*, 20 December 1901. Reprinted in a Dutch translation in het *Tijdschrift der Nederlandsche Maatschappij ter Bevordering van Nijverheid* (1 June 1902).

23 Van Winter, *Amsterdam en de opbouw van Amerika*, vol. 1: 12.

24 A.E. Zimmerman, *De consul generaal der Nederlanden te New-York Johannes Christian Zimmerman, 1789-1855, en zijne nakomelingen: genealogische aanteekeningen* [S.l. : s.n., ca. 1917]. J.C. Zimmerman was a member of the firm Ruysch & Zimmerman at Amsterdam. R.C. Burlage was a partner in the banking and trading firm of Bunge, Burlage and Company of New York (Gustav Bunge of Köln), (Veenendaal, *Slow Train to Paradise*, 72). J.R. Planten was proprietor of a pharmaceutical firm. H.J. Kiewiet de Jonge, 'Levensbericht J.R. Planten,' *Levensberichten Maatschappij Nederlandsche Letterkunde*, 1914, 152-153.

25 Westermann, *Netherlands and the United States*, 224-225.

26 Kloos, *Handelspolitieke betrekkingen*, 38.

27 Ibid., 97.

28 Nationaal Archief, 2.05.01 Ministerie van buitenlandse zaken, 1813-1896, inv. 3025 aanstelling consulaire ambtenaren, Folder 'Consulaat-generaal te New York' 1855-1870.

29 Ibid., Amsterdam, 11 April 1855, letter by Mr. Bunge to the Dutch Foreign Minister Van Hall.

30 Ibid., J.C. Gevers to Van Hall, 27 March 1855.

31 An Amsterdam Jew connected with a Swedish firm, the young son of Zimmerman, who had acted as vice-consul, the firm of Kerkhoven recommended Cornelis Buijs, Crommelin supported a mr. Alofsen, who had powerful relations. Stadnitski gave a reference to J.W. Van der Horst Kuyt. Ibid., Gevers aan Van Hall, 2 April 1855.

32 Ibid., Petitions of 20, 22, and 24 April 1855.

33 Message of R.C. Burlage to Dutch Secretary of State D.J. Gevers van Endegeest, 24 March 1857. The respect for the Zimmerman family was so high that Roest van Limburg proposed an unusual promotion of Zimmerman to vice consul general in 1860. But his career ended sudden with his death in 1874. Letter of 12 Mach 1860 to Foreign Secretary of State Baron van Gollstein, the promotion was effectuated on April 13. Zimmerman died in Egypt in 1874 (2.05.13. Gezantschap vs, inv nr 67 R.C. Burlage to B. Westenberg, 4 March 1874).

34 Ibid., 21 June 1855, Van Hall to Dutch minister in Washington Gevers.

35 *Verzameling van consulaire en andere verslagen en berichten over nijverheid, handel en scheepvaart*, 1865-1893. Uitgegeven door het Ministerie van Landbouw, Handel en Nijverheid. *Consulaire verslagen en berichten*, 1894-1906. Uitgegeven door het Ministerie van Buitenlandse Zaken. *Economische verslagen van Nederlandsche diplomatieke en consulaire ambtenaren*, 1907-1936. Uitgegeven door het Ministerie van Landbouw, Nijverheid en Handel, met medewerking van het Ministerie van Buitenlandse Zaken.

36 Ben Schoenmaker, 'Berichten uit de Bondshoofdstad. Politieke rapportage van de Nederlandse gezant te Washington, 1893-1917' (M.A. thesis Leiden University, n.d.[1987]) 10.

37 *Verzameling van consulaire en andere berigten en verslagen over nijverheid, handel en scheepvaart*. 1878: 524-530, and berigten till 1883. See also the failure for the largest Dutch inter-

national commercial firm to create a foothold in New York: W.J. Wensink, 'Te billijk en te nauwgezet. De mislukte poging van de Nederlandse Handelmaatschappij om een Agentschap te vestigen in New York 1879-1882,' *Aanzet* 11 (April 1993): 21-30.

38 *Het Nederlandsch Consulaatwezen*, p. 24.

39 2.05.13. Gezantschap vs, inv nr 67 R.C. Burlage to B. Westenberg, 4 March 1874.

40 *Statistiek van den in-, uit- en doorvoer* ('s-Gravenhage: Departement van financiën, 1877-1915). *Statistiek van den handel en de scheepvaart van het Koningrijk der Nederlanden* ('s-Gravenhage: Departement van financiën, 1869-1876). Preceding the U.S. as exporters were Prussia, Belgium, Great Britain, Russia, the East Indies, while these five and Hamburg and Italy imported more from the Netherlands.

41 Kennedy, *American Consul*, 217. Thanks to an able testimony of Elihu Root, the Senate accepted the bill but left the promotion to the president and removed the examination process. The House added the need for approval of the Senate in transfers of consuls of equal rank. What was left of the reform was a seven-layered scale for consul generals, a nine-layered one for consuls, American citizenship as a condition for consul earning more than $ 1,000, and a biennual inspection. Roosevelt added by executive order an examination for all lower ranks. Furthermore, Congress paid for the transportation of the consuls. In 1915 promotion could also take place by upgrading the rank and not by transfer to a place with a higher rank. The first inspection officer for the Dutch foreign service was appointed in 1954.

42 Richard Hume Werking, *The Master Architects: Building the United States Foreign Service 1890-1913* (Lexington: University Press of Kentucky, 1977), 111.

43 Frank D. Hill had a law degree from National Law School of Washington DC, had practiced law in Minneapolis, and read Spanish, French, Portugese, Dutch and some German. Hill to Assistant Secretary of State, 1 July 1906, M446 Reel 7.

44 National Archives, Washington DC. RG 59, Inspection Reports of Foreign Service Posts, 1906-1939. Rotterdam, 1913, 1916, 1920, 1923, microfilm edition Roosevelt Study Center (RSC).

45 NA RG Inspection Reports of Foreign Service Posts, 1906-1939. Amsterdam 1923, 12. (microfilm edition RSC)

46 Onno de Wit, 'From Europe to the United States and Back Again? Two Centuries of Inward Investments in the Netherlands' (October 31, 2003) published at www.bintproject.nl/textfiles/two_centuries.pdf. American products included technological inventions such as the telephone, typewriter, photo camera, sewing machine and the petrochemical industry.

47 Letter form the American consul general George E. Anderson to the Secretary of State, 27 February 1923 (inspection report 1923) microfilm RSC.

48 NA 2.05.38, inv. 1753. Letter of R. de Marees van Swinderen to Hr. Hanneman, 15 July 1909, see also the letter of 11 May 1909.

49 Salzmann, *Bedrijfsleven, overheid en Handelsbevordering*, 38.

50 Ibid., 46.

51 W.H. de Beaufort, 'Twee rapporten over het consulaatwezen,' *De Economist* 52 (1904): 5-21. J.P. de Valk and M. van Faassen, eds., *Dagboeken en aantekeningen van Willem Hendrik de Beaufort 1874-1918*, part 1 (Den Haag: Instituut Nederlandse Geschiedenis, 1993).

52 NA 2.05.13 Plaatsingslijst van het archief van het Nederlands gezantschap in de vs 1814-1940, inv. 383 '1919-1925'. The consulate moved to the Kerr Building and hosted the trade attaché. The staff was well adapted to the American situation (Jhr. Mr. De Beaufort to Mr. J. Nederbragt, chief of the departement of Economic Affairs of the Ministry of Foreign Affairs, 9 December 1921).

Tracy Metz

THE CITY PICTURESQUE: A BOON AND A BURDEN

Let me tell you about my house. I live just a few minutes walk up the street from here, on the Prinsengracht canal. It is a lovely house, I must say, that we rent from a small housing society called Stadsherstel, specializing in the restoration of dilapidated landmarks which that they then give back to the city, as it were, as living space. We have traced it on at least three of the photographs that Breitner took along the canals in the late nineteenth century, and from the previous inhabitants we inherited a photograph of the place when it was a shop. Not a trendy boutique like the ones the neighborhood is now filled with, but a simple shoemaker's shop. The Prinsengracht always *was* the 'working man's' canal, with the least grand houses and the most garages and workshops.

I was thrilled to be living on a canal – after all, that's really the only place *to* live when you've traded the aridity of Southern California for the watery reaches of Holland. Then after a few years we made a discovery that changed my whole attitude to the house. It was time to substitute the old carpet with something new. And what did we discover when we tried to put a drill into the floor: that it was made of concrete! This charming centuries-old waterside palazzo is a replica!

You can imagine: I was shattered. Here I am, a denizen of the New World who had willingly transplanted herself to the Old World, and I'm living in a replica! Disney meets Rembrandt. The story was, it later transpired, that the original house had burnt down in the sixties, leaving a gaping hole for many years, which Stadsherstel had conscientiously filled with a meticulous copy. Once I was over the shock I realized that it was really very funny. All my romantic ideas about authenticity and historic landmark buildings had been turned on their head – and that is always healthy. And practically speaking I realized that I was onto a good thing: I have the esthetic pleasure of an old house with a fraction of the maintenance. There *is* something to be said for concrete floors. Although the windows close just as poorly as they probably did in the seventeenth century.

So I admit, here for the first time in public, that when I arrived here as an anonymous tourist, I fell for the picturesqueness of this city. It fit my schoolbook idea of what a European city should look like, with cavernous old churches and winding streets with cobblestones and little shops where you could buy *hagelslag,* chocolate sprinkles, in a pointy paper bag.

A large part of the attraction, too, was that 'downtown' here is still 'downtown' in a sense that is long lost in most American cities (New York and San Francisco being the notable exceptions). In his fascinating book of the same title, 'Downtown', the American political scientist Robert Fogelson begins by describing how downtown disappeared from the lives of his own family. His father went downtown to work every day. Fogelson himself lives in a suburb and works at the university and goes downtown maybe twice a month for dinner and a movie. His son lives in a so-called 'edge city' and goes downtown maybe twice a year, if at all. In my youth in Los Angeles, downtown was synonymous – as in many cities – with crime, poverty and neglect. It was also in American cities that the so-called 'doughnut city' developed, as the economic and social life of the city moved in concentric rings away from the center.[1]

But not here. I found it extraordinary that people actually lived in downtown, in this charming picture-book decor. Downtown was not derelict, nor was it just a place where people came to work, or to visit, or to play, and then went home afterwards. The proof was right there in front of me, because as you have probably noticed the Dutch all leave their curtains open in the evening, allowing unlimited opportunities for gaping. I know no city that bears such a striking resemblance to an Advent calendar, where as Christmas approaches children are allowed to open a new little window every day.

The city's greatest landmarks, of course, are the canals, those ribbons of public space that are continually moving, shifting and changing, that sometimes shine and sometimes stink, that reflect the sky and the boats and the buildings, and whose pockmarked surface helps you gauge from your window several stories up how hard the rain is coming down. The canals give Amsterdam its unique urban structure and that also provide the riveting spectacle of barges dredging up dozens, hundreds of rusty bicycles. I always stop and wonder: how in the world did all those bikes get in there? I have lived here for may years and I have never once seen anyone throw a bike in the canal! Yet there they are. They are such an Amsterdam institution that the zoo, Artis, even incorporated a cross-section of a canal underwater into its new aquarium, barnacle-covered bike-wreck and all.

Living History

Amsterdam has charmed many a visitor before me. The American artist Whistler adored Holland, and painted and drew here copiously. The critic Jan Veth appreciated Whistler's work, but also felt reservations about his sentimental gaze, as he wrote in the magazine *De Nieuwe Gids* in 1891, as I paraphrase:

> He has poeticized the Snoekjesgracht or the Groenburgwal or the Kromboomssloot into warehouse idylls, he has composed cellar songs or sleepy serenades – they gave the refined artist the reverie of a decorative, tidy city, airy and sunny, rising slenderly from clear water, liberated from Holland's heaviness. He has lapped it up like a slightly exotic fairy tale décor. With the silky fineness of softly spun lines like the gold dust of the most delicate lacquer work, with the amber-scented bouquet of his illusions of s summery Holland, he paints a Venice-like Amsterdam, cleared in the dolce far niente of his artistic caprice.[2]

Nor was Whistler alone. In her book *Holland Mania* the American art historian Annette Stott shows that American visitors, for whom Holland held a particular fascination between 1880 and 1920, were really only interested in seeing a confirmation in three-D of the images they knew from Old Master paintings. They preferred the fishermen's folklore of Marken and Volendam to Amsterdam because it looked more like the seventeenth century – i.e., like the real thing. Stott concludes: 'Clearly the tourism that brought in welcome revenue was not an unmixed blessing. While it undoubtedly increased Americans' admiration and love for the Netherlands, it did not always increase their understanding. Instead, the tourist experience helped to confirm the old-fashioned 'windmills and wooden shoes' image of Holland....'[3]

The City Picturesque, then, is both a burden and a boon. That was the case a century and a half ago and that is still the case today. On the one hand history is an attraction, with any luck even a unique selling-point in marketing terminology. Conveniently packaged into heritage it is an increasingly saleable commodity in a world of global travel in which cultural tourism draws a public of millions. It is at the same time a high-maintenance commodity that also costs a lot of money, as the Landmarks Department of Amsterdam can testify. In this regard Amsterdam gets a free lunch: the spatial and architectural homogeneity of the canals and their tall, narrow houses make them instantly recognizable. They are, in short, a ready-made logo, the essence of the city's urban profile. On the other hand this is a trap. A logo is also a cliché. Marketeers prefer one-dimensional messages, and it is not easy to convey that you are both historic and dynamic at the same time.

New York

New York does not have that problem. Picturesque is *not* the word that comes to mind when you think of New York. The essence of New York – which, of course, was robbed of one of its logos on 9/11 – is its heterogeneity. Happily, there are still several 'logo's' left whose potency has been heightened by that awful event. For New York's landmarks, spread over the city as they are, this lack of cohesion can be a danger. The fact that they are stand-alone buildings, combined with the general American fascination with the new, makes them relatively easy prey for greedy developers and uninterested city bureaucrats. Remember, even Jane Fonda could not save Penn Station. On the other hand there have been heroic preservation efforts by neighborhoods and individuals that have rescued very characteristic elements of the New York streetscape, such as the cast-iron facades of Soho. And loft-living itself is an homage to the flexibility of spaces whose designers could never have dreamt that people would later work there and live there.

How far can a city go in (re-)creating the past as an attraction? Can you help history along, and how hard can you push before preservation becomes packaging? In 1996 I wrote a story for my newspaper about attempts to bring new life to Downtown, the tip of Manhattan that is graced with what Henry James so charmingly called 'a loose bouquet of architectural flowers'. One of the plans was to bring residents and tourists in, by converting empty offices into apartments for the former and by setting out a so-called Heritage Trail for the latter. This was an initiative of the wealthy philanthropist Richard Kaplan. His son, an architect of the same name, told me that until now, the way New York went about revitalization had been to build big projects: Chase Manhattan Plaza in the fifties, the World Trade Center in the seventies, Battery Park City in the eighties. Now, he said, it was time to take a more subtle approach and not to make new places, but to make better use of the places that were already there. One of Kaplan's ideas was a series of four Heritage Trails that would take in, among other things, the Stock Exchange, South Street Seaport, the new Museum of the American Indian, an early eighteenth-century burial ground of black slaves and a number of early twentieth-century skyscrapers. I must admit that I was surprised to see on internet that the trails still include the World Trade Center, so it would seem that they have fallen into disuse.

Ellis Island is in many ways a similar story. Perhaps it's not a landmark in the way a building is, but is a place of great significance for Americans, not just New Yorkers. As the granddaughter of an immigrant from Latvia I am glad that this significance has been recognized by making Ellis Island accessible, not as a maudlin attraction but as a place to visit for those with a personal or historical interest.

South Street Seaport, however, is a different kettle of fish, and a more difficult one. What you visit now is a vestige of the original fish hall, all gussied up with cute shops and delicatessens and nice restaurants and of course the mandatory South Street Seaport Multimedia Experience. Here I get the feeling that a historic location is only a vehicle for a commercial formula. But it clearly works, like most of the Rouse Company's waterfront leisure- en retail formulas of the eighties in a number of American cities. Even though the contemporary contents of South Street Seaport are not to my liking, I have to admit that the commercial and touristic activity there have brought liveliness, and money, back to this part of town that seemed to have disappeared forever.

Funzones

Increasingly, historic districts are becoming *funzones*. Events like the Uitmarkt, the Gay Parade and Queen's Day in Amsterdam draw crowds of 250.000, 500.000, 600.000 people to an area of town that normally houses 80.000 residents. Elsewhere in Holland the old city centers are being set apart even more emphatically for pleasure. In Maastricht and Groningen, for example, these are literally zones, with special paving stones, historic-looking streetlights, strict rules for the shops signs, sometimes even with enamel street signs, but also with signs warning you that your every move is being registered by closed-circuit camera's. The eastern town of Deventer has a Dickens-festival every year around Christmas, when the whole historic center is transformed into a theme park with everybody in period dress and street theatre and so on. On internet the city warns visitors that it can get so busy that you might have to wait at the 'entrance'. This historicized fun puts a whole new light on our concept of what public space is.

The phenomenon, or threat, of the historic city as a pleasure zone is certainly not limited to this corner of Europe: in his book *The Tourist Gaze* the English sociologist John Urry describes a terrifying plan for Tuscany's cultural Mecca of Florence. Already in the eighties the 500.000 residents had to accommodate 1.7 million visitors a year, and in desperation it was proposed to move the city's academic, commercial and industrial functions out of the center and turn it over completely to tourists. Disney meets Michelangelo.[4]

Not only history, but all aspects of daily life are being packaged and sold as a tourist attraction. We know the word 'museumization', in my book I add to that the word 'theatralization'. Of course the open air spectacle for which Amsterdam has long been best known is the red light district. And even in the Dutch climate the number of outdoor café terraces has grown enormously in the last, say twenty years. You'll notice that the chairs are not placed facing one another, but facing the parade on the street. I notice it, too, when

I sit out on my stoop in the summer and read the paper. The house of ours is such a faithful replica that we're not allowed to add a balcony or a roof terrace, so the stoop is the only option. As tourists walk by I can see them thinking: 'Oh look! There's real Amsterdammer, sitting on the stoop reading the paper! That's what daily life is like here.' Little do they know that I'm just as much a native as they are!

Authenticity
Cities searching to heighten cultural and touristic profile have a keen eye for the authenticity market too. The Hague offers an ethnic-culinary tour, and last summer Amsterdam let people sail along with the barges that pick floating trash out of the canals. Maybe this was meant as an antidote to the picturesqueness of the surroundings? Rotterdam has something called the City Safari, which takes visitors to places where you would probably never go on your own: the city's biggest mosque, a tattoo shop, a Turkish coffeehouse, an SM-club, an artist's studio, an asylum seeker's home (well, home … tiny apartment). After visiting this young man, a Christian from Iraq, our little group got into a very emotional discussion, about whether this was a disgusting and embarrassing form of voyeurism, or whether it was a good thing actually to meet and talk with a person who would otherwise be no more than a statistic in the papers. I was one of those who felt that this was a good thing. I had asked the Iraqi fellow if he did not find it an unpleasant confrontation, having gawking groups of people over who were generally white, middle-class and obviously much better off than he. He said: 'No, I like it. I'm very lonely here. It is difficult to make friends with the Dutch, and I can't trust the Iraqis here because the secret service is everywhere. I find it comforting that there are people who want to hear my story.' For me this was a completely new light on the phenomenon of urban tourism.

There can conceivably come a time when the marketing of the historic city center takes on such proportions that you can no longer distinguish the authentic historic environment from the open air museum and the theme park, filled with fun events and tasteful replica's – like my house. In his thesis on the 'The directors of memory,' Ad de Jong, who works as a historian at the Open Air Museum in Arnhem, observes with sharp humor that the museumization of the world outside the museum has undercut much of the uniqueness of the Open Air Museum. 'Is the historic city center of Amsterdam not really Holland's biggest open air museum?' he asks – only slightly rhetorically. 'Things that thirty years ago were enshrined in ethnological museums are now to be seen everywhere, *in situ*, not as originals but in a revitalized form. The museum, therefore, is no longer an illusion of reality – reality is itself a museum.'[5]

The charm of Amsterdam is that to a considerable extent it is still what it was meant to be: a real live city for real live people, not a calculated, commercialized, monocultural fun-zone, dusted with a layer of powdered sugar. My hope for the future is that it will not give in to a prettified but misguided idea of heritage.

Notes

1 Robert M. Fogelson, *Downtown: Its Rise and Fall, 1880-1950* (New Haven, CT: Yale University Press, 2001).

2 'Van de Snoekjesgracht of de Groenburgwal of de Kromboomssloot heeft hij pakhuis-idyl-len gedicht en kelderliedjes gecomponeerd of slepende serenades gedacht, – ze gaven den verfijnden kunstenaar de droomerijen van een sierlijke, nette stad, luchtig en zonnig, rank oprijzend uit helder water, bevrijd van Hollandsche zwaarte. Hij heeft met een delicieuze kennis van zijn zien verteld in ragfijn scherende strepen, schaduwende in zilveren ritse-lende kratsjes met de keurigste hand die ooit over het koper ging, prentend met de zijden fijnheid van zacht gesponnen lijntjes als in goudstof van het teederst lakwerk, het am-bergeurig boeket zijner geserreerde illusiën van een zomersch Holland, een Venetiaansch uitziend Amsterdam, een Noordelijk donkere achterstad, opgeklaard in het dolce far niente van zijn effen artistieke caprices.' *De Nieuwe Gids* (1891): 115.

3 Annette Stott, *Holland Mania: The Unknown Dutch Period in American Art & Culture* (Wood-stock, NY: The Overlook Press, 1998), 151.

4 John Urry, *The Tourist Gaze* (1990; rev. London: Sage, 2002).

5 Ad de Jong, *De dirigenten van de herinnering. Musealisering en nationalisering van de volkscul-tuur in Nederland 1815- 1940* (Nijmegen: SUN, 2001).

NOTES ON CONTRIBUTORS

DR. BOUDEWIJN BAKKER studied history and art history. He is chief curator for publications and exhibitions at the Gemeentearchief Amsterdam. In 1981, he was responsible for the exhibition *The Birth of New York* at the New York Historical Society. His most recent research project is called *Het aanzien van de stad*, on the image of the city of Amsterdam in the seventeenth century (the city in reality, in art and as a rhetorical concept). His own research is on Netherlandish topographical art and art theory. He published a.o. on Rembrandt as a landscapist and on the town plan of Amsterdam as a reflection of the humanist theories on the ideal city. In 2004 he published *Landschap en wereldbeeld van Van Eyck tot Rembrandt*, a study of early landscape painting and the philosophy of nature in the Low Countries.

DR. ELISABETH PALING FUNK attended the University of Amsterdam, moved to the United States, received a B.A. in English, cum laude, from Manhattanville College, Purchase, NY, and a M.A. and PH.D. in English from Fordham University, Bronx, NY, where she held a graduate assistantship and a teaching fellowship. She is an independent scholar and a free-lance editor and translator, and was, until June 1996, an adjunct assistant professor of English at Manhattanville College. Her articles on early American and Dutch-American literature have been published in the United States and the Netherlands. She is rewriting her dissertation, 'Washington Irving and His Dutch-American Heritage as Seen in *A History of New York*, *The Sketch-Book*, *Bracebridge Hall*, and *Tales of a Traveller*,' for publication as a book.

DR. JOYCE D. GOODFRIEND is professor of history at the University of Denver. She is the author of *Before the Melting Pot: Society and Culture in Colonial New York City, 1664-1730* (Princeton University Press, 1992) as well as numerous essays on the colonial Dutch and early New York history, including 'Writing/Righting Dutch Colonial History,' *New York History* (January 1999), 'Archibald Laidlie and the Transformation of the Dutch Reformed Church in Eighteenth-Century New York City,' *Journal of Presbyterian History* (Fall 2003), and '"Upon A bunch of Straw": The Irish in Colonial New York City,' in Ron Bayor and Timothy J. Meagher, eds., *The New York Irish* (Baltimore and London, 1996).

DR. GEORGE HARINCK is extraordinary professor of History at Kampen Theological University and director of the Historical Documentation Center for Dutch Protestantism, Vrije Universiteit Amsterdam. He is the editor of the collected works of the Dutch theologian K. Schilder, he edited books and articles f.e. about the *De Antirevolutionaire Partij, 1829-1980* with Roel Kuiper and Peter Bak (Hilversum 2001), and wrote a great number of books and articles about Dutch church history. He also edited a number of travellogs of Dutch travelers in the United States.

DR. JAAP JACOBS is post-doc research fellow at the Amsterdam Center for the Study of the Golden Age, University of Amsterdam, and Senior research fellow at the Amsterdam / New Netherland Center, affiliated with the Gemeentearchief Amsterdam. He is the author of *Een zegenrijk gewest. Nieuw-Nederland in de zeventiende eeuw.* [A Blessed Country. New Netherland in the Seventeenth Century] (Amsterdam, Prometheus / Bert Bakker 1999). This book was awarded the yearly Andrew Hendricks Manuscript Award 1999. A English translation of this work is under contract to Brill. He is currently working on a biography of Peter Stuyvesant.

DR. MARIKA KEBLUSEK is professor of the History of the Book at the University of Amsterdam, and directs the research project 'Double Agents: Cultural and Political Brokerage in Early Modern Europe' at Leiden University. In 1997, she published her dissertation *Boeken in de hofstad. Haagse boekcultuur in de Gouden Eeuw.* She was responsible for a number of exhibits at the Haags Historisch Museum and the Royal Library at the Hague and has published widely in book history and cultural history, most recently 'The Business of News. Michel le Blon and the Transmission of Political Information to Sweden in the 1630s,' *Scandinavian Journal of History* 28 (2003): 205-213. Her book *Minds of Winter: Book Culture and Literary Life of Royalist Exiles in the Netherlands, 1640-1660* is forthcoming.

DR. HANS KRABBENDAM is assistant-director of the Roosevelt Study Center in Middelburg. He published *The Model Man: A Life of Edward W. Bok, 1863-1930* (2001), articles on Dutch immigration history and edited several books on European (Dutch)-American relations. Among them are: coedited with Larry Wagenaar, eds., *The Dutch-American Experience: Essays in Honor of Robert P. Swierenga* (Amsterdam 2000), coedited with Hans-Martien ten Napel, *Regulating Morality: A Comparison of the Role of the State in Mastering the Mores in the Netherlands and the United States* (Antwerpen 2000), coedited with Marja Roholl and Tity de Vries, *The American Metropolis: Image and Inspiration* (Amsterdam 2001), and coedited with Giles Scott-Smith, *Boundaries to Freedom: The Cultural Cold War in Europe, 1945-1960* (London 2003).

DR. HENRY W. LAWRENCE is Associate Professor of Geography, Department of Geosciences, at Edinboro University of Pennsylvania. Edinboro, Pennsylvania. He holds degrees in history, landscape architecture and geography from Yale University, and the University of Oregon. He published widely on the history of urban landscapes in a comparative perspective, among others in 'National Differences in Urban Green Spaces: France, the Netherlands, Britain and America, 1600-1800,' *Planning History* 20.2 (1998): 20-28 and 'From Private Allée to Public Shade Tree: Historic Roots of the Urban Forest,' Arnoldia

57, no. 2 (1997): 2-10. He is presently working on a book called 'City Trees in Europe and America: A Historical Geography to 1900.'

DR. ROBIN A. LEAVER is Professor of Sacred Music at Westminster Choir College of Rider University, New Jersey, Visiting Professor of The Juilliard School, New York City, and the past-President of the American Bach Society. An internationally recognized hymnologist, musicologist, liturgical and Bach scholar, and Reformation specialist, Dr. Leaver, has written numerous books and articles in the cross-disciplinary areas of liturgy, church music, theology, and hymnology, published in the United States, England, the Netherlands, Germany, Africa, Korea and Japan. He has made significant contributions to Luther, Schütz and Bach studies, and authored articles for such reference works as the *New Grove Dictionary of Music and Musicians* (1980 and the second edition, 2001). His doctorate is from the Rijksuniversiteit Groningen, and a revised version of his dissertation was published by the Clarendon Press, Oxford, as *"Goostly psalmes and spirituall songes": English and Dutch Metrical Psalms from Coverdale to Utenhove 1535-1566.* Professor Leaver is currently at work on a history of American Church Music.

TRACY METZ, originally from the United States, is a journalist at the NRC *Handelsblad,* writing about architecture, city planning and landscape. She is (co-) author of *Snelweg/ Highways in the Netherlands, Nieuwe natuur; Reportages over veranderend landschap* en *Atlas van de verandering: Nederland herschikt (Atlas of Change: Rearranging the Nether- lands).* Her most recent book, *FUN! Leisure and landscape,* deals with the changes that leisure and the leisure economy have wrought on Dutch cities, the urban 'pleasure periphery' and the countryside.

DR. SIMON MIDDLETON is Lecturer in American history in the School of American Studies, University of East Anglia. He holds a PH.D. from the City University of New York, Gra- duate Center. He is the author of *Privileges and Profits: Tradesmen in Colonial New York, 1624-1750* (University of Pennsylvania Press, forthcoming) which was awarded the 2004 Andrew Hendricks Manuscript Award. He has published articles in *New York History, The Historical Journal,* and *The William and Mary Quarterly.* The latter article, 'How it came that the bakers bake no bread: a struggle for trade privileges in seventeenth-century New Amsterdam,' was awarded the 2001 Library Company of Philadelphia, Program in Early American Economy and Society (PEAES) Prize for early American economic history. His work in progress includes a study of economic and legal culture in eighteenth-century New York City and various edited projects (with Professor Billy G. Smith) including an anthology of essays entitled Class Formation and Class Identity in Early North America.

DIRK MOUW is a PH.D. candidate in history at the University of Iowa, Iowa City, Iowa, presently completing a dissertation titled: '*Moederkerk* and *Vaderland*: Religion and Eth- nic Identity in the Middle Colonies 1690-1772.' He held a Samuel Smith Fellowship for Research in New Jersey History, 2000-2001, and served as a visiting fellow at the Center for Reformed Church Studies New Brunswick, New Jersey during 2002-2003. He was an Iowa Fellow at The University of Iowa, 1992-1995, and 1998-1999, where he also taught in the History Department as Graduate Instructor from 1993-2002.

DR. CLAUDIA SCHNURMANN holds the chair of North American and Atlantic History at the University Hamburg, Germany. Her publications include: *Kommerz und Kluengel. Der Englandhandel Koelner Kaufleute im 16. Jahrhundert* (Goettingen 1991, PhD thesis), *Atlantische Welten: Englaender und Niederlaender im amerikanisch-atlantischen Raum, 1648-1713* (Cologne 1998, Habilitation, second thesis) awarded the Foreign Language Book Prize for the Best Book on the American Past 2000 by the *Organization of American Historians* in 2001, *Europa trifft Amerika: Atlantische Wirtschaft in der Fruehen Neuzeit, 1492-1783* (Frankfurt/Main 1998), and *Vom Inselreich zur Weltmacht. Die Entwicklung des englischen Weltreichs vom Mittelalter bis ins 20. Jahrhundert*, Stuttgart 2001. Her present projects include: the editing of a new series entitled *acs = Atlantic Cultural Studies* which will be published by LIT Verlag Hamburg.; she is presently working on a monograph entitled *"God's own country": Land und die USA, 1750er-1890er"*, and on a study of the extensive transatlantic academic networking of Francis Lieber, 1820s-1860s.

ACKNOWLEDGMENTS

The origins of this volume lie with a conference held in Amsterdam in January 2003 to commemorate the first city charter of Nieuw Amsterdam/New York, issued 350 years ago on February 2nd, 1653. This event offered the perfect opportunity to transcend the past three centuries and a half by zooming in on a variety of political, economical, social, intellectual, artistic, and religious aspects which compared old and new Amsterdam and put the Dutch legacy of New York in a long historical perspective.

This conference was the result of a fruitful cooperation of the Roosevelt Study Center, a research institute on twentieth-century American history located in Middelburg, the Netherlands, the Amsterdam Municipal Archives, and institutes at the two Amsterdam universities: the Vrije Universiteit and the University of Amsterdam.

The conference organizers Boudewijn Bakker, George Harinck, Jaap Jacobs, and Hans Krabbendam greatly benefited from the support of Jan Boomgaard, director of the Amsterdam Municipal Archives and Kees van Minnen, director of the Roosevelt Study Center, the promotional expertise of André Hirs and Gabriëlle Dorren, the editorial skills of Dagmare Houniet and Hans Seijlhouwer, and the indexing abilities of Ruben Vroegop.

Financial support was granted by the Royal Netherlands Academy of Arts and Sciences, the American Embassy in The Hague, the Amsterdam Municipal Archives, the Jan Wagenaar Stichting, the Historical Documentation Center for Dutch Protestantism at the Vrije Universiteit Amsterdam, the Amsterdam Centre for the Study of the Golden Age at the University of Amsterdam, and the Roosevelt Study Center.

Hans Krabbendam and George Harinck

INDEX